THE INTERIOR CASTLE

EXPLORING A SPIRITUAL CLASSIC AS A MODERN READER

ST. TERESA OF ÁVILA

EDITED BY
LAUREL MATHEWSON

WHITAKER
HOUSE

Unless otherwise indicated, all Scripture quotations from the Psalms are taken from *The Book of Common Prayer and Administration of the Sacraments and Other Rites and Ceremonies of the Church: Together with the Psalter or Psalms of David According to the Use of the Episcopal Church* (New York: Seabury Press, 1986). Public domain. Unless otherwise indicated, all other Scripture quotations are taken from *New Revised Standard Version, Updated Edition* (NRSV), copyright © 2021 National Council of Churches of Christ in the United States of America. Used by permission. All rights reserved worldwide. (https://nrsvbibles.org/). Scripture quotations marked (KJV) are taken from the King James Version of the Holy Bible.

THE INTERIOR CASTLE:
Exploring a Spiritual Classic as a Modern Reader

laurelmathewson.com

ISBN: 979-8-88769-092-6
eBook ISBN 979-8-88769-093-3
Printed in the United States of America

Whitaker House
1030 Hunt Valley Circle
New Kensington, PA 15068
www.whitakerhouse.com

Library of Congress Control Number: 2024930176

1 2 3 4 5 6 7 8 9 10 11 31 30 29 28 27 26 25 24

CONTENTS

INTRODUCTION TO *THE INTERIOR CASTLE*

When there are so many books on prayer, why choose one written almost 450 years ago? One answer: *especially now,* in our age of excessive information from almost-always dubious sources, it's worth looking at any teaching, and any teacher, that has withstood the test of time. Teresa of Ávila has proven herself to be a helpful guide on the Christian spiritual journey through a vast, centuries-long variety of historical settings and theological moods. Out of all the books and letters where we might meet this trusted teacher, *The Interior Castle* is widely recognized as her masterpiece: a late-life creative synthesis of her autobiography and teachings on prayer. To enter *The Interior Castle* is to put yourself in the hands of an extraordinarily certified mentor in faith. Perhaps this is enough for you to begin.

Yet maybe you're still thinking, "There are lots of 'classics' out there written by saints—what's special about this one?" All these years later, Teresa herself answers this question best: while there are many books about prayer and what *we* do to pray, or pray better, there are relatively few that focus on what *God* does in prayer—the sometimes wild and inexplicable ways that God gives us (mere mortals!) experiences of love, healing, strength, insight, companionship, and knowledge of God's presence in and will for our lives. These are the "supernatural" gifts we experience in our human hearts, minds, and bodies.

But then, how do we discern what is genuinely good? What is of God? What do we do with—and in the wake of—such marvelous gifts? And what is it all about, or *for*? Here, Teresa shines brightest, and *The Interior Castle* pulls ahead of the competition as an essential guidebook for the continuing journey. Those who've experienced something spiritually "extraordinary" often feel a bit alone and even disoriented, despite the peace and gratitude such gifts from God bring. Through *The Interior Castle,* Teresa sketches a trustworthy survival map of the spiritual landscape, while also assuring her reader that these gifts are real—and the reader is not alone in receiving them.

For those who don't identify with this path, *The Interior Castle* still offers plenty of riches; it is a framework for reflecting on the depths of our discipleship and how this is manifest in our lives. Teresa herself is very clear that extraordinary gifts in prayer or conscious experiences of the Spirit are not necessary to achieve the deepest states of union with God. But it doesn't hurt our faith—or it shouldn't, she insists—to learn about some of the ways that God sometimes *does* help and strengthen people through such experiences.

You can enter *The Interior Castle* without knowing anything about Teresa of Ávila. But mostly, we humans struggle to love what we do not know. To love—or at least appreciate—Teresa's voice and humor, it helps to know a bit about who she was, what she did with her life, and the context in which she wrote the text.

Introducing Teresa de Jesus, a.k.a. "Teresa of Ávila"[1]

I could be wrong, of course, but I get the feeling that for those who grew up going to Roman Catholic schools or receiving a parish education, Saint Teresa of Ávila is as familiar as the early American presidents—which is to say that her name and stature as an "important person" are well known by

1. This portion is excerpted from the "Introductions" section of Laurel Mathewson's memoir *An Intimate Good: A Skeptical Christian Mystic in Conversation with Teresa of Avila* (New Kensington, PA: Whitaker House, 2024). Used by permission.

almost everyone, but the particulars of her life and teachings are still pretty obscure to those who have little interest in history. Like the early presidents, however, she is wonderfully "knowable" to those who do seek out deeper knowledge of her person, her thoughts, and her time thanks to her prolific writings and all the great thinkers who have reflected on her life and legacy. For my part, growing up as a mainline American Protestant, I remained wholly ignorant of Teresa until the summer between my freshman and sophomore years of college, when I stumbled across an old Penguin edition of *The Interior Castle* and tried to read it because it was lauded as "a classic of Western spirituality," "a masterpiece on the life of prayer." At that time, I found it utterly unintelligible, and I distinctly remember struggling with and abandoning the text after only a couple of days of reading it at the front desk of the Stanford Alumni Center, where I was working as a fill-in receptionist. The contrast between the (to my mind) dark medieval imagery of shadowy rooms with slithering serpents and the sunlit palm trees through the wall of glass doors before me was too great; I could not enter Teresa's world.

My intent now is to at least introduce you to Teresa enough that you might be open to her words and to the ways in which her experiences and writings still shed light on things that happen in *our* world, *so* different from hers in many ways but still filled with human beings struggling to be in relationship with one another and God. To that end, as we embark on the world of ideas she presents in *The Interior Castle,* I'd like to briefly present Teresa to you as a controversial reformer, a writer under obedience, and a "grounded mystic." All of these identities are bound together, of course; but, for the sake of simplicity, I'll address them in turn.

As a means of orienting you to Teresa in relation to these essential aspects of her life, I want to first offer the briefest of biographical sketches—which feels as absurd as writing a few sentences of introduction to the life of George Washington or Queen Elizabeth I. But, assuming you may have little to no knowledge of Teresa, I hope this brief summary provides a basic framework while still allowing us to move quickly into conversation with her teachings on Christian spirituality.

In stark terms, then, in a form that might be given at a cocktail party or over coffee, who is Teresa of Ávila?

Teresa (1515–1582) was a sixteenth-century Spanish Carmelite[2] nun, long honored by the Roman Catholic Church as a saint.[3] In 1970, she became the first woman to be called a "doctor of the church," a title through which the Vatican recognizes contributions to theology and teaching. (Since then, three other women have been added to this esteemed list.) Interestingly—by her own admission—her "early" spiritual life was very uneven: she suffered a prolonged illness just a few years into her vocation as a nun, which she began at age twenty; and, in the wake of this illness, she entered an arduous period of struggle with prayer and authenticity that lasted through the rest of her twenties and most of her thirties. In 1554, when she was thirty-nine years old, she had a decisive moment of reconversion and began in earnest the work that would leave such a formidable legacy. For the next twenty-eight years, until her death at the age of sixty-seven, she dedicated herself to prayer, establishing a reformed Carmelite religious order, and writing. *The Interior Castle* is her best-known text.

TERESA THE CONTROVERSIAL REFORMER

What most surprised me when I began to seek out Saint Teresa as a spiritual guide was not her descriptions of rapture (though there is plenty to surprise there) but rather the active, administrative, political, and public nature of much of her work. As Raimundo Panikkar says, "There is…not a little difficulty in classifying Teresa of Avila. If we class her as contemplative because she reached the highest degree of fruition of God and union with Him, we forget that she led an extremely active life. If we rank her among the teachers, we overlook the fact that she was also a reformer…as well as a poet."[4]

I knew nothing of Teresa the reformer. I knew of her only as a contemplative and a teacher. And yet, in reading Teresa the teacher, we find an undeniable emphasis on the balance between what we now might call "the life of contemplation and the life of action." She says that the worth of any

2. For those unfamiliar with Roman Catholic religious orders, the Carmelites are a branch of the church family known for their commitment to a deep contemplative prayer practice, although, as with all organizations, the expression of this initial (founding) commitment can be unsteady, which is precisely what Teresa tried to address in her day through her reform work.

3. Since 1622, just forty years after her death.

4. Raimundo Panikkar, preface to *The Interior Castle*, by Teresa of Ávila, trans. Kieran Kavanaugh, O.C.D., and Otilio Rodriguez, O.C.D. (New York: Paulist Press, 1979), xiii.

prayer is measured by the extent to which it results in more loving action (demonstrable action) in our lives. In her case, this loving action centered on reforming the religious order that she loved, seeking to establish small, simpler communities of eleven sisters in contrast to the large community of 180 she herself had joined as a novice. I will not recount here the political sagas and struggles that accompanied her reform work, but if there is any mythical image of "Teresa of Ávila, set apart from the real world" in your imagination, simply know this: in her determination to establish a new kind of Carmelite house, one that reflected more truly the original simplicity and austerity of the Carmelite rule, she established *fifteen* houses across Spain in the last two decades of her life, often in the face of bitter opposition from civic and religious authorities. Despite all the discomforts of sixteenth-century travel, she spent her last years traversing the country, writing letters, and meeting with opponents and supporters, fighting for the conditions under which future Carmelite sisters might dedicate themselves seriously to the contemplative life.

TERESA THE AUTHOR, UNDER OBEDIENCE

That Teresa wrote is no surprise; *why* she wrote, or under what circumstances, is more intriguing. Apart from her letters, Teresa composed six works. The texts of most interest to a general audience are probably her autobiography, *The Book of Her Life* (sometimes retitled today as *The Autobiography of Teresa of Avila*); *The Way of Perfection* (instructions and observations about prayer for her Carmelite sisters); and *The Interior Castle* (again, in many ways a synthesis of her autobiography and *The Way of Perfection*). Although a full picture of authorial motives will always elude us, it seems quite clear that Teresa began writing in earnest about her prayer life and the "state of her soul" because she had to.

In an era highly suspicious of claims of spiritual authority (to put it mildly), Teresa needed to share openly with her spiritual directors (male priests) and other church authorities about what was happening in her and how she understood it if she hoped to continue her work on many levels—chief among her endeavors being the establishment of a newly reformed order and the supervision of her Carmelite sisters. Her first proposal for a new Carmelite house "aroused hostile gossip about Teresa's circle," as scholar Rowan Williams puts it,[5] and at least two officials suggested that she defend herself through a description of her spiritual experiences and her methods of prayer. The resulting text, *The Book of Her Life*, mostly satisfied the authorities; early reactions were favorable, and she was allowed to continue with her reforms. However, eventually, in reaction to a negative report by a widowed princess with a personal vendetta against Teresa (really!), the Inquisition offices swept up the original manuscript and all copies of it. Although the manuscript was later deemed acceptable, it was never returned to Teresa.

This background is pertinent to the creation of *The Interior Castle*. About three years after the Inquisition seized all copies of her autobiography, Teresa was in conversation at one of her newly formed houses with a supportive superior, a priest named Father Gratian, who also served as her confessor at the time. According to his own notes, while discussing matters "concerning her spirit" and the continued need for teaching certain insights to the nuns under her supervision, Teresa became a bit frustrated, saying, "Oh, how well this point was described in the book about my life, which is in the Inquisition!" In response, Father Gratian observed that the manuscript wasn't likely to come back any time soon, and he ordered her, in essence, to write it again (about ten years later), this time a bit more cautiously, in order to share the teaching "in a general way without naming the one to whom the things you mentioned there happened."[6]

Thus, once more, Teresa found herself compelled to write, in a way that might be hard for those of us unfamiliar with lives of vowed obedience to understand. While she observed that there were benefits to writing such a reflection anew, particularly because there were things that she had come to better understand through the past decade, it made her task no less of a dreaded chore, and an ill-timed one at that. In 1577, when Gratian ordered her to write this "new" book, she was sixty-two years old and plagued not only by physical maladies but also by serious political assaults on her reform work, exemplified by one series of events that took place in the middle of her writing project. Teresa was elected as prioress of the Monastery of the Incarnation in Ávila, but a church superior who opposed her reforms

---

5. Rowan Williams, *Teresa of Avila* (London and New York: Continuum, 2000), 42.
6. Introduction to *The Interior Castle*, by Teresa of Ávila, trans. Kieran Kavanaugh, O.C.D., and Otilio Rodriguez, O.C.D. (New York: Paulist Press, 1979), 15–16.

annulled the valid election. In response, in the reelection, the nuns once more voted for Teresa—and were all promptly excommunicated! In the months before and after this drama, Teresa wrote her book on the sublime mysteries of prayer, the friendship of God, and visions of the Holy Trinity—but, perhaps unsurprisingly, given this context, never in a way that loses sight of the realities and challenges of life on this earth with other humans.[7]

TERESA THE GROUNDED MYSTIC

It is partly Teresa's constant connection with, and concern for, communities in this world that leads me to underscore this third feature of her life and legacy: while it may be evident from even the briefest descriptions of her active reform work, a mindset that wants to segregate "mystical spirituality" from the thorny complexities of real relationships in a dysfunctional world will be constantly challenged by Teresa. She would have found the terms *mystical* and *spirituality* foreign in more ways than one. It was her constant turning from prayer to active love, and the way in which she did this—with so little delusion about what that means—that has caused me to think of her as a "grounded mystic." She was down-to-earth in her prose, her witty and candid teaching, and her lived experience.

It could be argued that every "true" mystic or saint is grounded, or has some element of both the active and contemplative life. That is right, in a sense, but Teresa still strikes me as having been remarkably and robustly balanced in a way that her basic reputation as a mystic sometimes betrays. She was notably resolute in both her defense of the reality of "supernatural" prayer experiences *and* her insistence that this loving movement of God to an individual must then extend *into* the world rather than curve in on itself. What we might call her "grounded" nature even extended into her prayer dialogues with Jesus: once, when complaining honestly to Christ about her many struggles, she heard a response to this effect: "Don't be troubled; so do I treat my friends." Her tart response? "I know, Lord—but that's why you have so few friends!"[8] In many of her waking days, she worried that Christ had so few "good friends" and tried to encourage her

7. Introduction to *Interior Castle*, trans. Kavanaugh and Rodriguez, 17–18. The Monastery of the Incarnation was also Teresa's initial home as a nun.
8. There are many and various accounts of this exchange, with slightly different wording, but I first encountered this story in Raimundo Pannikar's preface to the 1979 Kavanaugh and Rodriguez translation of *The Interior Castle*, page xvii.

contemporaries to become better friends of God. But she was clear-eyed and honest about the things that stand in the way of that friendship, from within and from without.

Introducing Teresa's Dwellings, a.k.a. The Interior Castle

Now that we know a bit about this work's author, Teresa, and the context in which she wrote, it's time to introduce the text itself. What is it actually about? How is it organized? Who is the audience?

The Interior Castle is a book about prayer, spiritual progress, and what it means to be a soulful creature with the inherent capacity to encounter God through Christ who dwells within. Yet it must be admitted that even Teresa's central metaphor for the soul is a bit alienating: a series of rooms in a castle, subdivided into seven "layers," surrounding a central chamber where God dwells—all within us. Right away, we stumble. A castle? Unless we are among the few who live in landscapes dotted with castles, this is already a strain for our imagination. And then, even if we are relatively familiar with castles as physical structures, the whole social system reflected by the rooms she describes—with the King, frequently described as "His Majesty," at the center—has shifted. But for me, much of the difficulty is resolved by one simple translation change. Although, in English, this work has long been titled *The Interior Castle*, in Teresa's Spanish, the title is much more humble and accessible: *Las Moradas*, which means "the dwellings," or even more simply, "the houses."

Although Teresa does use the image of a grand (crystal!) castle at one point in describing the soul, the dominate landscape she creates, and refers to, is the biblical image from John 14 of a vast house or even compound, owned and occupied by God ("my Father's house"), within which there are many rooms, homes, or dwellings.[9] Since most of humanity does not live in

9. In John 14:2, Jesus says, "In my Father's house there are many dwelling places," but the word in Greek that is "dwelling places" was first commonly translated into English as "mansions." There is a similar ambiguity with the words Teresa uses to describe these spaces within our soul. Some translators point out that the word rendered as "room" (*aposentos*) is more like "apartment," and translators have always needed to decide if they want the English word for *moradas* to be "mansions," "dwelling places," or simply "dwellings." To use the "fancier" translation option, like "mansions," points to the dignity and richness of the place. But this term can also be unnecessarily complicating, distracting, and distancing from many people's lived realities of small, humble homes.

grand spaces, I think it is more helpful to talk about these various spaces as "dwellings," not mansions—keeping in mind as we do so, however, the beauty and dignity of this whole compound (and every room within it). We all know that the places where we literally and figuratively "live" in the course of our life often look and feel very different from one another. Most simply put, Teresa wants us to explore the "spaces" we inhabit as we seek to draw closer to God.

From the beginning, we notice that Teresa is not exploring these "dwellings" in a haphazard, random way. To create structure and order for her metaphor, she divides them into seven categories or levels of spiritual progress. Even she is aware that this tempts our lazy minds into thinking of them as singular and linear, one lined up after another, and warns against such oversimplification. She tries to scramble the linear image by introducing the circular concept of a palmetto seed surrounded by many layers of leaves: imagine then that the "outer leaves" are the first dwelling places, the circle of leaves a bit closer to the center are the second dwelling places, and so on, until at last the soul rests in the heart of the palm with God in the seventh dwelling places. This is a helpful way to remember that each "level" of her seven stages includes a great many different rooms, not just one or a few.

For those less-botanically inclined, another way to think of this might be to look at a map of Paris, France, and the city's numbered neighborhoods, or *arrondissements*. They start with the number one in the center and work their way up and out in a spiral, snail-shell pattern away from the oldest, central part of the city. For Teresa's seven *arrondissements*, each filled with many dwelling places, the numbers would work in reverse: those called the "first" would be on the outside, and as a person traveled toward the center (perhaps in a spiral), they would move through the second, third, and so on, until they reached the heart of the city—the "seventh"—in the center.

Teresa also reminds the reader throughout that these stages and our movement through them are by no means one way; our continual progress toward communion with God in the center is not assured, and, if we are not careful, we can easily wander or slide back toward the outer rooms or layers.

Right away, the modern reader notices that Teresa is addressing her audience directly and often, starting in the first paragraph of the first dwellings: "Considered in this way, *sisters*, the soul of a person attentive to God's ways is a paradise."[10] As we know from the origin story of the book, as well as her own preface, *The Interior Castle* was written with a specific audience and purpose in mind: to help fellow nuns in the Carmelite order with the challenges of prayer. She calls these women who have taken on the shared life and disciplines of their religious order "sisters" as well as "daughters," and if we don't remember Teresa's teaching context and aim, we might understandably feel left out of the intended audience. (For those readers who are Carmelite sisters today, I imagine the effect is more powerfully inclusive!)

We might walk more comfortably with Teresa as she teaches her fellow nuns if we remember two things: First, some of our best learning happens when we feel that we are "overhearing" the truth (not being addressed directly), and thus making deductions for ourselves about how it applies to our lives.[11] Secondly, there are hints throughout the text that Teresa knows her *actual* (if not intended) audience extends beyond the circle of Carmelite sisters. She had already written books on prayer "for her sisters" that were widely circulating beyond the convents. In her humility, Teresa probably wouldn't have guessed at how widely she would be read after her death (although who knows what God revealed to her about this), but with her characteristic practicality, she surely knew that her writings would reach others outside those in the cloisters. It's as if she is giving a tour to our interior dwelling places that is indeed primarily crafted and executed with the nuns in mind, but she is aware of the many people on the edges who have joined the crowd; she frequently broadens her horizons and her rhetoric to include the whole audience. Throughout her life, Teresa mentored and taught friends who were outside religious orders as well as those within; beyond her in death, through the gift of her writings, we all might be included in those who consider her a teacher of faith. We can think of ourselves as those who are lucky enough to hear about and join this tour.

10. *The Interior Castle*, 1.1.1. Emphasis added. Abbreviations identifying the location of quotes from the "Dwelling Places" sections of *The Interior Castle* will be used periodically in the footnotes of this book. For example, "1.1.1." refers to "First Dwellings," chapter 1, section 1.

11. Jesus employs this "method" of indirect teaching in his parables; Fred Craddock brought this insight (via Søren Kierkegaard) to a new generation of American preachers through his book *Overhearing the Gospel*.

Common Stumbling Blocks (and Aids to Keep Walking)

If Teresa is our guide, and the *Interior Castle* is the tour we've decided to join (we've heard so many interesting things about it!), there are a few things we should know that might help us stick with it to the beautiful end. First, we can't completely forget or deny that our guide is 450 years older than we are and is from another time and place. She thinks about certain things differently, both theologically and politically, based on the particular life and context God gave her.

For example, Teresa was reared as a Spanish Roman Catholic in the age of a powerful church and monarchy. I was reared as an American Protestant in an era of institutional decline; given the depth of my training in democratic ideals and simplified (often weakened) church hierarchies, I can probably never understand the depth of feelings and perspective implied when Teresa refers to the Lord as "His Majesty," though, over time, I can get a sense of the warmth and love that infuses her use of this term.

Or, to offer another example of this gap: there is a depth of humility, self-deprecation, and verbalized submission to authority throughout Teresa's writings that many modern readers find difficult to understand. Why is she so hard on herself? Why is she constantly insisting she is "wretched," or, as I have rendered it in this version, "pathetic"? Answering those questions with nuance could fill articles and books (and already has), but one short answer to keep in mind throughout is simply this: historical context plus personality. As a woman garnering attention, resources, and power through her reform work, Teresa needed to constantly broadcast that she wasn't "getting too big for her britches"—that she knew her weaknesses and her place within the church hierarchy; *and* I think she felt genuine remorse for her lapses and imperfections, especially during the time in her twenties and thirties when she was not particularly focused on prayer or genuine spiritual progress.

Another thing to know in advance about our guide: she loves to explain concepts through images and metaphors. This is natural, understandable, and the hallmark of many great teachers (including Jesus!), but despite the apparent "order" to the tour, described as seven levels, we can't expect all of the images, or paintings, to be neatly arranged. Sometimes she jumps from one image to another quite quickly: the soul is a paradise, a garden, then it's a castle, then it's a palmetto, then it's a pearl—and she's moving through the images as if thinking out loud, searching for the one that is just right and yet realizing all the while that none of them is perfectly adequate to the task. Sometimes she lingers with an image or metaphor for quite some time, trying to draw out the complex implications of the "painting" she's attempting to use as a teaching tool. Inevitably, eventually, the text will stop in a room or in front of a painting that you neither understand nor have much interest in. My encouragement for a first-time reader is to not get stuck or fixated on any particular image, especially if it's one that doesn't make much sense to you. Don't try to force a logical connection between all of the images; allow each to speak for themselves in time. Like the many images in the gospel of John—where Jesus is Word, Light, Bread, Good Shepherd, Gate, Life, to name just a few—Teresa's metaphors are always seeking to point beyond themselves. So, hold them, look at them, but don't get obsessed with them. Keep moving. You can always return to a perplexing one later.

Finally, my competitive husband pointed out to me that few readers can enter *The Interior Castle* without some degree of preoccupation with their own "place" or "level" within it. I think he's right. No matter what our level of competitiveness, the subtext as we read along can easily become self-assessment: "Am I still in the first dwelling places? The third? Have I 'made it' to the fourth or fifth, or even sixth?" The framework of the seven dwelling places can be a helpful tool that facilitates self-awareness and self-reflection about various seasons and times in our lives, including the present. But, as with the images, I encourage first-time readers not to cling too tightly to the labels, boundaries, and supposed "status" of each section. Although continued progress and increased spiritual maturity is the general template, Teresa frequently describes ways that we can move about this porous landscape (with many doors and many rooms) in a more dynamic fashion. This includes not only the ever-present danger of "backsliding" but also the unexpected God-given gifts in prayer that are "above" our supposed category. So, once again, keep walking—even if you feel that the tour has entered territory that is "above you." There may be a moment, still around the corner, when you suddenly realize that Teresa is now talking about a topic you *do* know or *have* known something about, but you didn't know how to place it. And, if not, you will still be tracing the contours of the Christian contemplative prayer landscape with a fascinating firsthand guide, learning about the paradoxical blend of perils and peace that await those who persevere to sojourn there, with God's help and by God's grace.

What Is "Modernized" about This Edition of The Interior Castle?

Before finally joining Teresa in her walk through the soul's dwelling places, I want to offer a few clarifications about what this version is (or strives to be), and what it is not. This modernized edition seeks to stylistically update the English language versions currently available to the reader in the public domain, with the aim of helping Teresa's teachings reach a new generation and broader audience. To that end, the foundational text for this edition is the English translation of Teresa's original Spanish manuscript created by the Englishman E. Allison Peers in 1942. Peers was a professor of Hispanic studies at the University of Liverpool who literally published *volumes* of translations of Spanish works, including all of those by Saint John of the Cross (in three volumes) and Saint Teresa of Ávila (in five volumes). I felt my work in updating the English for this publication, more than eighty years after Peers wrote, was primarily to dust off some linguistic cobwebs, knowing that his academic work of translation from Teresa's original text was sound. In my efforts to accurately render Teresa's teachings and sentiments with greater clarity for a twenty-first-century reader, I also consulted other English language translations of the text—both those in the public domain from 1852 (translated by Fr. John Dalton) and 1921 (translated by the Benedictines of Stanbrook and edited by Fr. Benedict Zimmerman), and those still under copyright, like Kavanaugh and Rodriguez's 1979 translation. I looked at the Spanish text throughout to see where every translator had to make choices about adding words to make concepts clearer and breaking up sentences when possible. This was most helpful for seeing how sparse and fluid Teresa's language often is—it feels like she is writing in a hurry, with a waterfall of thoughts and little time to clarify or restate which previous noun she is referring to, or to pause for a break using a period (her preferred form of punctuation, even between many sentences, is a comma!). But I am not a scholar of sixteenth-century

Spanish; I stand with gratitude on the broad shoulders of the dutiful and talented academics who labored with the original text before my time.

Perhaps an example from a time when Saint Teresa herself writes about clarity in writing will give greater clarity about the nature of this edition. Here is a paragraph from Teresa's preface as translated by Peers:

> I was told by the person who commanded me to write that, as the nuns of these convents of Our Lady of Carmel need someone to solve their difficulties concerning prayer, and as (or so it seemed to him) women best understand each other's language, and also in view of their love for me, anything I might say would be particularly useful to them. For this reason he thought that it would be rather important if I could explain things clearly to them and for this reason it is they whom I shall be addressing in what I write—and also because it seems ridiculous to think that I can be of any use to anyone else. Our Lord will be granting me a great favour if a single one of these nuns should find that my words help her to praise Him ever so little better. His Majesty well knows that I have no hope of doing more, and, if I am successful in anything that I may say, they will of course understand that it does not come from me. Their only excuse for crediting me with it could be their having as little understanding as I have ability in these matters if the Lord of His mercy does not grant it me.

I have edited Peers' translation to read this way:

> The person who commanded me to write told me that Carmelite nuns need someone to help solve their difficulties in prayer. Because—it seemed to him—women best understand the words of other women, and because they love me, I might be particularly helpful to them. He emphasized that I try to explain things clearly to them, and so I'm addressing the nuns in this work. It seems ridiculous to think that I can be of use to anyone else! It would be a great gift from God if a single nun finds my words help her to praise Him even a little better. God knows that I don't hope to do more than this. If I am successful in writing things of use, they must understand that it doesn't come from me. They could only

give me the credit if they are lacking understanding—lacking it as much as *I* lack the ability to say anything of use if the Lord does not grant it to me by His mercy.

I have tried to simplify sentence structure and convey the essential meaning with as little redundancy as possible. That said, this modernized version is not an *abridged* edition; it was not my intent to leave out any of Teresa's insights, even if they seem at times to the modern reader to be meandering and "beside the point." Even in more contemporary parlance, Teresa may sometimes still seem too "wordy" for our attention spans, which have been shaped and shortened by Internet scrolling, quick content streaming, and screens in general. But I owe too much to her words and her work, personally, to feel comfortable removing anything; even her asides help us know her a bit more as a person and a teacher.

I have retained some of Teresa's central word choices that might initially seem foreign (like references to "His Majesty") because they are characteristic of her voice and this work. As a general rule of thumb, however, in the face of a word that is no longer commonly used, even in religious circles—such as "wretched"—I looked for a word that would convey the sentiment (in the case of "wretched," sometimes this was "pathetic," other times "miserable"). Teresa dances around with tenses and voice—sometimes using the impersonal third person ("a soul"), sometimes the second person ("you") or first-person plural ("we"). I gave myself the liberty of dancing around in these voices, too, seeking the greatest coherence, clarity, and directness for a given point, and trusting that the "voice" of the teaching was not its essence. Finally, to supplement where clarity within the text might still be lacking, I've offered brief chapter overviews, essential footnotes, section breaks with headers, and questions for reflection. (Because I have included brief chapter overviews, I have excluded the even shorter bullet-point-style introductions to each chapter that were in the original book).

In the end, there is no way to make a sixteenth-century text completely digestible to the modern reader without losing or damaging aspects of its character, nuance, and constitution. And this is probably doubly so for a text about mystical prayer. I have tried to balance my deep desire for others to be fed by Teresa, as I have been, with my concern to minimize such losses. So, to be honest, certain parts of *The Interior Castle* remain challenging to navigate (I'm looking at you, "Sixth Dwellings"!). And there are probably areas, on the flip side, where I have erred in my attempts to make things easier. I ask forgiveness for any unintentional distortions and place my trust in the God who knows my intention. I pray others can find this work by Saint Teresa to be a means of life-changing and transforming grace, to God's greater glory, as it has been for me.

Overview of the Prologue

Here we learn from Teresa herself about the basic context of writing *The Interior Castle*: she has been ordered to, and she understandably complains about the task. She is busy and not feeling well. Yet she ultimately trusts that God will help her. Talking about "other books" she has been commanded to write, she demonstrates annoyance that she doesn't have access to her previously written autobiography; at that time, all the copies had been swept up for review by the Inquisition. Knowing that this book will face similar scrutiny, she makes clear that she has no desire to say or teach anything contrary to the teachings of the Church. Finally, she names her audience and the immediate reason for writing: to help her sisters in Carmelite convents with their lives of prayer. With humility, she acknowledges that God must help her if this work is to be a "success," which she defines (modestly) as helping even a single sister to praise God a little more fully.

Prologue

There are few things commanded of me that have been as difficult as this current assignment to write about prayer: because I don't feel the Lord has given me either the spirit or the desire to do it; and because, for the last three months, I have been suffering from headaches and other mental distractions. It's even hard to write about necessary business, let alone prayer!

But I know that there is a strength that comes from obedience, and it has a way of simplifying things that seem impossible. So I gladly resolve to try, though even thinking about the prospect seems to make my body weak. The Lord has not given me enough strength to wrestle continually with sickness and with all the work I must do without really feeling it in my body. May He who has helped me before in doing other—and more difficult—things help me do this, too. I put my trust in God's mercy.

I really think there's little left for me to say that I have not already said in other books that I've been commanded to write. In fact, I'm afraid that I will do little but repeat myself. I write literally and with repetition, like parrots. They only know what is taught to them and what they hear, and then repeat the same things again and again. If the Lord wants me to say anything new, His Majesty will either teach it to me or draw my memory to what I have said before. I would be quite satisfied with this, because my memory is so bad that I would be delighted if I could manage to write down even a few of the things that people appreciated in the past, in case they've been lost. If the Lord *doesn't*[12] help me in this way, I will still be better off for having tried (even if this act of obedience tires me out and makes my head worse, and if what I write is of no use to anyone).

And so: I begin to complete this task on this Day of the Holy Trinity [June 2],1577, in the convent of St. Joseph of Carmel in Toledo. This is where I currently live, submitting myself and all that I say to the judgment of the people who have commanded me to write. They have great learning. If I should say anything that is not in line with the teachings of the holy church, it is only out of ignorance and not malice. You can be sure of my good intentions. I am, always have been, and will always be obedient to the church. May God be forever blessed and glorified. Amen.

The person who commanded me to write told me that Carmelite nuns need someone to help solve their difficulties in prayer. Because—it seemed to him—women best understand the words of other women, and because they love me, I might be particularly helpful to them. He emphasized that I try to explain things clearly to them, and so I'm addressing the nuns in this work. It seems ridiculous to think that I can be of use to anyone else! It would be a great gift from God if a single nun finds my words help her to praise Him even a little better. God knows that I don't hope to do more than this. If I am successful in writing things of use, they must understand that it doesn't come from me. They could only give me the credit if they are lacking understanding—lacking it as much as *I* lack the ability to say anything of use if the Lord does not grant it to me by His mercy.

---

12. There are no italics or underlining in Teresa of Avila's original Spanish text of *The Interior Castle*, although there are exclamation points and question marks, which help to provide a sense of her voice. In this edition of *The Interior Castle*, I added all of the italics as I modernized the text, to facilitate greater comprehension.

FIRST DWELLINGS

Overview of Chapter One

Teresa divides this section into two "chapters." In chapter one, she introduces her primary and *foundational* metaphor for the entire text: the soul as an interior castle, or series of "dwellings" of great grandeur, beauty, and value. It is worth noting that in Teresa's theological worldview, the soul's complex layout is a gift, or capacity, given to all of humanity in creation. It is part of our being made in the "image and likeness of God," Teresa says, using a key phrase from the book of Genesis. She recognizes with sadness that not all people believe they have been given the capacity, or "spaces," in their very selves and souls where they might meet God. Then she moves into an aside about God's gifts in the various dwelling places of this castle. She refers to the particular gifts, often translated as "favors," that God sometimes gives in prayer. This is, frankly, a detour from a strict or logical outline: later she will acknowledge that God doesn't usually give such gifts in the first dwelling places! But this shows the weight of these divine gifts in her heart and head as she begins this work; she knows that she is going to be talking about them eventually, and she wants to clear the air right away about the benefits of doing so when she knows full well that they are not universal experiences. Returning to the immediate questions and concerns of the first dwelling places, she addresses the nuts and bolts of entering the castle, explaining that we access these spaces where we encounter God's light through the door of prayer.

Chapter One (1.1)

THE SOUL AS AN INTERIOR CASTLE

1. While I was praying today that God might speak through me (since I was severely struggling to even begin this task of writing), a thought came to me. It's a foundational image on which I might build. I started to think

of the soul as being like a castle made of diamond or crystal, with many dwelling places—as there are in heaven.[13]

Considered in this way, sisters, the soul of a person attentive to God's ways is a paradise, a beautiful place; the One who created it delights in it.[14] What do you think a place would be like that delights One so powerful, wise, pure, and full of goodness? There's no adequate image for the beauty of the soul and its vast capacity! No matter how smart we are, we can't understand our depths any more than we can understand God: for we are created in God's image and likeness, as He Himself says.[15] Given this connection, there's no point tiring ourselves out trying to understand the beauty of this vast castle, our souls. There remains a clear difference between the soul and God; like any aspect of creation, the creature is not the same as the creator. But the fact that His Majesty *says* the human soul is made in His image means we can hardly conceive of its dignity and beauty.

2. It's sad, really, and a shame: through our own inattentiveness, we don't understand ourselves, or know who we are. Imagine how ignorant we would consider a person who could not say who he was, who his parents were, or what country he came from. That seems unbelievably obtuse—but our own ignorance is far greater if we don't even try to discover what we really are: if we live our lives thinking only of ourselves as our bodies. Because we've heard it said, and because faith tells us so, we know that we have souls. But we rarely consider their qualities, their precious value, or who dwells there, and so we don't bother to care for them. We fixate our attention on the rough setting of the diamond, or the outer wall of the castle—in other words, our bodies.

GOD'S GIFTS IN THE VARIOUS DWELLING PLACES OF THIS CASTLE

3. Imagine, again, that this castle contains many dwelling places all around: above, below, and to each side; in the center of them all is the

13. In Spanish, this is a clear reference to Jesus' words in John 14:2: "In my Father's house there are many dwelling places."
14. Proverbs 8:30–31: "Then I was beside him, like a master worker; and I was daily his delight, rejoicing before him always, rejoicing in his inhabited world and delighting in the human race."
15. Genesis 1:26: "Then God said, 'Let us make humankind in our image, according to our likeness.'"

central dwelling place where the most secret, hidden exchanges take place between God and the soul. Take time to think about this comparative image; maybe God will use this metaphor to show you something of the various gifts He gives to souls. I'll do my best to explain them. There are so many different gifts that no one can possibly understand them all, especially someone as simple and deplorable as I. If the Lord gives you these gifts, you'll have the consolation of knowing that such things really are possible. If not, you'll have the consolation of praising God's goodness in giving them at all.

It doesn't hurt us, spiritually, to think of those blessed to be enjoying God's presence in heaven—it can actually bring us joy, too, and inspire our perseverance. In the same way, there's no harm in seeing that it is possible even here on earth for our glorious God to commune with the foul-smelling worms we humans are and for us to love God all the more for this goodness and mercy. Anyone who is offended by even the thought of God giving such gifts to others must be lacking in both humility and love. How could we not rejoice that God offers such grace to one of our family members? Especially when these gifts to others do not hinder the possibility that they will be given to us! His Majesty grants an understanding of His greatness to whomever He wants. Sometimes it's simply to reveal His power, as He said at the healing of the blind man when asked if the man was born blind due to his own sins or those of his parents.[16] He gives these gifts not because the *recipients* are holier than those who do not receive them, but so that *His* greatness may be made known. We see this dynamic in the lives of Saint Paul and Mary Magdalene. The point is that we might praise God for His works in His creatures.

4. Some might say that such gifts from God seem impossible, and that it's better not to talk about them because they only serve as a distraction or even a stumbling block to the weak. But less is lost by such disbelief than by the missed opportunity to strengthen those who have known such gifts. Such readers will rejoice and will awaken others to a renewed love of the God who so generously gives such mercies and whose power and mercy are so great. Anyway, I know that the sisters I'm writing to will not fall prey

16. John 9:2–3: "His disciples asked him, 'Rabbi, who sinned, this man or his parents, that he was born blind?' Jesus answered, 'Neither this man nor his parents sinned; he was born blind so that God's works might be revealed in him.'"

to this scandalized doubt, because they know that God gives even greater evidence of His love than what is described here. I *am* sure that if anyone doesn't believe such gifts are possible, she will never learn it by experience. For God doesn't want us to limit the possibility of God's works. So don't set such limitations on God's actions or gifts to others, sisters, if the Lord does not lead *you* by this road.

ENTERING THE CASTLE

5. Let's return to the beautiful castle. How can we enter it? This seems a silly question, because if this castle is the soul, and we are the castle, we are, in a sense, already in it! But there are many ways of "being" in a place. Many souls remain in the outer court of the castle, which is occupied by guards. They are not interested in going inside, and they have no notion of the wonders it holds, how many rooms it has, or who lives in it. Some books on prayer advise "entering within oneself" or "searching within," and this is the interior shift I'm trying to get at.

6. Recently, a learned man told me that those without prayer might be compared to those who suffer from paralysis: they have feet and hands, but no control over them. There are souls so weak, so used to keeping busy with outside affairs, that nothing can be done. It seems they are incapable of entering within themselves. They have gotten so used to living with the reptiles and other creatures in the outer courts[17] that they have become somewhat like them. Although they are naturally endowed with the power to converse with God Himself, nothing can be done *for* them. Unless they seek to understand their pitiable condition and change it, they will be transformed into lifeless pillars of salt for not looking within themselves, just as Lot's wife was because she looked back.[18]

7. As far as I can tell, the way into this castle is through prayer and meditation. I'm not saying mental prayer *rather* than spoken prayers, because all prayer must include internal meditation. If someone is not mindful of whom they are addressing, what they are asking, and who *they are* in asking, that's not prayer at all, no matter how much the lips move.

---

17. Because Teresa uses this image of "reptiles" repeatedly, I wanted to include it at least a few times. She is speaking metaphorically of all the unhelpful, dangerous, distracting elements and values from the world that slip into our prayers.
18. Genesis 19:26: "But Lot's wife, behind him, looked back, and she became a pillar of salt."

True, sometimes we can pray without paying direct attention to all these things, but that's only because we have considered these matters before. To regularly talk to God as if talking to a servant, never questioning oneself, while merely saying words memorized through constant repetition—I do not call that prayer at all! I pray that no Christian may ever speak to God like that. Anyway, sisters, I hope in God that none of you will, because we are used to considering interior matters. It's a good way to avoid such empty practices that deny our God-given depths as humans.[19]

8. Let's not talk anymore about these paralyzed souls. Unless the Lord Himself commands them to rise, they are like the man in Scripture who laid beside the pool for thirty-eight years.[20] They are quite unfortunate and living in danger. Let's consider those souls who *do* eventually enter the castle. These, too, are absorbed in worldly and exterior affairs, but their desires are good. Sometimes—though infrequently—they turn to our Lord. They think about the health and state of their souls, but not very carefully. Filled with a thousand preoccupations, they pray only a few times a month. Generally speaking, they are mentally consumed by the affairs of their life to which they are most attached: where their treasure is, there is their heart also.[21] From time to time, though, they shake off these mental shackles. It's significant progress when they know themselves well enough to realize they aren't heading toward the castle door at all. Eventually, they enter the first rooms on the ground floor, but so many reptiles slip in along-side them that they can't appreciate the beauty of the place or find any peace there. Still, they have achieved a fair amount just by entering.

9. You might think this is irrelevant, daughters, since, by the grace of God, you are not such a beginner. But you need to be patient, for there's no other way to explain to you some ideas I have about the interior dynamics of prayer. May the Lord give me the ability to say something about them, because what I'd like to explain to you is very hard to explain unless you have had personal experience. And anyone with such experience *still* must address subjects that we pray, by God's mercy, will never concern or apply to us.

---

19. Literally, Teresa says, "That is a good way of keeping oneself from falling into such bestiality," sometimes translated as "animal-like habits" (Peers) or "carrying on like brute beasts" (Kavanaugh and Rodriguez).
20. John 5:5: "One man was there who had been ill for thirty-eight years."
21. Matthew 6:21: "For where your treasure is, there your heart will be also."

Overview of Chapter Two

In chapter two, Teresa takes time to consider the state of souls separated from the light of God. This is an important part of working out the implications of her foundational metaphor: If we all have been given the gift of the light of God's presence, somewhat "accessible" within us by virtue of being made in God's image, how do we make sense of those people who are obviously living lives of darkness, opposed to God's will and God's ways? Teresa does not make sin something "other people" do; as she introduces the concept that sin "covers"—but never removes—the light of God's presence, she reminds her readers that we should be mindful of the particular kinds of pitch that prevent God's light from shining more fully in and through *us*. The metaphor also invites humility about the true source of any goodness, or light, that we do share with the world.

Following this topic of sin, Teresa expands upon her foundational metaphor from the first chapter to help the reader imagine the nonlinear spaciousness of the soul, focusing on how vast and diverse this metaphorical compound of dwelling places truly is. She then moves into an extended reflection on the importance of true and balanced self-knowledge. *Self-knowledge*, while not a common term in many churches today, refers to the still-common Christian practice of reflecting on your particular weaknesses, temptations, and patterns of failure to love God and love others well in both word and deed, in things done and left undone. It is an honest and ever-broadening awareness, with God's help, of our own limitations. In Teresa's day (and ours, too, to a lesser extent), the good work of "self-knowledge" could be compromised by an unhealthy fixation on one's sins and weaknesses. Thus, she emphasizes the importance of these spaces of honest self-reflection but urges her readers not to get stuck in them, reminding us to balance such meditations with time spent focusing on God's goodness, glory, light, love, forgiveness, and character. This is healthier, and more helpful.

Finally, she concludes by describing the general struggles and experiences of the first dwelling places, which center on the many distractions and distortions from our lives and the world that we carry with us into prayer. Here, it's helpful to remember that Teresa is not advocating a spirituality that forgets the material world or the concrete ways we must love and serve others. But she is very clear that learning to pray, learning to focus on the light and life of God, is very hard work at first because we are so distracted, preoccupied, and confused by all those things that compete for our energy and attention, even when we want to focus on God, or that which is "most essential." She advises simplifying our lives as much as possible—as much as our "state in life" allows—and asking for God's help to become less entangled in and more detached from everything that draws us away from our own desire to come closer to God, where we might perceive more of God's light in our lives.

Chapter Two (2.1)

SOULS SEPARATED FROM THE LIGHT OF GOD

1. Before moving along, I want you to think about what happens to this beautiful and grand castle, this pearl, this tree of life planted in the living waters of life—in God!—when the soul commits a willful sin. There is no thicker darkness. You need to know just one thing: although the Sun Himself is still there, as the giver of all this splendor and beauty, it is as if He were not there. The soul doesn't experience Him, although it is still as capable of enjoying Him (like a crystal is inherently capable of reflecting the sun). While in such a state, the soul cannot improve or grow. While the person is engaged in willful sin, no good works they might do will bear fruit or bring glory, because they won't be rooted in God, the only source of true virtue. And because such a soul has separated itself from God, God cannot look upon it with pleasure. After all, the *intention* of a person who engages in willful sin is *not* to please God, and in choosing darkness, the soul takes on darkness.

2. I know someone to whom God showed what a soul was like in this state of willful sin.[22] She says if people really grasped this, they wouldn't sin at all. They would rather take on the greatest troubles imaginable than knowingly sin. She wanted everyone to see this! Daughters, may you be just as concerned. Pray earnestly for those in this state of deep darkness.

When enveloped in grace, the works of a soul please both God and humanity, because they *come* from the spring of life. Just like the little streams that branch out from a clear spring are beautifully clear, so it is with a soul rooted in God. A tree without such a source of water cannot give shade or yield fruit; the spring sustains it, brings fruitfulness, and prevents desiccation. When a soul willfully abandons this spring and tries to draw life from a pool of black, foul-smelling water, it naturally produces ugly hardships.

3. Take note: it's not the spring, or the brilliant sun in the center, that loses splendor and beauty. Nothing can remove or diminish this central loveliness. But if you place a black cloth over a crystal in the sunshine, it obviously will not reflect the sun's light.

4. O souls redeemed by the blood of Jesus Christ, learn to understand yourselves and pity yourselves! Surely, if you truly understand your own natures, you can't help but strive to remove the pitch that occludes the crystal? Remember, if your life were to end now, you would never enjoy this light again. O Jesus, it's so sad to see a soul without abundant light! The rooms of the castle are in a sorry state. The senses are so distracted. The mental and physical faculties (which are like the governors, servants, employees) are so blind, out of control, and poorly managed! But what kind of fruit can one expect to come from a tree rooted in rebellion against God?[23]

5. A wise and spiritual man once said to me that he was less astonished by what a soul engaged in willful sin does than by what they *don't* do. May God mercifully save us from such evil. Because this, above all else, deserves to be called evil, since endless evil follows from it. We *should* fear this kind

22. This is Teresa herself, but she had been advised to cloak and depersonalize her experiences.

23. Literally: "rooted in the devil." I have translated it as "rebellion against God" (or God's ways) because this is the primary feature of the devil, the Satan, the adversary or accuser, in the Christian tradition.

of sin and earnestly ask God to keep us from it. "If He doesn't guard the city, all our efforts are for nothing."[24]

The woman I mentioned—given a vision of a soul in willful sin—said that this gift from God taught her two things: first, to fear offending God. (She continually pleaded in prayer to not be allowed to fall, because she saw what terrible things came of it.) Secondly, the image brought humility to the way she saw herself, because she realized that any good we do is not rooted in *ourselves* but rather in the spring. The soul, like a tree, owes all its fruitfulness to the clear waters in which it is planted and the radiance of the sun. This was so clear to her that whenever she did anything good or witnessed any true good, she turned her attention and thanks to the Source. Realizing that, without God's help, we are powerless to create good, she turned her praise to God and generally avoided any self-congratulations when her actions *were* good.

6. If we can remember these two takeaways, sisters, then the time spent writing and reading about this will not be pointless. Wise and educated men know this well, but we women, without education, need instruction in many things. Perhaps it is the Lord's will that such metaphors and comparative images be brought to our attention. May He in His goodness give us the grace to understand them.

7. These interior topics are so difficult to grasp that anyone—like me—with little formal education will circle around the point, saying a lot more than I need to, in order to get to the point. Readers must be patient with me, just as I've tried to be patient with myself in writing about topics about which I feel ignorant. Sometimes I feel like a perfect fool when I face the blank page, not knowing where to begin or what to say. Yet I realize the importance of explaining certain interior topics as well as I can. We hear all the time what a good thing prayer is, and our vows and rules for living as nuns mean that we must engage in prayer for many hours daily. But these guidelines don't tell us anything except what *we* have to do. They say very little about the work that *the Lord* does in the soul—I mean supernatural work. So, as I describe what He does and give explanations of these things, keeping in mind this celestial building within will be helpful. It is so poorly understood by mortals,

24. A reference to Psalm 127:1: "Unless the Lord builds the house, those who build it labor in vain. Unless the Lord guards the city, the guard keeps watch in vain."

even though many visit it often. And although God has thrown light on many of the topics I've written about before, I don't think I understood them then—especially some of the difficult subjects—as well as I do now. But, as I said, before I can get to these topics, I have to explain more well-known and basic things. This necessity follows from my simplicity of mind.

THE NONLINEAR SPACIOUSNESS OF THE SOUL

8. Let's return to our castle with its many dwelling places. Don't imagine these dwelling places as neatly lined up in a row, but focus instead on the center. This is the room or grand dwelling place—a palace—occupied by the King. Imagine a palmetto, with layers of leaves surrounding and enclosing the central kernel within (which have to be removed to see and eat the kernel). In the same way, around this central room are *many* more rooms, and many more above it, too. The soul must always be thought of as spacious, vast, lofty. There is no danger of exaggeration, because the soul's capacity is greater than we can imagine. And the Sun, from within the central palace, reaches every part of it. Whether one prays a little or a lot, it's very important that there is no false sense of constraint or limitation. Because God has given each soul such dignity and value, each must be allowed to roam freely among these dwelling places—above, below, from side to side. A soul must not be forced to stay for a long time in a certain room...well, unless perhaps it is in the room of self-knowledge.[25]

THE IMPORTANCE OF TRUE AND BALANCED SELF-KNOWLEDGE

Listen closely: this room is essential, even for those whom God keeps close in His very dwelling place! No matter how high a state a soul may have known, self-knowledge is necessary. One can never neglect it, even though one might want to. Humility must always be at work, like a bee busy making its honey in the hive: without humility, all will be lost. Still, it's helpful to remember that the bee flies constantly from flower to flower. In the same way, the soul must sometimes leave the room of self-knowledge

25. Again, self-knowledge refers to the practice of humble self-reflection: knowing ourselves truly, with all of our patterns and particular strengths and weaknesses. Teresa is pointing out that we never spiritually outgrow the need to look at ourselves and our lives critically, lovingly, and truthfully, with God's help.

and soar into places of meditation on the greatness and majesty of its God. This is actually more helpful in seeing our own basic and simple nature than pondering our weaknesses directly. It also liberates a person from some of the reptiles of the first rooms (like self-knowledge). Because, while it is true that reflective self-knowledge is actually a great *mercy* of God, too much of a good thing is still too much, as the saying goes.[26] Trust me—we grow to greater heights in virtue by thinking about the goodness of God than we do if we tie our attention down, looking only at our own little plot of dirt.

9. I'm not sure I have made this clear: self-knowledge is so important that even if you were drawn directly into heaven in prayer, I wouldn't want you to relax your practices of humble and honest self-reflection. As long as we live on earth, nothing is more important than humility. So, I say again that it is an *excellent* thing to start off in the space where one learns humility, instead of flying off to other rooms. That's the path to progress. If we have a safe, level road to walk on, why do we want wings to fly? Let's try instead to get the most out of walking.

And yet, from my perspective, we'll never truly know ourselves unless we seek to know God. Thinking of His greatness returns us more clearly to our own small and limited nature; looking at His purity, we see more clearly our marked flaws; meditating on His humility, we see how far we are from being humble.

10. There are two advantages to [seeking knowledge of God alongside self-knowledge]: First, anything white looks whiter against something black, just as black looks blacker against white. Secondly, if we turn from self toward God, our understanding deepens; our will and courage to embrace the good strengthens. We weaken ourselves if we never raise our eyes above the muck of our painful limitations and patterns.

We were just talking about the polluted streams that flow from souls in willful sin. Although it's not exactly the same thing (God forbid!), as long as we stay buried in the ugliness and smallness of our earthly nature, our streams will never be clear of the pollutants of self-protective cowardice, timidity, and fear. We'll constantly be looking around, saying: "Are people watching me or not? If I take this path, will it actually be harmful?

26. Literally: "Excess is as bad as defect."

Do I dare start? Is it prideful of me to even try? Can anyone as broken as me actually pray? Will my reputation be better if I don't follow the crowd?" Or saying: "Well, extremes are not good, even in trying to do good…and I'm such a sinner that if I fail, I'll only fall farther. Maybe I won't make any progress, and then I'll only be harming good people by trying. No need for someone like me to try to do or be something special."

11. Oh, God, help me! The adversary must have wrecked so many souls this way! They imagine that these misgivings—and others—come out of humility, but they really come from a *lack* of self-knowledge. If we never stop thinking about ourselves, we get a distorted idea of our own nature. Unsurprisingly, it leads to such fears and other even worse ones. This is why I say, daughters, that we need to set our eyes upon Christ our Good, from whom we learn true humility, and upon His saints. Then our understanding is enriched, and self-knowledge will not make us creep along timidly, content with a low standard. This is important, because although this is only the first dwelling place, it holds riches of great value. And anyone who can evade this room's characteristic trip-ups[27] will surely progress further. The adversary uses terrible and very tricky means to keep souls from truly knowing themselves and understanding his distortions.

THE GENERAL STRUGGLES AND EXPERIENCES OF THE FIRST DWELLING PLACES

12. About these first dwelling places I can share some useful information from my own experience. Think of them as being not just a few rooms, but a million. Souls enter them in many ways, always with good intentions. But the adversary, with intentions that are just as consistently bad, has many evil spirits in each room in order to prevent souls from moving around. We, poor souls, fail to realize this and get tricked by all kinds of deceptions and distortions. The adversary has less success with those closer to the King's dwelling place, but early on, the soul is still consumed by worldly affairs and pleasures, still filled with concerns for worldly reputation and ambitions. As a result, its servants or employees—the senses, the mental and physical faculties given by God as part of human nature—are weakened and easily defeated, though the soul

27. Literally: "reptiles."

might desire *not* to offend God and might perform good works. Those in this state need to turn to His Majesty for help every chance they get, and take His blessed mother and His saints as intercessors on their behalf, since their self-defense is weak. In reality, in every state of life, our help must come from God. May His Majesty grant us such help, in His mercy. Amen.

13. How miserable is this life of ours! Daughters, I've often talked about the harm that comes to us because we don't properly understand the concept of humility and self-knowledge, so I'm not going to say more here, even though it's very important. May something I've said be of use to you, God willing.

14. Notice that the light from the central palace, where the King dwells, hardly reaches these first dwelling places. Although the rooms are not completely without light (like when the soul is in a state of sin), they are dim and cannot *really* be seen by those in them. It's hard to explain. This is not because anything is wrong with the room, but because so many bad things[28] have entered the room *with* the soul that they prevent the light from being seen. It's like if someone were to go into a place that was flooded with sunlight, but their eyes were so caked with dust and dirt that they could barely be opened. The room is light enough, but the person can't enjoy the light because these wild beasts and animals[29] force the person's attention to remain on *them*. This seems to be the condition of a soul that is not in a bad state but is so completely absorbed and consumed by the things of the world—possessions, honors, business—that it is prevented from opening its eyes more fully to gaze at the beauty of the castle, even though it would like to. It's entangled, and seems both wrapped up and trapped by all the things. It's good advice for everyone who wants to enter the second dwelling places to try to put aside all *unnecessary* affairs and business—as much as your state in life allows. For those hoping to reach the central dwelling place, this is an essential and necessary first step. And even though a soul has entered the castle, it's not free from danger while inhabiting this dwelling place, because you can't avoid being bitten occasionally when you live among poisonous things.

28. Teresa specifies "snakes and vipers and poisonous creatures," which are images of deception, distraction, destruction, and weakening.
29. Again, these "wild beasts and animals" are images of destructive distractions in prayer.

15. Daughters, we are free from these entanglements and have already entered much farther into the castle, but what would happen if—by our own fault—we returned to these crowded distractions? Our sins have led many people who have received gifts from God to relapse into this sad state. We in our convents are free from outward concerns; may it please the Lord to keep us free internally and deliver us from evil. Be on guard against cares that have nothing to do with you. Remember, we are actually free from struggles with deceptive and distracting forces[30] in *few* of the interior castle's dwelling places. In some of the places, the "guards" (our physical and mental faculties) have strength to fight, but we must remain watchful for the adversary's tricks. He can deceive us in many ways, including by *appearing* to be good.[31] His entrance is subtle and gradual; we often do not notice until the harm is done.

16. Like I said, he works smoothly and silently, and we must be on guard from the start. Here are several illustrations to explain: He inspires a sister with yearnings to greater acts of generosity in service and prayer;[32] she has no peace unless she's completely putting herself out for God.[33] Alone, this may be fine for a time. But if her superior has ordered that no extra devotions be done without permission, and yet the sister secretly arranges her life to make her continued extra work and prayer possible (thinking it's okay because they are "good"), and then burns out and is completely unable to follow even the basic faith practices of the community, you can see where this seemingly "good thing" has led. Another sister is inspired toward perfection. Again, this is fine on its own. But it may lead to her thinking that *any* little fault by anyone in the community is a serious failure. She may then obsessively look for and report faults to the superior. In her zeal for everybody "doing things right," she may be blind to her *own*

30. Literally: "devils."

31. I love the elegance of Peers' translation: "Lest he deceive us in the guise of an angel of light." Second Corinthians 11:14 says, "And no wonder! Even Satan disguises himself as an angel of light."

32. Literally: "penance." The twentieth-century Carmelite sister Ruth Burrows helpfully describes the heart of penance as actions of greater *generosity* toward God and others than typically understood as normative or required: "In her day penances, that is voluntarily accepted forms of self-denial such as fasting, wearing hair shirts, vigils, were the accepted signs of generosity, of the desire to give all, to go beyond what was asked." (*Interior Castle Explored* (Mahwah, New Jersey: HiddenSpring, 2007), 31.

33. Literally: "torturing herself."

faults. Other sisters will probably not take this perfectionism well, regardless of her good intentions.

17. The adversary's true target here is no small thing: he's aiming to diminish love and understanding within the community, and any "success" in this regard is extremely harmful. Let us see clearly, my daughters, that true perfection is made up of the love of God and of our neighbor. The more perfectly we observe *these* commandments, the more perfect we will be. All our rules are nothing but tools and supports to help us love more perfectly. It's better if we resist the urge to try to make sure everyone is doing right all the time, and instead focus primarily on ourselves. I'll not say more, because I've said a lot about this in other communications.

18. The grounding in mutual love is so important: I never want you to forget it. If you go around looking for faults in others (which may not even be faults, just misperceptions based on ignorance of the full picture!), you lose your own peace and disturb the peace of others. This is a high price for perfection. The adversary might also tempt the community's leader[34] in this way, which is even more dangerous. Great care and thoughtfulness is needed in such a case: if she's going against the community's Rule of Life, this is serious, and someone must talk to her about it. If she doesn't change her ways, someone above her must be told, as an act of compassion for all. This also applies to the humblest community members[35] when there is a *serious* (not trivial) fault. Not saying anything in such a case because one fears it is a temptation is its own temptation. To prevent the adversary working in such circumstances, though, gossip *must* be avoided, because it easily leads to false claims and misinformation about others. Any concerns must be discussed *only* with the person whose behavior is concerning. We keep almost continuous silence in our communities so that the opportunity for gossip does not often come (glory be to God!). Still, we must be careful.

34. "The prioress" in Teresa's context.
35. "The sisters."

Questions for Reflection

1. What are the strengths of Teresa's foundational image of the soul as an interior castle or collection of dwelling places with God at the center? Are there other images or metaphors—given by her or found elsewhere—that you find more helpful?

2. How does Teresa's teaching about what sin is and does compare to what you've learned or thought about sin in the past?

3. How would you explain the importance of self-knowledge and humility on the spiritual journey?

4. What have been the "reptiles" in your life of prayer in the past or present?

SECOND DWELLINGS

Overview of Chapter One

There is only one chapter in the second dwellings section, and, as a whole, it is the shortest of the seven dwelling places outlined in the book. This seems to be a conscious and intentional choice by Teresa because this is the "stage" of spiritual progress that both she and others have already written about extensively: the times in our lives when we really do want to pray, really do want to draw closer to God, and yet doing so feels like such a struggle (including the basic act of prayer!). At our most self-aware, we recognize our inconsistency and our battling priorities, but we still wonder how we will ever find a place of greater steadiness and peace. Teresa names the good and beautiful origin of this inner agitation: it is because we are hearing the Lord's call and seek to respond.

Because there are so many powerful competitors for our energy, devotion, and allegiance in this world (many of which very subtly and seductively claim ultimate value for our lives), the spiritual sojourner enters a season marked by inner conflicts, perseverance, and progress. Teresa emphasizes the need for perseverance in order to make the progress we desire and realistically advises humble expectations for prayer as a solid foundation: we should not expect the gifts that God (typically) gives later on, but this lack of "tangible" feedback in prayer does not mean that we are not spiritually maturing. In slow, steady ways, as if you are undertaking the most grueling and rewarding hike you can imagine, you will indeed be moving toward peace in your own house. This is a great gift, and Teresa encourages the reader by assuring them that the tormented sense of inner conflict that marks these dwelling places will not last forever. With further kindness, she closes by offering some general teaching about prayer in the second dwelling places: she reminds those familiar with her teachings that, when we encounter distractions during prayer, we must persevere in prayer but face our distractions gently. We may feel embattled, but we will make more progress by gentleness and patience than by getting fixated on "the enemy." And lest we think prayer isn't worth all this effort if it's going to be so difficult, she reminds the reader that this interior journey to know ourselves and God is necessary, and we must be willing to engage in its inherent work.

Chapter One (2.1)

1. Let's now turn our attention to those who enter the second dwelling places, and what happens there. I don't want to say a lot about this, because I've written about it at great length elsewhere.[36] It will be impossible for me not to repeat much of this material, because I can't remember exactly what I said. If it could be presented in a different way, I'm sure you wouldn't mind, though. We don't get tired of books that talk about this subject, even though there are so many.

HEARING THE LORD'S CALL

2. This chapter concerns those who have begun to practice prayer and who see the importance of not staying in the first dwellings but can't yet quite bring themselves to leave for good...and don't avoid occasions of sin that keep drawing them back. This a dangerous condition. It's a great mercy when they manage to escape from the destructive, distracting elements,[37] even if it's only long enough to see that it's good to get away from them. In some ways, these souls have it harder than those in the first dwellings. But, in reality, they are in less danger because they now seem to *understand* their position. There is great hope they'll be able to go further into the heart of the castle. I say it's harder for them because those in the first dwellings are like those who are unable to speak but also unable to hear, so their lack of speaking ability is not particularly frustrating. Those in the second dwellings are like those who can hear others speaking but cannot talk themselves. This is much more difficult, more frustrating. But that's no reason to envy those who can't hear. After all, it is a wonderful thing to be able to hear and understand what is being said to us.

---

36. For more of Teresa's teachings about prayer in these spaces, see *Life*, chapters 11–13, and *Way of Perfection* (various places throughout).
37. Literally: "snakes and other poisonous creatures."

These souls *can* hear and understand the Lord when He calls them. They are getting closer to the central place where His Majesty dwells, and He is a very good Neighbor as they approach. His mercy and goodness are so great that even when we are engaged with our worldly activities, business, pleasures, and struggles, as we are falling into sins and getting back up again (because the deceptive and destructive elements are so active, it would actually be a miracle *not* to stumble and fall while in their midst), still this Lord of ours deeply wants us to love Him and seek His companionship. And so He calls us again and again, ceaselessly, to come closer. And His voice is so sweet and obviously good that the poor soul is grief-stricken because such obedience, such progress, feels impossible. This is why I say it suffers more than it would if it could not hear Him at all.

3. I do not mean here that He speaks to us and calls us in the way I'll describe later. His invitations to draw nearer come through words heard from good people, or through sermons, or as we read good books, or through sicknesses and trials, or through truths God teaches us when we are praying. (However weak our prayers may be, God values them highly.) There are many other ways God calls us, as you know. You must not underestimate this initial gift of perceived calling, sisters, or despair if you don't respond immediately. His Majesty is willing and ready to wait for many days, even years, especially when He sees our desires are good and that we keep trying. This combination of perseverance and good intentions is the most necessary thing here; if we have it, we cannot fail to make progress.

INNER CONFLICTS, PERSEVERANCE, AND PROGRESS

Still, the forces of distraction, deception, and weakening[38] now attack the soul in all kinds of ways, and it's terrible. The soul suffers more than in the previous dwelling places. There, it was unable to hear or speak—or, at least, it heard very little—and so it didn't resist the attacks much, like one who has lost hope of ever winning. Here, the understanding is sharper, the faculties more aware, and the clash of the battle is so loud that the soul cannot help hearing it. For here, the forces against spiritual progress[39] show you the things of the world, and pretend that earthly pleasures are practically eternal. They remind you of your reputation, your friends and

38. Literally: "the devils."
39. Again: "the devils."

relatives, the way in which your health and strength will be endangered by any generous act of self-sacrifice (which one always wants to do upon entering this dwelling place), among thousands of other kinds of stumbling blocks.

4. Oh, Jesus! These forces bring such confusion. The poor soul is greatly troubled and doesn't know if it should continue on farther or go back to the room it just left. But then, on the other hand, there are forces that help: Reason tells you that earthly things are of little value compared to what you are truly seeking (and it's a mistake to think otherwise); faith teaches what you must do to actually find satisfaction; memory reminds you how all these earthly goods come to an end, drawing to mind the death of those who enjoyed such things greatly (their sometimes sudden deaths, and then how quickly their lives can be forgotten by all, these formerly prosperous people, now buried…how we walk carelessly over their graves, reflecting on their bodies, filled with worms, as we pass by!); the will moves us to love One in whom it has seen so many acts and signs of love—desiring to return some of the same. In particular, the will shows you that this true Lover never leaves but is always present, giving life and being. Then the understanding comes along and helps you realize that you could never in your lifetime hope to have a better friend: the world is full of deceptions, and the alluring "goods" coming to mind bring difficulties, burdens, and annoyances. Understanding also tells you that security or peace will surely never be found outside this castle, and says to stop wandering from one house to another, searching for satisfaction, when your own home is full of good things—if you would only sit down to enjoy them. How fortunate to be able to find everything one needs at home and to have a Host who will give and share all sorts of good things with us—unless, like the Prodigal Son, we want to leave the house and find ourselves eating pig food![40]

5. Reflections like this overcome the forces acting against our spiritual progress. But oh, my Lord and my God, how the whole world's habit of getting involved in worthless vanities ruins everything! Our faith is so lifeless that we want what we can see with our eyes more than the things faith tells us about—though what we *actually* see is that people who chase

40. Luke 15:15–16: "So he went and hired himself out to one of the citizens of that country, who sent him to his fields to feed the pigs. He would gladly have filled himself with the pods that the pigs were eating; and no one gave him anything."

after these visible vanities ultimately find only misfortune. All this confusion and deception is the work of the "poisonous creatures" we've been describing. If a viper bites a man, his whole body swells up from the poison; this happens to souls, and yet we aren't careful! Obviously, we need a lot of medical attention to be cured of such venom, and only the mercy of God will save us from death. One thing is sure: you will suffer great trials in the second dwelling places, especially if the adversary notices that you have the character and habits needed to progress. Then all the powers of hell will combine to try to drive you back again.

6. Ah, my Lord! We need Your help here; without it, we can do nothing. In Your mercy, do not allow us to be deluded and led astray when our journey has just begun. Give us light to see how our complete well-being is to be found in the continued exploration of the castle, and enough insight to avoid evil companions. Associating with others who are walking in the right way is very helpful; don't just mingle with those in the same rooms where you find yourself, but with those whom you know have progressed to rooms nearing the center. They will help you greatly, and, in your drawing close to them, they will draw you along toward the center, too. Fix your determination *not* to be beaten. If the adversary sees that you have firmly resolved not to return to the first room—and are willing to lose your life, peace, and everything he tries to offer rather than fall back—he'll soon stop troubling you. The soul must be courageous and composed, not like those who fell down on their knees to lap the water directly from the stream when going to battle (I forget whom).[41] Be determined going into this battle, knowing there is no better weapon than the cross.

HUMBLE EXPECTATIONS FOR PRAYER AS A SOLID FOUNDATION

7. There's one thing so important to say that I will knowingly repeat myself here.[42] At the beginning, one must not think of such things as spiritual gifts or favors, for that's a very shabby way of starting to construct such a large and beautiful building. If one begins to build on sand, it will all

41. Judges 7:5: "So he brought the troops down to the water; and the Lord said to Gideon, 'All those who lap the water with their tongues, as a dog laps, you shall put to one side; all those who kneel down to drink, putting their hands to their mouths, you shall put to the other side.'"
42. *Life*, chapter 11.

collapse.[43] Souls that build in this way will *never* be free from annoyances and temptations. Because it is not in these dwelling places that it rains manna, but in the ones farther on. Once there, the soul has everything it wants, because it only wants God's will. It's an odd and funny thing: here we are, coming across barriers, stumbling, and suffering from imperfections by the thousand, with newborn virtues so undeveloped they can't even walk (God granting they have even come to life at all)—and yet we are shameless about wanting consolations in prayer and complain about periods of dryness. Sisters, don't let this be true of you: embrace the cross that your Spouse carried on His shoulders and realize that this cross is yours to carry, too. The one who is willing to suffer for Him, and is capable of bearing this suffering, has the reward of true freedom. Everything else is secondary, extra. *If* the Lord does grant you such consolations or gifts in prayer, give heartfelt thanks.

8. You might think that you *would* be full of determination and able to better handle the challenges of your life…if only God would give you inward gifts in prayer. But His Majesty knows best what is right and good for us; it's not for us to boss Him around about what to give us, for He can rightly respond that we don't really know what we're asking for.[44] All the beginner in prayer needs to do is to work, to try, resolutely preparing himself as much as possible to bring his will into alignment and conformity with the will of God. As I'll say later, you can be assured that the greatest perfection attainable on the spiritual road lies in this conformity. The more fully you align your will with God's, the more you receive of the Lord, and the greater progress you make on the journey. We don't need sophisticated terms or efforts in spiritual practices we don't understand. All our well-being is found through seeking conformity to God's will. If we stray from this path right away, waiting for the Lord to do *our* will and lead us in the ways *we* want, how can this building possibly have a firm foundation? Do as much as you can to avoid such poisonous deceptions.[45] Often the Lord wills that such evil thoughts or periods of spiritual dryness challenge us. Sometimes He even allows them to really get to us,[46] so

43. See Matthew 7:26–27.
44. See Matthew 20:22.
45. Literally: "venomous reptiles."
46. Literally: "bite us."

our defenses and awareness might grow for future challenges. Such "falls" also reveal if we are really troubled when we go against God.

MOVING TOWARD PEACE IN OUR OWN HOUSE

9. So, if you sometimes fall, don't lose heart or stop trying to progress. Even from your fall, God will bring good. It's kind of like a man selling a medicinal antidote to poison who personally demonstrates its power by drinking a little of the poison himself. If we can't "naturally" see what pathetic creatures we are and how much we hurt ourselves by scattered desires and wasted energy, this internal battle might be enough to show us—and lead us back to recollection.[47] Can any evil be greater than that which we discover in our own house? How can we hope to find rest in other people's homes if we can't rest in our own? No friend or family member is as close as our own faculties. We always have to live with them, whether we like it or not. Yet our own faculties seem to create inner conflicts, as if they resent the conflicts created by our bad choices. But sisters: the Lord said "Peace, peace" to His apostles, again and again. Trust me, unless we have peace and strive for peace in our own home, we won't find it elsewhere. Let this inner war cease. By the blood of Christ, shed for us, I beg you—those who haven't even started this inward journey and those who have just begun—don't let such inner conflicts and confusion turn you away from prayer or cause you to retreat. Falling twice is worse than falling once, and turning back leads only to greater destruction. Place your trust in the mercy of God, not in yourself, and you *will* see how His Majesty can lead you on from one set of dwelling places to another. Eventually, He sets you on safe ground where such beasts can't bother or hurt you. The beasts will be put in their place, and you will even be able to laugh at their attempts to harm. Then—even in this life!—you enjoy many more truly good things than you could ever ask or imagine.

GENERAL TEACHING ABOUT PRAYER IN THE SECOND DWELLING PLACES

10. As I said at the beginning of this chapter, I've already written a lot about how you should respond when you're tormented by mental

47. "Recollection," for Teresa, is a state in which we have the ability to attentively listen to (and for) God in prayer. It's a term for a state of prayer that she will describe more fully in the fourth dwellings.

distractions and emotional disturbances in prayer. Remember: recollection can't begin through hard work or mental fighting. It must come *gently*, and eventually you'll be able to experience this quiet prayerfulness for longer stretches of time. So, I won't say anything more now, except that talking with experienced mentors at this stage is important. Otherwise, you might imagine that you are seriously failing in the normal and necessary work of prayer. If you don't abandon your efforts, the Lord will help you benefit, even if you don't find a teacher. There's no solution for the temptation to give up on prayer except to start again at the beginning. May God help you see that you lose a little more each day you don't even try.

11. Some might think: if turning back is so bad, maybe it would have been better not to have begun at all, and to just have stayed outside the castle. I told you at the beginning, though—and the Lord Himself says this—that you lead to your own demise when you throw yourself into danger.[48] And the only way we can enter this interior castle is through prayer. It's crazy to think we can enter heaven[49] without first going into our own souls—without getting to know ourselves. We must reflect on the weakness of our nature and what we owe God, and ask continually for His help. The Lord Himself says, "No one will ascend to My Father, but through Me"[50] (I'm not sure if those are the exact words) and "He who sees Me, sees My Father."[51] Well, if we never look at Him, or think of what we owe Him, or ponder the death He suffered for our sakes, I don't see how we can get to know Him (or do good works of service for Him). How valuable is faith without works? And how valuable are works, if they are not united with the works of Jesus Christ, our Good? And how else can we come to love this Lord? May it please God to give us this understanding: how much we cost Him, that the servant is not greater than his Lord, and that to enjoy His glory we must work. We need to pray for this understanding so that we don't keep entering into temptation.[52]

---

48. Ecclesiasticus 3:27: "A stubborn mind will be burdened by troubles, and the sinner adds sin to sins."
49. It helps here to remember that a basic understanding of heaven is to see it as the place where we experience the presence of God, the place where we share in *God's* dwelling place.
50. See John 14:6.
51. See John 14:9.
52. Matthew 26:41: "Stay awake and pray that you may not come into the time of trial; the spirit indeed is willing, but the flesh is weak."

Questions for Reflection

1. What are some of the ways that you have experienced or heard the Lord's call to you? Teresa describes how this often occurs through the words of others (though not always): "His invitations to draw nearer come through words heard from good people, or through sermons, or as we read good books, or through sicknesses and trials, or through truths God teaches us when we are praying." Are there particular instances when you have "heard" the Lord beckon you closer in some of these ways?

2. What are the forces, values, or elements of the world that compete most often in your life with your desire to love and serve God? Have they changed over time? If so, how?

3. Teresa reminds her sisters that we always have the potential to return to previous (and more conflicted) dwelling places, even after we have known seasons of "peace in our own house." If you've known such a movement back and forth, what would you say about why and how such a "regression" or cycle happens?

THIRD DWELLINGS

Overview of Chapter One

As we enter the third dwellings, Teresa begins by addressing a topic that is particular to those who are making significant spiritual progress and think of themselves as committed to God and God's ways: the illusion of self-made "security" through our own "goodness." Thus, she spends some time addressing the precarious nature of our faithfulness and virtue. She draws from her personal experience, obliquely using her own story as an example and lamenting that she has not been as perfect as the sisters might hope. We don't know the fullness of what she is referring to in terms of her past lapses. But it *was* well-known through her own admission that she had abandoned prayer and seriously "relapsed," spiritually, for many years during her twenties and thirties, leading up to her "reconversion" at age thirty-nine.

After this, Teresa tackles another typical sticky point for those in these dwellings: often we are willing to keep all the commandments and live a righteous life—up to a certain point, where we lack boldness and reveal our ultimate attachment(s) to something else. Here, she makes comparisons to the story in the Gospels about the rich young man to help the reader understand this dynamic of having both faithfulness toward God and a desire to preserve certain aspects of self-will. Finally, she speaks about spiritual dryness and the need for humility. Here she's pointing directly at an often-unacknowledged element in the lives of those who are "doing right and being good": there is an undercurrent of works-righteousness where we think that if we are good, then God will reward us spiritually and otherwise. The flip side of this false coin is the indignation, irritation, and impatience that can then come if we feel that we are being good but are *not* being rewarded, in prayer or otherwise. Teresa reminds her readers that God owes us nothing for our faithfulness, and that in assuming we deserve rewards, we actually reveal our lack of humility.

Chapter One (3.1)

1. To those who have overcome these battles, by God's mercy, and with perseverance have entered the third dwelling places, what can we say, except "Happy are those who fear the LORD"?[53] Because I'm not educated in Latin and the Scriptures, it's no small thing that His Majesty enabled me to understand the meaning of this verse. We are right in calling such persons blessed, or happy, because unless they turn back, they are on the path to salvation (as far as we can tell). Sisters, here you see how important it is to have experienced *overcoming* past battles. I'm convinced that the Lord always gives a person who has overcome inner strife a certain security, a peace of conscience, which is no small blessing. I say "security," but that's probably the wrong word because nothing is completely "secure" in this life. Whenever I say it, please know I mean and imply "unless they stray from the path they've begun."

THE PRECARIOUS NATURE OF OUR FAITHFULNESS AND VIRTUE, DRAWN FROM TERESA'S PERSONAL EXPERIENCE

2. Life is truly terrible when we live like those with enemies at the gate, not able to put aside our weapons while sleeping or eating, always afraid of being surprised by a sneaky intruder. Oh, my Lord and my Good! How can you possibly want us to find such a life desirable? If not for our hope that we might lose our life for Your sake, or spend it completely in Your service (and finally realize Your will for us), it would be impossible to keep from begging You to end our time on earth. If it is Your will, then may we die with You, as Saint Thomas said.[54] Because without You, life is nothing but death many times over, and constant fear that You might be lost to us forever. So, daughters, I think the happiness we should pray for is the complete security of the blessed. Given these fears, what else can we hope for than that our deepest happiness comes from pleasing God? Remember, though, that this kind of happiness could be seen in some of the saints, and yet they fell into serious sins. We can't be sure that God will give us His hand to help us turn back again.

---

53. Psalm 112:1: "Praise the LORD! Happy are those who fear the LORD, who greatly delight in his commandments."
54. John 11:16: "Thomas, who was called the Twin, said to his fellow disciples, 'Let us also go, that we may die with him.'"

3. Truly, daughters, this topic of lapsed faithfulness fills me with fear even as I write.[55] Whenever I think of it, which I do often, I hardly know what to write, or honestly how to go on living. Earnestly pray that God might always live within me, my daughters, because what other security can there be in a life like mine, so misspent? Don't be depressed to realize that I wasted so much of my life; I've seen your sadness when I've talked about it. You want to think that I have always been holy, and, frankly, I'd *like* to say the same thing. But what can I do? The truth is, I lost so much through my own fault. I won't complain or cast blame, saying God stopped giving me all the help I needed to be as holy as you wish I had been. I can't say this without crying, realizing that I'm writing for those who are capable of teaching *me*! Writing this text as an act of obedience is difficult work in more ways than one.[56] May God grant that you benefit at least some from this work, since it's being done for His sake.

Please ask Him to pardon me, a pathetic and foolish woman. But God knows well that I rely on His mercy. Since I can't help having been what I have been, there's nothing to do but approach God and trust in the saving work of His Son, and in the prayers and goodness of the Virgin, His mother. (We all wear her habit, unworthily.) Praise God, daughters, that you are really the daughters of Mary, our Lady—not me. When you have a Mother as good as she, there's no reason for you to be scandalized by my mistakes and unworthiness. Imitate our Lady. Consider her greatness and the goodness of having *her* as our Patroness. Even my sins—my being what I am—haven't tarnished our sacred order.

4. But I must warn you: even though you're in this order and have such a Mother, don't be too sure of yourselves. After all, David was a very holy man, but you know what kind of man Solomon became.[57] Don't put too much stock in the fact that you are cloistered [cut off from the temptations and distractions of general society] and live very simply. You shouldn't be overly confident just because you're always talking about God, engaging in prayer, and separating yourselves from the things of this world and (as much as one can) seeing them as worthless. All that is good, but it's not

55. Again, this is a tender and personal topic for Teresa because she herself abandoned prayer for a long time as a nun, even after she had known great zeal for God and experienced many gifts from God in prayer.
56. Literally: "Rigorous obedience [it] has been." She seems contextually to be referring to the layered difficulties of writing for nuns whom she knows might be more steadfast and purehearted than she herself was over the years when she neglected prayer.
57. Seemingly a reference to Solomon's turning away from God.

enough to justify a complete lack of fear, a settled self-satisfaction. Keep this verse in mind, repeating it often: "Happy are those who fear the LORD."

5. I forget what I was saying—I indulged in a long digression. When I look at myself, my life, I feel like a bird with a broken wing who cannot possibly fly well enough to offer you something good. So, I'll leave this topic for now, returning to what I started to explain about souls that have entered the third dwelling places.

COMPARISONS TO THE GOSPEL STORY ABOUT THE RICH YOUNG MAN

By enabling these souls to overcome their initial challenges, the Lord has given no small mercy but a very great one. Through God's goodness, I believe there are many such souls in the world, people earnestly desiring not to offend God. They avoid committing even small, unconscious sins; love to give of themselves generously and sacrificially, and to make up for it when they do wrong; spend hours in prayer and meditation; use their time well; practice works of charity toward their neighbors; and act very thoughtfully and intentionally in their speech and dress and in the management of their households, if they have one. This is certainly a desirable state. There seems no reason why they should be denied access to the final dwelling places. And the Lord will not deny this movement, if they *truly* desire it—such a desire is excellent preparation for the granting of every kind of favor.

6. Oh, Jesus! How could anyone ever say they have no desire for such a wonderful thing? Especially when they've gotten through the troubled stages leading up to this? Surely, no one could, or would. We all *say* we want to live fully with and in God—but if the Lord is to take complete possession of the soul, more is necessary. Words are not enough, just as they were not enough for the young man at the moment when Jesus told him what he needed to *do* if he wanted to be perfect.[58] Ever since I started

58. Matthew 19:16–22: "Then someone came to him and said, 'Teacher, what good deed must I do to have eternal life?' And he said to him, 'Why do you ask me about what is good? There is one who is good. If you wish to enter into life, keep the commandments.' He said to him, 'Which ones?' And Jesus said, 'You shall not murder. You shall not commit adultery. You shall not steal. You shall not bear false witness. Honor your father and mother. Also, you shall love your neighbor as yourself.' The young man said to him, 'I have kept all these; what do I still lack?' Jesus said to him, 'If you wish to be perfect, go, sell your possessions, and give the money to the poor, and you will have treasure in heaven; then come, follow me.' When the young man heard this word, he went away grieving, for he had many possessions."

to talk about these third dwellings, I've had that young man in mind, for we are exactly like him. Generally speaking, this is the source of our long seasons of dryness in prayer (though there are other causes, too). I'm not talking at all here about interior trials, which disturb many good souls to an intolerable level, and through no fault of their own, nor am I referring to those who suffer from depression and other illnesses. The Lord always provides a rescue, to their profit. In these cases, and all others, we must let God be the judge.

I've been referring to what *usually* happens. Souls in the third dwelling places know that nothing would persuade them to seriously defy God in sin—many of them would not even commit small sins intentionally or knowingly—and they make good use of their lives and their possessions. But then they can't be patient when the door [to the inner rooms of the castle] is closed to them and they can't move to the King's presence. They consider themselves to be God's dedicated servants, and, in fact, they are. But even an earthly king might have many devoted servants, and not all of them get to enter into his personal room. Enter within yourselves, daughters, as far as you are able. Stop circling around your petty good works. These—and more!—are your basic duties as a Christian. It's enough to serve God; don't try to get so much that you achieve nothing. Look at the saints who have entered the King's chamber, and you'll see the difference between us and them. Don't ask for rewards you don't deserve. For we all grieve God in some way. However faithfully we serve Him, we shouldn't think we *deserve* anything.

ABOUT SPIRITUAL DRYNESS AND THE NEED FOR HUMILITY

7. Oh, humility, humility! I don't know why I'm tempted to judge in this way, but whenever I hear people making a big deal about their times of spiritual dryness, I can't help thinking that they're lacking in this virtue. Again, I'm not referring to the great interior trials I mentioned earlier, because of course this kind of "dryness" is about much more than a lack of devotion. Let us prove ourselves, sisters, or allow the Lord to prove us. He knows how to test [our depths of faith], although we often refuse to understand Him.

Let's return to these carefully ordered souls and think about what they actually do for God, because then we see how wrong they are to complain. If God tells us what we must do in order to be perfect, and we then turn our backs on Him and go away sadly, like the young man in the gospel story, what do you expect His Majesty to do? The reward that He will give us must be somewhat proportionate to the love we demonstrate. And this love, daughters, can't be just in our imaginations. It must be proved by actions. Yet at the same time, don't think God has any *need* of our works; what He needs is our resolute and determined will.

8. To us nuns, it might seem like we have already done everything: we've taken on the religious habit by our own will and left everything we had, all the things of the world, for His sake (even if we left behind relatively little, like Saint Peter, who left only his nets behind). To those who give everything they have, it seems like a lot...and that, already, all the sacrifice is done. This is indeed a great *start*. If we continue on with perseverance—if we do not go back, even in our heart's desires, to keep company with the distractions and deceptive worldly attractions of the first rooms, and persist continually in this detachment and abandonment of everything—we shall achieve our goal.

But I'm warning you, this can only happen when we see ourselves as servants to whom nothing is owed (as we hear from either Saint Paul or Christ[59]) and realize that our Lord is in no way *obligated* to give us such gifts. On the contrary, the more we've been given by God, the more deeply we are indebted to Him. What can we do for such a generous God—who died for us, created us, gives us being—without considering ourselves simply fortunate to be able to repay *something* of what we owe Him for the way He has served us? I write this word ["served"] reluctantly, but it's true. All the time He lived in the world, He did nothing but serve. So, can we serve without asking for *more* gifts and favors?

9. Daughters, think carefully about these things I've said, even if it's been in a rather mixed-up way. I can't explain them better, but as you ponder them, the Lord will give you clarity, so that these times of spiritual dryness might lead you toward humility, and not restlessness (which is what the adversary wants). You can be assured that when true humility

59. Probably a reference to Luke 17:10: "So you also, when you have done all that you were ordered to do, say, 'We are worthless slaves; we have done only what we ought to have done!'"

is present, even if God never gives gifts in prayer, He *will* give peace, and resignation to His will. With this peace, a soul may be more content than others are with such gifts. Often, as you've read, it's to the *weakest* that His Divine Majesty gives extra gifts in prayer. I don't think we would ever trade these gifts for all the natural strength given to those who continue to make progress without them, journeying through spiritual dryness: we are more fond of spiritual sweetness than crosses. O Lord, you know the truth. Test us, that we may know ourselves.

Overview of Chapter Two

In continuity with the challenge to the rich young ruler she referred to in chapter one, Teresa describes the kinds of tests of trust and detachment for those living well-ordered lives that often come at this point in the journey. She describes how easily we can deceive ourselves into thinking that we have fully abandoned our will to God, and how changes in circumstance or threats to our "good" reputation can test the true locus of our faith. From here, she moves to a different sort of problem for those in the third dwellings, talking about the downsides of excessive carefulness and caution. In addition to being risk-averse and lacking boldness, souls here can develop a stilted self-obsession with being perfectly good, which detracts from their humility and makes their lives generally miserable. Teresa wants us to avoid (or escape) this "safe-goodness" trap. Then she returns to the theme of spiritual favors in these dwelling places and beyond, noting that while there are many rewards and much goodness to be found here, they're probably not of the sort that will be described later.

Pointedly, she reminds the reader that no one should begrudge others receiving divine gifts that they themselves don't happen to receive—another echo of the humility theme. Acknowledging, nevertheless, that those in the third dwellings are indeed strong Christians with the potential to "fly" even higher, she points to the value of spiritual direction from experienced mentors in the faith. From them, we are inspired to keep walking and not feel so bogged down by the complexities of faithfulness. Finally, she issues a stern reminder about avoiding temptation and judgment, telling the "good Christian" in these spaces not to get too smug about their moral or spiritual strength, which they can easily overestimate to their own detriment and that of others. Addressing a different sort of temptation, she notes that these folks are often the most tempted to judge others and over-function as helpers and teachers, and she urges refraining from both forms of meddling where we ought not.

Chapter Two (3.2)

TESTS OF TRUST AND DETACHMENT FOR THOSE LIVING WELL-ORDERED LIVES

1. I've known a few souls—I think I'd even say a lot of souls—like this: they've reached the third dwellings, and as far as anyone can tell, they've lived an upright and carefully ordered life both in soul and body for many years. Then, just when it seems like they must have achieved mastery over the world (or at least must be completely detached from it), His Majesty sends them tests that are not particularly rigorous...and they get so worked up and depressed in spirit that they drive me crazy! It even makes me afraid for them. And it's no use offering them advice, for they've been practicing "doing good and being good" for so long that they think they're capable of teaching others—and, honestly, they have good reason for feeling this way.

2. I've never found any way of comforting such people. All I can do is express sadness for their troubles, which I really do feel when I see them so distressed, so miserable. It's useless to argue with them. They brood about their woes and decide that they're suffering for God's sake, and so they never really understand that the depth of their disturbance is their *own* imperfection. In people who have made so much progress, this is another mistake. Their suffering itself is not really a surprise, but I think this kind of suffering should pass quickly.

It is often God's will that His chosen ones should be aware of their pitiful limitations, and so He withdraws His help from us a bit. (Nothing more is needed to make us recognize our limitations very quickly.) At this point, we realize that this is a way of testing us, because we see our own shortcomings more clearly. Sometimes the *realization* that we're grieving the loss of insignificant earthly things is even more painful than the "issue" that's causing grief. This kind of process is a great mercy from God; in seeing our faults, we can grow in humility.

3. With the other people I've been talking about, it's different: they see their conduct and feelings as saintly, and they want other people to think so, too. I'll give you some examples so that we might learn to understand and test *ourselves* before God tests us. It's extremely helpful to be prepared in this way and to know ourselves and our limits deeply beforehand.

4. A childless rich man, with no one to leave his money to, loses part of his wealth, but not so much that he doesn't have enough for himself and his household. He still has enough money, and some to spare. If he starts to get worked up and anxious, as if he didn't have a crust of bread left to eat, how can our Lord ask him to leave everything for His sake? *Maybe* he's suffering because he wants to give the money to the poor. But I think God would rather have us be resigned to what He does—and keep our peace of mind and heart—than [desire to] perform an out-of-reach act of charity. If this man can't resign himself to his new situation because the Lord has not led him that far on the journey, that's fine; but he should *realize* that he lacks this freedom of spirit. Then he can pray for it and prepare himself to receive it from the Lord.

Another person with enough means to support himself—and actually an excess of resources—sees an opportunity to acquire more property. Let him take the opportunity, certainly, if it comes to him. But if he strives for wealth, and then, after getting it, strives for more and more, he doesn't need to fear ever rising to the dwelling places that are nearest to the King. It doesn't matter how good his intentions may be (and they must be good, because, as I've said, these are all virtuous, prayerful people).

5. It's the same thing for people who are in the third dwelling places who suffer some disrespect or loss of reputation. God often grants them grace to bear it well [publicly], because He loves to help people be virtuous in front of others. Perhaps this is so that the virtues they *do* possess won't be diminished in the minds of others, or perhaps God gives them this help because they have served Him (our Beloved is good indeed). But then they become agitated and worked up inside; they can't quickly shake or subdue these feelings, even though they'd like to. God help me! Aren't these the same people who have meditated for a long time now on how the Lord suffered, and on what a good thing it is to suffer, and who even *wanted* to suffer? And yet they'd like their life to be untroubled, surrounded by people living as well-ordered lives as they do. We can only hope that they won't start to imagine that their ongoing distress is someone else's fault and begin to see these troubles as praiseworthy.

6. You might think, sisters, that I'm wandering from the point of this writing, and am no longer speaking to you—that these things have

nothing to do with us. We don't have any wealth, we don't want it or strive after it, and nobody disrespects us. It's true that these examples are not *exactly* applicable to our monastic life, but we can deduce other examples from them that *would* apply. It's unnecessary and would be inappropriate for me to explicitly describe them. From such situations, you find out if you are really detached from the worldly things you've left behind. Small challenges and troubles do come up that give you the opportunity to test yourself and discover if you have mastery over your passions. Trust me, what matters most is not whether or not we wear a religious habit; it's whether we strive to practice the virtues of our faith, surrender our will to God in all things, and bring our lives into alignment with what God wants for them. In all things, we need to desire that not our will, but His, be done.[60] If we honestly haven't made it this far, then—humility! as I've said. Humility is healing ointment for our wounds. If we are truly humble, then (even if there is a delay) God, the physician, will eventually come to heal us.

THE DOWNSIDES OF EXCESSIVE CAREFULNESS AND CAUTION

7. The sacrifices of service[61] done by these persons [in the third dwelling places] are as carefully balanced as their lives. They strongly want to be generous so that, through their generosity, they might serve our Lord. There's nothing wrong with that. Yet they are so *careful* about their acts of generosity and service, not wanting to put themselves out too much. You never need to fear that they will kill themselves, because they are very reasonable folks! The strength of their love has not yet overwhelmed their reason. I wish *our* reason would make us dissatisfied with this way of serving God, step-by-step and at a snail's pace! We'll never get to the end of the road that way: we're walking along, getting fatigued all the time—because it is an exhausting road—and then we're just lucky if we don't get lost. Daughters, if we could get from one country to another in a week, do you think it would be a good idea to take *a year* to make the journey, through winds and snow and floods and bad roads? Wouldn't it be better to get the journey over and done with? For

60. Luke 22:42: "Father, if you are willing, remove this cup from me, yet not my will but yours be done."
61. Literally: "penances."

all of these obstacles are indeed present, plus dangers of misperception and deception.[62] Oh, I could tell you so much about this! I pray to God that I've moved beyond this stage, though often enough it seems to me that I haven't.

8. When we move with so much caution, we find stumbling blocks everywhere. We're afraid of everything and don't dare to go further. It's as if we think we can arrive at these dwelling places by letting others tread the path for us, but this is impossible. For the love of our Lord, we must make a real effort to move ahead, leaving our reason and our fears in His hands. Let us forget our natural [bodily] weakness, which causes us so much anxiety. Let our superiors oversee and concern themselves with the care of our bodies; *our* task is only to journey at a good pace so that we may see the Lord. Although we have few or no comforts here, we make a big mistake if we worry too much about our health, especially because our worry doesn't help anything. I know that our progress has nothing to do with the body; it's the thing that matters least. The journey I'm referring to demands great *humility* most of all; it's the lack of humility that prevents progress. We should think of ourselves as having advanced only a few steps, and see our sisters as more advanced (and progressing more quickly) than we are. Furthermore, we should truly want our sisters to consider us to be the most pathetic spiritual cases.

9. If we do this [strive to move ahead with humility and determination], this state [of the third dwellings] is a most excellent one. If we lack humility and are too mindful of our own progress, we might spend our whole lives in it and suffer in a thousand ways. If we don't fully abandon our self-interests, these dwelling places are very difficult and oppressive: like walking while weighed down with the mud of our human misery. Those who reach the later dwelling places are relieved from this load.

SPIRITUAL FAVORS IN THESE DWELLING PLACES AND BEYOND

In the third dwelling places, the Lord rewards us justly—even generously. He *always* gives us more than we deserve, giving a deeper joy much more satisfying than we can get from the pleasures and distractions of life. But I don't think that He gives many spiritual delights [in these rooms],

62. Literally: "snakes."

except when He occasionally gives us a glimpse of what happens in the remaining dwelling places, so that we might prepare ourselves to enter them.

10. You might think that spiritual delights and consolations are the same thing and be wondering, "Why is she using two different terms?" To me, it seems that these gifts are very different, though I might be wrong. I'll tell you more of what I think about this in the fourth dwellings (the dwellings directly following these), because I'll need to talk more about the spiritual delights God gives there. The distinction might seem unhelpful at first, but it may actually be of some use. Once you understand the nature of each one, you can strive for what is best. Learning about the spiritual favors ahead is a relief and comfort to many of those God has brought this far. If they are humble, they will be moved to give thanks [for the existence of such gifts]. If they think they already have everything, they will feel shame and confusion. Because if they don't experience these things, they feel discouraged. This is quite unnecessary, though, because perfection doesn't come through spiritual delights but through the increase of love. Our growth in love, combined with our actions of justice and truth, is what determines our reward.

11. If this is true—and it is!—you might wonder why I am discussing these interior favors and explaining them. I don't really know—you should ask the person who commanded me to write. I'm doing this under obedience to my superiors, and it wouldn't be right for me to argue with them. What I *can* honestly say is this: back when I had had none of these favors, and didn't know anything about them by my own experience, I actually never *expected* to know anything of them, personally, in my lifetime. This was an appropriate expectation, though don't get me wrong—it would have been the greatest joy for me to know, or even have hints, that I was in any way pleasing to God. Still, [at that time], when I read in books *about* these favors and consolations that the Lord gives to souls serving Him, it would give me the greatest pleasure and lead me to offer fervent praises to God. Now, if someone as terribly flawed[63] as I am did that, surely those who are good and humble will praise Him even more. Even if it only brings a single person to praise God once, I think it will have been worth it to talk about these things. It's also good to realize what happiness and delight we

63. Literally: "so worthless."

lose through our own fault. This is especially important because, if these spiritual gifts come from God, they come to us carrying love and strength for the journey, which helps us progress more easily and grow in good works and virtues. So, don't think that it doesn't matter whether or not we do what *we can* to have such experiences! But if it's not your fault, [and you still don't have them,] know that the Lord is fair: what His Majesty denies you in this way, He will give you in other ways. Because of His deep and hidden knowledge, what He does [or does not do] will be the thing most suitable and best for us, without a doubt.

THE VALUE OF SPIRITUAL DIRECTION FROM EXPERIENCED MENTORS IN FAITH

12. What I think is most helpful to those who are in this state, by God's goodness, is that they seriously seek to practice obedience. (It's no small mercy to be here, on the brink of rising higher.) Even if they are not in a religious order, it would be extremely beneficial for them to have someone they can go to for advice and direction. This can prevent them from following their own will [rather than God's], which is how we usually harm ourselves. They shouldn't look for someone with the same overly cautious approach to the spiritual journey—they should pick a person completely lacking in illusions about the things of the world. In learning to know ourselves, it's very helpful to have a conversation partner who sees the world [and human nature] for what it is.

It's also very encouraging to see that things that we thought were impossible *are* possible for others, and even come easily. It makes us feel that we might eventually fly ourselves, like they do. Like young birds, we may not be ready for great flights, but we can gradually learn by imitating our "parents." This is a huge benefit, I know.

AVOIDING TEMPTATION AND JUDGMENT

No matter how much those [in the third dwelling places] are determined not to offend the Lord, it's better if they don't put themselves in circumstances that give them the opportunity to offend. They are so close to the first dwelling places that they can easily return to them; their moral strength is not built on solid ground, like the steadfastness of souls who are practiced in suffering. Such tried-by-fire people are familiar with the storms of the world, and realize that one doesn't need to fear them. They aren't allured by worldly satisfactions. If those I'm talking about in the third dwelling places had to suffer great trials and persecutions, they *might* return to worldly sources of satisfaction (and the adversary knows how to stir up these provocations to do us harm.) People [in the third dwellings] might be pressing ahead spiritually with great enthusiasm, and even trying to help others not to sin...yet they might be unable to resist temptation when it comes their way.

13. Let's look at our own faults and leave other people's faults alone. Those who live such carefully ordered lives are apt to be shocked by everything. Yet we might actually learn very important lessons from the people who shock us. Maybe our self-control and behavior is better than theirs; this is good, but it's not the most important thing. There's no reason we should want everyone to travel by the same road we do.

Similarly, we shouldn't set out to teach the spiritual path to someone who perhaps doesn't know what such a thing is. Even in our God-given desires to help others, sisters, we can make many mistakes. It's better to try to do what our Rule tells us: to strive to live always in silence and in hope. The Lord will take care of His own. If we don't neglect to ask God to enable us to do this, we *will* be able to do much good, with His help. May He be blessed forever.

Questions for Reflection

1. The story of Jesus and the rich young ruler is a key comparison for Teresa in illuminating the "state" of those in the third dwelling places. How do you relate to this story or see yourself in it, either from present or past experiences? What do you feel Christ has asked you to abandon for the kingdom of God? When have you boldly accepted the risks, and when have you "walked away, sadly"?

2. Teresa has many examples of potential stumbling blocks and spiritual sticky points for those (genuinely) "good Christians" leading "well-ordered lives." Where and how do you see these dynamics playing out today, whether for yourself or for those in your church, family, or community?

3. Who are the mentors and guides in your life who have been essential to your progressing on the spiritual journey? What do think Teresa means by a person who is "lacking in illusions about the things of the world"?

4. In 3.2.13, Teresa writes, "Those who live such carefully ordered lives are apt to be shocked by everything. Yet we might actually learn very important lessons from the people who shock us." When or how have you learned important lessons from people who (initially) "shocked" you?

FOURTH DWELLINGS

Overview of Chapter One

As she begins her general introduction to the fourth dwellings, Teresa asks for the help of the Holy Spirit anew because "supernatural experiences begin here, and this is extremely difficult to explain." In her attempt to explain, however, she begins by teaching about the difference between consolations and spiritual delights: in short, one starts in us and ends in God, while the other starts in God and ends in us. Another way of determining the difference, she writes, is that in and through spiritual delights, we experience our heart somehow being "enlarged" by God.

Acknowledging that the fourth dwelling places represent a state where the natural and supernatural comingle, she then addresses the continuing challenge of wandering thoughts for those seeking peace and progress in a life of prayer. Offering one frame of understanding that might help us avoid getting too fixated on, or frustrated with, our wandering thoughts, she essentially tells us to think of our thoughts as somewhat independent of our intellect and will, which will allow us to be more "patient in this regard." A determination to love and serve God is much more important than a perfectly trained or focused mind in prayer, she assures us.

Chapter One (4.1)

GENERAL INTRODUCTION TO THE FOURTH DWELLINGS

1. Before I start talking about the fourth dwellings, I must once again commend myself to the Holy Spirit. I beg the Holy Spirit from now on to speak for me so you might understand what I'm going to say about the dwelling places not yet addressed. For supernatural experiences begin here, and this is extremely difficult to explain unless His Majesty takes it in hand (like He did when I described my knowledge of the subject, up to

that point, about fourteen years ago).[64] Although I think I now *understand* these favors that the Lord gives to some souls better than I did then,[65] knowing how to explain them is a different matter. May His Majesty work in and through these explanations if there might be some benefit to them; otherwise not.

2. These dwelling places are getting close to the place where the King dwells. As a result, they are tremendously beautiful and contain such exquisite treasures that the intellect simply cannot describe them accurately. Those without any experience of them might find the descriptions obscure. Still, if something is well put, they might gain some understanding, and those with personal experience—especially a lot of it—will likely understand the descriptions very well.

It does seem that a person must have lived in the other dwelling places for a long time in order to reach these spaces. As a rule, you need to have been in the third dwellings, but there is no *infallible* rule: as you've probably heard before, the Lord gives when He wills and as He wills and to whom He wills. Because the gifts are His own to give, there's no injustice to anyone in this.

3. Poisonous creatures rarely enter these dwelling places. If they do, they're quite harmless, or can even do the soul good. For, in this state of prayer, it's better for them to come in and challenge the soul [with some distractions]; if we have no temptations, the adversary might mislead us with regard to the spiritual delights God gives. This can open up doors to greater harm than comes through basic temptations. The soul would also be hampered, because it would lose all opportunities for demonstrating and strengthening integrity, living in a state of permanent blissful absorption. When someone is continually in a state like this, I don't consider them to be spiritually "safe" at all. I actually don't think it's possible for the Spirit of the Lord to remain in a soul continuously, like this, during our life of exile.

THE DIFFERENCE BETWEEN CONSOLATIONS AND SPIRITUAL DELIGHTS

4. Getting back to what I was saying I would describe here: the difference between consolations and spiritual delights. It seems to me that

64. A reference to *Life*, chapters 11–27.
65. Literally: "I have now a little more light upon these favors."

we can describe "consolations" as those experiences we get from our meditations and petitions to the Lord that come from and through our own nature. Of course, God plays a part in this process (we must always keep in mind that we can do nothing apart from Him), but consolations arise from our actual virtuous efforts and actions. It seems we have earned the consolations by our work, and we are right to feel such satisfaction through virtuous effort. But when you think about it, the same feelings of joyful consolation and satisfaction can come through many experiences on earth: when we suddenly receive a valuable inheritance; when we suddenly come across someone we love dearly; when we bring an important piece of work to a successful conclusion, and those around us are pleased with our work and speak well of us; when we have been told someone we love is dead, and they come back to us, actually alive. I have seen people cry with joy over such great consolations; in fact, I've even done so myself at times.

It seems to me that the feelings of consolation that come to us from divine things are as purely natural as these examples, but their source is more noble. (These worldly joys aren't bad, though.) To summarize: consolations begin in our own nature and end in God; spiritual delights begin in God, but our human nature feels and enjoys them as much as it does consolations, and indeed much more. Oh, Jesus! I wish I could be clear about this! I can see a very marked difference between these two things, but I'm not clever enough to describe it very well; may the Lord explain it for me.

5. I've just remembered a Scripture verse that we say at the end of the last psalm at Prime.[66] The closing words are: *cum dilatasti cor meum* ("when You enlarged my heart").[67] For those with a lot of experience, this [line] is sufficient for explaining the difference between the two. To those who have not, more explanation is needed. Consolations do not enlarge the heart; in fact, they seem to oppress it somewhat. The soul experiences joy when it realizes what it is doing for God's sake, but then come a few bitter tears that seem in some way to be the result of passion. I don't know much about these passions

---

66. This is the office—or daily time—of community prayer typically said at 6:00 a.m.
67. Teresa only includes the Latin; I added the translation when modernizing the text. She's referring to Psalm 119:32: "I will run the way of thy commandments, when thou shalt enlarge my heart" (KJV).

of the soul. If I knew more, maybe I could make it clear, explaining what comes from sensuality and our human nature. But I am very uneducated; I could explain this only if I could analyze and understand my own experience of it. Knowledge and education are very helpful in all things.

6. My own experience of this state—these gifts and consolations in meditation—was like this: if I began to weep over the passion, I couldn't stop until I had a splitting headache. When I wept over my sins, the same thing. This was a great gift given by our Lord. I won't pause here to examine which of these two [kinds of tears] is better. What I want to be able to describe is the difference between them. In the state I'm describing, tears and longings sometimes arise, in part, from our own nature and disposition; still, as I've said, they eventually *lead* us to God. And this is an experience to be treasured...as long as we also stay humble, understanding that these feelings don't make us any more virtuous. For it's impossible to be certain that these feelings are the effects of love. When they are, it is God's gift.

For the most part, souls in the dwellings already described [the first, second, and third] have these consolations that arise in and through spiritual devotion. These souls work continually with their intellect and reason in their meditations. This is appropriate, because nothing more has been given to them. It would be good for them, though, to spend a little time in other practices: praising God, rejoicing in His goodness and that He is who He is, and desiring that God receive honor and glory. They should do this as much as they can, because it awakens the will greatly. When the Lord gives them such feelings or acts of praise, they would be well-advised not to put them aside to finish their usual meditations.

7. Because I've written at length about this topic elsewhere,[68] I won't repeat myself here. I just want you to be well aware that to progress a long way on this road, and to rise to the dwelling places you'd like to find yourself in, the important thing is not to think much but to love much. Do whatever most stirs and awakens you to love. Yet maybe we don't know what love is. Learning this wouldn't surprise me, because love is not found in the greatest pleasure or happiness but in the greatest determination to please God in

68. *Life*, chapter 12; *The Way of Perfection*, chapters 16–20.

everything, and to try in every way possible not to offend Him, and to pray that He advances the honor and glory of His Son and the Church. These are the signs of love; don't imagine that the most important thing is to never think of anything else (and that if your mind gets slightly distracted, all is lost!).

THE CONTINUING CHALLENGE OF WANDERING THOUGHTS

8. Sometimes, I've been terribly oppressed by this turmoil of thoughts. Just over four years ago, I came to understand through experience that our *thoughts* (or, to clarify, our imaginations) are not the same thing as the *intellect*.[69] I asked an educated man about this, and he said I was right, which gave me no small satisfaction. Since the intellect is one of the faculties of the soul, I couldn't see why it was sometimes so timid and restless.[70] Thoughts generally fly so fast that only God can restrain them, by giving us the sense, somehow, of being freed from the body. It seems to me that I have seen how the faculties of the soul [the intellect] can be occupied with God and recollected in Him, while, on the other hand, our thoughts remain rowdy. This drove me crazy.

9. O Lord, take into account how much we must suffer on this road [of prayer] due to our ignorance! The worst part is that, because we don't think there is anything to know except "we must think about You," we can't ask those who know more. We often don't even have any idea of what we might ask them. So, we suffer terribly because we don't understand ourselves; we worry over what we think is very wrong—when it is not bad at all, but actually good. This is where many of the hardships and complaints of "interior trials" come from for people who practice prayer, especially if they are uneducated. This can lead them to hopelessness, declining health, and even abandonment of prayer altogether; they fail to realize that there is an interior world right there, inside them.

Just as we can't stop the motion of the heavens, moving and spinning with such speed, we cannot restrain our thoughts. When we try

69. The Spanish word *pensamiento* I have rendered as "thoughts," while *entendimiento* is the word Teresa uses that is translated as "intellect."

70. The Spanish phrase here, *tan tortolito*, is colorful: "so like a little turtledove." In other words, as Peers puts it, "not only timid, but irresolute and apparently stupid, like an inexperienced fledgling."

to, sending all the faculties after the soul in pursuit, thinking we are lost, we misuse the time we are spending in the presence of God. The soul might be wholly united with Him in the dwellings very near His presence, while our thoughts remain in the outskirts of the castle, suffering the attacks of a thousand wild and poisonous creatures, growing in virtue through this suffering. So, this must not upset us, and we must not give up the struggle, as the adversary intends. For the most part, these anxieties and struggles come from the fact that we don't understand ourselves.

10. As I write, the noises in my head are so loud that I'm beginning to wonder what's going on. As I said when I began, they've been making it almost impossible to obey the command to write. My head sounds like it's full of rivers, and then like all the water in those rivers suddenly came rushing down. On top of this, a flock of little birds seems to be whistling—not in my ears, but in the upper part of my head. (This is where they say the higher part of the soul is. I have held this view for a long time, since the spirit seems to move upward with great speed and power. Please, God, may I remember to explain the cause of this when I write about the later dwelling places, because it doesn't fit in well here.)

I shouldn't be surprised that the Lord wants to send me this trouble in my head so that I understand it better. Nevertheless, all of this physical turmoil doesn't hinder or damage my prayers or what I'm saying now; rather, my soul is whole and unaffected in its tranquility, love, desires, and clear knowledge.

11. But if the higher part of the soul is in the upper part of the head, how can it not be disturbed? I don't know, but I do know that what I'm saying is true. I suffer when my faculties are not suspended while I pray. (When the faculties are suspended, I feel no pain until the suspension is over.) But it would be terrible if this obstacle forced me to give up praying entirely. It's not good for us to be disturbed by our thoughts or to worry about them. If the adversary is responsible for them, and yet we aren't anxious or overly preoccupied with them, they will stop. If they come—as they do—from the basic human weaknesses we inherit from the sin of Adam, let's simply have patience and bear all these limitations for the love of God.

After all, we are also subject to the need to eat and sleep, and we can't escape it; this is a big burden.[71]

12. Let's recognize our frustrating limitations and desire to go where "no one will taunt us." Sometimes I recall hearing these words the bride says in the Canticles.[72] I really believe there's no place in our lives where these words apply more, because I don't think that all the scorn and trials we may have to suffer in life are as bad as these interior battles. Any unrest and war can be endured, as I've said, if we find peace where we live. We want to have a break from the thousand trials that afflict us in the world, and the Lord *wants* to prepare such a rest for us; the fact that the obstacle to such tranquility lies *within* ourselves cannot help but be very painful—almost unbearable. Because of this, Lord, take us where these weaknesses will not taunt us, because they sometimes seem to be making fun of the soul. Even in this life, the Lord will free the soul from these miseries when it reaches the last dwelling place, as we'll explain (God willing).

13. These weaknesses won't give everyone as much trouble and misery—or seem to attack as violently—as they did me for many years. Because I was *so* terrible and pathetic,[73] it seems like I wanted to take revenge on myself. Since it's been troublesome for me, it might be for you, too. So I'm just going to talk about it here and there, hoping that I might make you realize how unavoidable it is, and prevent you from growing restless or distressed. We must let the clacking old mill [of our thoughts] keep on going around while we grind our flour, not stopping our work with the will or intellect.

14. This trouble will sometimes be worse, and sometimes better, depending on our health and age. The poor soul might not be to blame

71. This is a sentiment that is often very surprising to the modern reader. Peers translates Teresa here as saying, "they are a great burden to us," while Kavanaugh and Rodriguez say, "is quite a trial." Either way, they agree that Teresa is speaking of the unpleasant work of caring for our bodies, which consumes time and energy we might otherwise devote to loving God and others more "completely."

72. Song of Solomon 8:1: "O that you were like a brother to me, who nursed at my mother's breast! If I met you outside, I would kiss you, and no one would despise me."

73. The Spanish word here for pathetic is *ruin*, which can be translated in so many different ways, such as "wicked," "wretched," "dastardly," "mean," and "vile." Since none of these words is frequently in use in how we describe ourselves, even at our worst, I tried to capture Teresa's sense of failure and disappointment with herself.

for this, but it will still suffer. We have other faults, so it's right for us to be patient in this regard. We are so dense that even reading and receiving advice (to not be overly concerned with these thoughts) is not enough to really teach us. So, it doesn't seem to me a waste of time to go into it a bit more, consoling you. Ultimately, though, this is of little help until the Lord wants to enlighten us. But it is necessary—and His Majesty wants us—to *try* to understand ourselves, and then not blame our souls for the work of our weak imagination, our nature, and the adversary.

Overview of Chapter Two

In this chapter, Teresa returns to teaching about the favors, gifts, or graces we might begin to experience in prayer in the fourth dwellings. To help us recognize and understand both consolations and spiritual delights, she employs water images. With consolations, it is as if we are working hard to draw the blessing of water to ourselves; with spiritual delights, it's as if the blessing of water rises up from within us, without straining or striving on our part. After trying to illuminate this distinction, Teresa offers further explanation of spiritual delights, or the prayer of quiet. In this description, she again employs the concepts of dilation or expansion, but she adds the image of the soul receiving blessings it can't really understand, with the effects often extending to the body. Knowing that her sisters (and other readers) might be eager to grasp for these holy gifts, Teresa closes the chapter by giving many reasons that one should *not* strive for them. Paradoxically, the genuine humility of not striving for them or not expecting them is perhaps the best preparation to receive such gifts.

Chapter Two (4.2)

1. God help me in this work that I've started on. I'd forgotten what I was writing about, because administrative work and health challenges forced me to postpone any progress until a better time. Since I have a poor memory, it may be confusing as I start again, for I can't read it over again. Maybe everything I say is confusing...at least that's what I'm afraid of!

UNDERSTANDING CONSOLATIONS AND SPIRITUAL DELIGHTS WITH THE HELP OF WATER IMAGES

I think I was talking about spiritual consolations and how they are sometimes intertwined with our passions, or deep emotions. They often cause intense sobbing; I've actually heard that, for some people, they lead to a constricted chest and uncontrollable flailing, the force of it all enough to produce a nosebleed or other disconcerting symptoms. I can't say anything about this because I haven't experienced it. But there must be some comfort in these kinds of consolations, because they still lead to a desire to please God and to enjoy His presence.

2. The experiences I call "spiritual delights of God"—which, in other places, I've called "the prayer of quiet"—are of a very different kind, as those of you who have experienced them by the mercy of God already know. To better understand, imagine that we're looking at two water fountain basins. (There are certain spiritual things that I can't explain better than through the metaphor of water. I'm uneducated, my natural wit doesn't help, I'm fond of water, and I've observed it more than anything else. In everything created by such a great and wise God, there must be many secrets and meanings that we can benefit from—and those who understand them do benefit. I believe that, in every little thing created by God, there is more than we realize—even in creatures as small as a tiny ant.)

3. These two large basins are filled with water in different ways: the water in one comes from far away, through many pipes[74] and human ingenuity; the other basin has been constructed at the very source of the water and fills without making any noise. If there is an abundant flow of water, which is the kind of situation we're talking about, an overflowing stream continues to run off from the fountain basin after it has been filled. No skill is needed; no pipes need to be created; the water is always flowing from the spring. In my opinion, the water coming through the pipes is comparable to the spiritual *consolations* that are produced by meditation. This water reaches us through our thoughts; we meditate on created things and tire our minds; when it finally comes through our great efforts, the satisfaction it brings to the soul *does* fill the basin, but it does so rather noisily, as I've said.

4. With the other fountain, the water comes directly from its source, which is God. When it is His Majesty's will, and He wants to give us some supernatural gift, it comes with the greatest peace and quietness and gentleness within ourselves—I can't say where it comes from, or how. And this kind of content and delight is not felt in the heart, as earthly consolations are. I mean it's not felt there *initially*, because later the delight fills

74. Literally: "aqueducts." The point is clearly the partnership of human effort and ingenuity with the water's flow.

everything...this water overflows through all the dwelling places and our faculties until it comes to our body. That's why I say it begins in God and ends in ourselves. Truly, as anyone knows who has experienced it, the whole "exterior" part of ourselves enjoys this spiritual delight and sweetness.[75]

5. As I wrote this, I was just thinking about the verse I already quoted, *Dilatasti cor meum,* which refers to the heart expanding. Yet I don't think that this kind of experience is born in the heart, as I've said. It arises from a much more interior part, something very deep. I think this must be the center of the soul, as I came to realize and will explain later. I certainly find secret things within us that often amaze me—and how many more there must be! My Lord and my God, how wondrous are your wonders![76] We're wandering around like simpleminded little shepherds, thinking we are learning something about You, and yet the most we can know amounts to nothing because, even in ourselves, there are secrets we don't understand. When I say "amounts to nothing," it's because of the many, many mysteries that are in You, not because the signs of greatness that we *can* see in Your works are insignificant—they are extraordinary.

SPIRITUAL DELIGHTS, OR THE PRAYER OF QUIET

6. Returning to this verse [*Dilatasti cor meum*], what it says about the *expansion* of the heart may, I think, be helpful. For as this heavenly water flows from its source—our very depths—it then swells and spreads within us, causing an interior dilation and producing ineffable blessings. The soul itself cannot understand all that it receives. Let's say that for now it's as if the soul perceives a fragrance, as if, in those interior depths, there was a basin of coals beneath an offering of sweet incense: the light can't be seen, nor the place where the fire-pan dwells, but the fragrant smoke and the warmth penetrate the entire soul, and, very often, as I've said, the effects extend even to the body. Listen and understand me well here: no heat is felt, nor is any fragrance perceived. It is more delicate than that; I only put it this way so that you might understand it. People who have not experienced it must realize that it actually does happen; when it

75. Teresa uses the term "all of the exterior man" (*todo el hombre exterior*), but the emphasis is on the "exterior" (the body), as distinguished from "the interior" (the soul). Here she is affirming that the body often shares in the gifts given to the soul.

76. Literally: "how great are your grandeurs!" Given the next few sentences, it seems the emphasis is not only on magnitude but on our relative awe and humility before them.

happens, it is capable of being perceived, and the soul becomes aware of it more clearly than I can express here. It is not a thing that we can imagine, because no matter how diligently we strive, we cannot acquire it. From that very fact, it is clear that it is not made of human metal but of divine wisdom, the purest gold. I think that, in this state, our faculties are not in union, but they become absorbed, looking in amazement and wonder at what's happening to them.

7. It's possible that, in writing about these interior things, I'm contradicting what I've said elsewhere, before. This wouldn't be surprising, since almost fifteen years have passed since then.[77] In that time, the Lord might have given me a clearer understanding of these matters than I had initially. Both then and now, of course, I might be mistaken about all of this—but I cannot *lie* about such things (by the mercy of God, I would rather die a thousand deaths). I describe it as I understand it.

8. The will certainly *seems* to be united in some way with God's will, but it's the effects of this prayer—the actions following it—that test the genuineness of the experience. There's no better crucible for testing prayer. It's a great gift[78] from God if the person receiving the gift recognizes it, and a *very* great one if he doesn't turn back.

I know you'll now want to try to attain this way of prayer, my daughters, and this is right and good. As I've said, the soul can't fully understand the gifts that the Lord gives there or the love with which He draws the soul nearer to Himself. Clearly, it's desirable to try to understand how to reach, or attain, this gift. I'll tell you what I've learned about it.

9. We'll leave aside the times when the Lord wants to give these gifts because He wants to and for no other reason. He knows why He does this,

---

77. Teresa is referring to writing her autobiography, *The Life of St. Teresa de Jesus*. She finished the first manuscript of her *Life* in 1562 and is writing these pages of *The Interior Castle* in the latter part of 1577. Ever an astute administrator, she is well aware of the markers in our earthly years!

78. The word here in Spanish is *merced*, which is often translated as "favor" in English. The word itself has connotations of a gift, grace, or mercy from someone with more power or wealth. Although "favor" is accurate, in recent years, its use has increasingly reflected the shady, not benevolent, side of power dealings. Even when used more neutrally ("a neighbor is doing me a great favor"), there is a bit of a transactional edge to the term. "Gift" remains more pure in spirit, at least for now. I interchangeably use "favor," "grace," "mercy," or "gift" for *merced*.

and it's not for us to interfere. So then: in addition to doing what should be done by those in the previous dwelling places—humility! Humility! It's through humility that the Lord allows Himself to be conquered with regard to anything we ask of Him. The first way to see if you have humility? If you do have it, you don't think you deserve these gifts and spiritual delights of God, or that you'll receive them in your lifetime. "But how," you'll ask, "can we get them if we don't go after them?" My answer is that, for the following reasons, there's no better way than the one I've described—of not striving for them:

First, because the most essential thing is that we love God without any motive of self-interest.

Second, because we lack humility by thinking that in return for our pathetic service, we might obtain something so great.

Third, because the true preparation for receiving these gifts is a desire to suffer and to imitate the Lord, not to receive consolations, for we have often offended Him.

Fourth, because His Majesty has not promised to give them to us, as He has [promised] to grant us glory if we keep His commandments. (We don't need these gifts to be saved, and He knows better than we do what is good for us and who among us truly loves Him. This is a certain truth. I also know people who walk along the road of love as they should—*only* in order to serve Christ crucified, and not only do they not ask for spiritual delights, but they don't want them, and they even ask God not to give them in this life. This is true.)

Fifth, because we would be laboring in vain: this water doesn't flow through constructed pipes, like the other kind does, so we gain nothing by tiring ourselves out if the spring doesn't want to flow. What I mean is that no matter how much we practice meditation and try to squeeze or press ourselves, even to tears, we can't produce this water in this way. It is given only to those whom God wills to give it, and often when the soul is not thinking of it at all.

10. We are His, sisters. May He do with us as He likes and lead us along as He pleases. I'm sure that if any of us achieve *true* humility and detachment, the Lord won't fail to give us this gift and many others that we

don't even know how to desire. (I say "true" because it can't be in thought alone. Our thoughts often deceive us; it must be total detachment.) May He be praised and blessed forever. Amen.

Overview of Chapter Three

In the final chapter of the fourth dwellings, Teresa jumps "backward" to explain the prayer of recollection, which might be described most simply as the gift of supernatural focus or attentiveness to God; she says it's as if God suddenly brings us into the spaces of our interior life where we are attuned to the presence of God and less distracted than usual. To this end, she goes on to talk about the prayer of recollection as a foundation for listening deeply to God. With the help of this prayer, we are actually able to listen with some stillness and to receive the wisdom, guidance, or gifts that God wants to give us. Teresa acknowledges that she's placed this teaching a bit out of order and should have started the fourth dwelling places with it, because the prayer of recollection usually happens in a person's life or experience *before* the prayer of quiet, or spiritual delights. Then she jumps "forward" again, taking time to describe the effects of spiritual delights, or the prayer of quiet. "This gentle movement and interior expansion," she writes, "is seen in that it leaves a person less constricted or uptight than before in terms of serving God; there is more freedom." Teresa concludes by offering a few key warnings for those who experience the prayer of quiet, despite its accompanying growth in both freedom and the virtues: in short, don't turn away from prayer, and don't get so caught up in the experience (or seeking it) that you languish and neglect your active life or responsibilities.

Chapter Three (4.3)

THE PRAYER OF RECOLLECTION

1. There are many effects of this kind of prayer [the prayer of quiet], and I'll explain some of them. But first, I'll say something about *another* kind of prayer, which almost always begins before this one. (I won't say much, since I've talked about it elsewhere.)[79] It's a form of recollection that

79, In *Life*, chapters 14–15, and *Way of Perfection*, chapters 28–29.

seems supernatural to me, because it doesn't involve staying in the dark or closing your eyes—it isn't dependent on any exterior thing. The person involuntarily closes her eyes and desires solitude; it seems that, without any human effort, a building is being constructed in which she can experience the prayer already described. The senses and all external things seem to gradually lose their hold because the soul is recovering what it had lost.

2. Some say that "the soul enters *within* itself," while other say "it rises *above* itself." I can't explain things in that kind of terminology; I don't have any expertise in it. But I think you'll be able to understand what I *can* tell you, though maybe it will only make sense to me.

Let's suppose our senses and faculties—the inhabitants of the castle—have left the castle and have been hanging out for days and years with people who are opposed to the well-being of the castle.[80] Then, realizing how much they've lost, they move back toward the castle. They don't actually go inside, because the habits they've picked up are strong and make reentry difficult. But they aren't traitors, or *against* the castle anymore, and they're wandering around the outskirts of the castle. The great King, who dwells within the castle, perceives their good will. In His great mercy, He desires to bring them back to Him. So, like a good shepherd, with a whistle so gentle it is *almost* imperceptible, He teaches them to recognize His voice; He stops them from going off and getting lost and brings them back to their dwelling place. This Shepherd's call is so powerful that they abandon the exterior things that were causing such alienation and enter the castle.

3. I don't think I've ever explained this as clearly before. When we're seeking God within ourselves, it's a great help if God gives us this favor, this mercy.[81] (God is found more effectively and helpfully *within* than in other creatures, to quote Saint Augustine, who found Him within after looking for Him in many other places.)[82] Don't presume that the intellect can *attain* this sort of recollection simply by thinking about the fact that God is within, or trying to imagine Him there. This is a good habit, and

80. Teresa uses the word *enemiga* (enemy) yet interestingly doesn't say they are enemies of the castle directly but enemies of (or against) the well-being of the castle (*del bien de este castillo*).
81. Again the word is *merced*: a gift, a mercy, a "favor" from someone more powerful than we are.
82. A reference to Augustine's *Confessions*, X, chapter 27, or perhaps pseudo-Augustine's *Soliloquies*, chapter 31.

an excellent meditation, for it is founded upon a truth: that God *is* within us. But it's not the kind of prayer I have in mind now, because anyone can do this on their own (with God's help, as we understand is the case for everything).

What I'm describing is quite different: in these cases, people are sometimes brought inside the castle before they've started thinking about God at all. I can't say where they entered, or how they heard their Shepherd's call—it definitely wasn't with their ears, because outwardly such a call isn't audible. But they sense a noticeable yet gentle drawing inward; anyone who experiences this will find out what I mean. I can't explain it better. I think I've read a comparison to a hedgehog or a tortoise withdrawing into itself—and whoever wrote that must have understood it well. However, these creatures enter within themselves in this way whenever they like, but for us it is *not* a question of our will. It only happens when God wants to give us this gift.[83]

Personally, I believe that His Majesty gives this gift to people who are already leaving the things of the world. I don't mean married people need to actually leave "the world" [or their spouse]—they can't—but leave in terms of desire. He calls such people especially so that they will be attentive to their interior life. I really believe that if we desire to make space for His Majesty, He won't give only this to those whom He is already calling to more.

RECOLLECTION AS A FOUNDATION FOR LISTENING DEEPLY TO GOD

4. Anyone who's aware that this [drawing inward] is happening within should praise God—rightly recognizing what a gift it is.[84] Giving thanks also helps prepare the soul for greater gifts. And this state, or disposition, enables us to *listen* as certain books advise. Instead of running after God through reason and words, the soul is intent on discovering what the Lord is doing. But if His Majesty hasn't yet begun to absorb us, I can't understand how *we* can stop our thoughts in a way that doesn't bring more harm than good, although this has been a topic of continual discussion among spiritual people. I confess my lack of humility in saying that, personally,

83. Again: *merced*.
84. Once more the word translated as gift is *merced*.

their arguments have never seemed good enough to lead me to accept what they say. Someone told me about a book by the saintly Friar Peter of Alcantara—at least, I believe he's a saint!—that definitely would have convinced me, because I know how knowledgeable he is. We read it together and found that he says exactly the same thing that I do, but in different words: he clearly says that love must already be awakened [to listen in this way]. I could be wrong, but my position is based on the following reasons.

5. First, in this work of the spirit, the person who thinks less, and desires to do less, actually does more. Here's what we have to do: beg like a needy and poor person before a powerful and rich emperor, and then lower our eyes to the ground and wait with humility. When we seem to realize (through the secret signs He gives us) that He *is* hearing us, it's good for us to remain silent, since He's allowed us to be near Him. It wouldn't be wrong to try *not* to work with our intellect—that is, if we even can work with it. But if we aren't sure that the King has heard us, or sees us, then we must not hang around like fools.[85] The soul remains really foolish when it tries to grasp this kind of quiet prayer; it experiences more dryness, and the imagination is perhaps even more restless due to the forceful effort to "think nothing!" The Lord just wants us to ask things of Him and to remember that we are in His presence; He knows what is most fitting for us. I can't persuade myself to use human effort in matters where it seems His Majesty has set a limit and wants to leave the action in such places for Himself. There are lots of other things not reserved in this way that we *can* do (with His help), like sacrificial generosity,[86] good works, and prayer—as much as our weak human nature is able to do.

6. Second, all these interior activities are gentle and peaceful. To do anything difficult and distressing is harmful, not helpful.[87] By "anything difficult and distressing," I mean anything that we try to *force* ourselves to do, just as it would be distressing to hold our breath. We must simply rest in God's hands and do what He wants us to do, with the greatest disinterest to our own benefit possible, and with great resignation to the will of God.

---

85. Peers translates this line with the very evocative phrase "stay where we are like ninnies."
86. Literally: "penance."
87. The single Spanish word translated here as "difficult and distressing" is *penosa*, which has many meanings and has been translated by others as broadly as "painful" or "arduous." I chose two words to carry the broadness of the term in context.

Third, the same careful effort we make—trying to cease all thoughts—might awaken our minds to thinking even more.

Fourth, the most important and pleasing thing in God's eyes is that we are mindful of His honor and glory, forgetting ourselves and our benefits, comfort, and pleasure. And how can someone be forgetful of himself when he's being *so* careful not to stir—not even allowing his intellect or desires to stir for God's glory, or allowing himself to rejoice in the glory God already has? When His Majesty wants the intellect to stop, He occupies it in another way. He leads it into a state of absorption, and in this state—without knowing how—we are much better instructed than we could ever be through our efforts not to use our intellect. Since God gave us our faculties to work with (and in this work is their reward and satisfaction), there is no reason to try to cast a spell over them—they need to be allowed to function as intended until *God* gives them something better to do.

7. As I understand it, anyone who has been led into this dwelling place by the Lord will do best to act as I've been describing. Without forcing itself, let the soul try to rein in the wandering, rambling intellect, but not entirely suspend it or one's thoughts (it's good to be mindful of God's presence and who this God is). If this feeling leads to a state of absorption, well and good, but it shouldn't try to *understand* the nature of this state, because it's given to the will. Let the soul enjoy it, without any efforts except offering a few loving words. Although in such a case you might not be trying to "think nothing!" often the churning of the intellect *will* be paused, even if only for a brief moment.

8. I have explained elsewhere that the reason this happens in this kind of prayer—the kind that is like a naturally flowing spring, where the water doesn't come through pipes—is that the mind freezes and gets confused, realizing it can't understand what it wants, then wanders around in bewilderment. (Here, I'm referring to the kind of prayer that I talked about in the beginning of the fourth dwelling places. I've added the prayer of recollection in between, which I should have mentioned first, because the prayer of recollection is much less intense than the spiritual delights of God I've been talking about, but it's often the beginning, the first step toward them. In the prayer of recollection, meditation and the work of the intellect do not need to be set aside.) The will is so firmly fixed in and upon its God that

this bewildered condition of the mind causes it distress, but it must not pay any attention to this clamor and confusion because, in doing so, it will lose a great part of what it's enjoying. One must let the intellect go, simply abandon oneself into the arms of love. His Majesty will teach the soul what to do next; pretty much, the soul's only job at that point is to recognize its unworthiness to receive such a great good, and to focus on giving thanks.

THE EFFECTS OF SPIRITUAL DELIGHTS, OR THE PRAYER OF QUIET

9. In order to talk about the prayer of recollection, I skipped over the effects or observable signs in souls to whom God our Lord has given this prayer [of quiet]. Clearly, a dilation, enlargement, or expansion of the soul happens, as if the water coming from the spring simply cannot spill over and be lost—as if the fountain had a way of making sure that the more freely the water flows, the more space there is to receive it. It's like this with this kind of prayer. God works many more wonders in the soul, gradually enabling it to retain everything He gives. This gentle movement and interior expansion is seen in that it leaves a person less constricted or uptight than before in terms of serving God; there is more freedom. For example, the soul is not weighed down by the fear of hell, because even though it desires more than ever not to offend God, it loses all servile, groveling fear here. There is a firm confidence that the soul will enjoy God's presence. One who used to be afraid of devoted acts of generosity[88] due to worries about ruining his health now trusts that, in God, he can do everything—and he has a greater desire to do such things than before. The fear of trials he used to have is tempered. His faith is more alive, and he realizes that if he endures challenges and hardships for God's sake, His Majesty will give him the grace to bear them with patience. Sometimes the soul even desires challenging trials, because he still has a strong desire to do something for God. As he comes to know God's greatness more fully, he considers himself all the more pitiful and measly.[89] Having tasted the spiritual delights of God, he sees that the pleasures of the world are like garbage in comparison. Bit by bit, he withdraws from their grasp and thus becomes more and more his own master. In summary, there's improvement in all the virtues. Such a soul will continue to improve unless he returns to offending God.

88. Literally: "doing penance."
89. The Spanish word here is *miserable,* often translated as "miserable" or "wretched."

When that happens, everything is lost, no matter how close the man might have been to the mountain's summit. Don't understand me to mean that all these things happen just because God has given a soul this gift once or twice; you must persevere in receiving [these gifts], for in this perseverance is all our good.

WARNINGS FOR THOSE WHO EXPERIENCE THE PRAYER OF QUIET

10. There's one serious warning I have to give those who find themselves in this state: take the greatest care not to put yourself in the situation of offending God. Because, at this point, the soul is not even weaned but is like a child just beginning to suckle at the breast. If it turns away from its mother, what can be expected but death? That, I'm so very afraid, will be the case for anyone to whom God has given this favor who turns away from prayer. Unless he has an exceptional reason, or returns to it quickly, he will go from bad to worse. I know well that this is a legitimate fear; I've been seriously grieved by seeing what I'm describing in people I know. They've left One who, with great love, was desiring to give Himself to them as a friend, and proved it through actions. I seriously warn such people to guard against occasions of sin, because the adversary tries much harder for one soul in this state than for many others who have not received these gifts. Because those who are in this state attract others, they might really benefit God's church and thus potentially do the adversary great harm. Even if there's nothing but seeing that His Majesty shows this soul particular love, this is enough for the adversary to wear himself out trying to make sure this soul becomes lost. The conflict is thus more intense for such souls, and if they are lost, they are more lost than others.

Sisters, as far as we know, you are free from such dangers. May God free you from pride and vanities, and not allow the adversary to counterfeit these gifts. Such counterfeits are recognizable, though, because they won't produce these effects, but opposite ones.

11. There's another danger I want to warn you about (though I've talked about it in other places). I've seen people inclined to prayer fall into this, especially women. Since we are weaker, we are at greater risk of what I'm going to describe. Here it is: some women, due to prayer, vigils, severe penances, and other reasons, have poor health. When they experience any

spiritual gift, their physical nature is overwhelmed. As soon as they feel an interior joy, a physical weakness and languor comes over them, and they fall into what they call a "spiritual sleep" (a bit more intense than the prayer of quiet I've described). Thinking this to be the same thing, they abandon themselves to this absorption. The more they succumb to this, the more they feel almost intoxicated, because their physical condition continues to weaken. It seems to them that they are being carried away in rapture, but I call it being carried away in foolishness.[90] They're not doing anything but wasting their time and ruining their health.

One person was in this state for eight hours, not unconscious...but at the same time not conscious of anything concerning God. She got rid of this stupor by following instructions to eat more, sleep more, and do less penance. Although she'd involuntarily misled herself, her confessor, and others, one person understood her. I think the adversary is willing to work to gain some ground, and here he was beginning to get more than a little.

12. You have to understand, though, that when this state really comes from God, there is no stupor or lifelessness in the soul, though there might be interior and exterior quiet or inactivity. The soul has deep feelings as it finds itself near God. The experience lasts only a short while, but the soul might become absorbed again. As I've said, this type of prayer doesn't go so far as to overwhelm the body (except in cases of physical weakness) or bring any such external sensations. If you experience this kind of lifeless languishing, tell your superior and distract yourself from it as much as you can. The superior should assign such people fewer hours of prayer (very few!) and make sure they sleep and eat well until their exhausted physical strength comes back. If their constitution is so weak that this doesn't do the trick, they'll know with clarity that God isn't calling them beyond the active life. There's room in convents for all kinds of people; let someone like this keep busy with active duties and not be left alone very much (which might cause her to lose her health completely). This will seem like a mortifying punishment to her, but the Lord wants to test her love for Him by seeing how well she bears His absence. After a while, He may be happy to give her back her strength. If not, her vocal prayers and life of obedience

90. There is a wonderful and piquant play on words in the Spanish here: *arrobamiento* is "rapture"; *abobamiento* is "foolishness."

will give her as many benefits as she might have gotten through contemplative prayers, and maybe more.

13. There might also be some who are so weak in their heads and imaginations that they believe they actually *see* everything they imagine; I have known such people. This is very dangerous. Perhaps I'll address it later, but I won't say anything more here. I have written a lot about this dwelling place since it's the one that more souls enter, and since the natural and supernatural are joined here, the adversary can do more harm. In the dwelling places not yet described, the Lord doesn't give him as much leeway. May He be praised forever. Amen.

Questions for Reflection

1. When have you experienced the prayer of recollection, or something like it? Teresa reminds us that this can happen both in prayer and when we're not even thinking about God. How might thinking of the *ability* to listen deeply to God as a gift in and of itself change your understanding of these experiences?

2. Based on Teresa's images and comparisons for spiritual delights, or the prayer of quiet, do you think this is a grace God has given you at some point in your life? If so, which aspects do you most relate to? Would you describe it any differently?

3. If you've never experienced anything like the prayer of quiet, or spiritual delights, how do you feel about the concept? Is it something you desire? Why or why not?

4. What do you make of Teresa's persistent warnings not to fall back, turn away, or grow complacent in the spiritual life?

FIFTH DWELLINGS

Overview of Chapter One

In this first of four chapters addressing the fifth dwellings, Teresa once more reminds the reader that what she's venturing to describe is indescribable. She then encourages her sisters—and, by extension, all her readers—not to grow weary in prayer and faith because, although we cannot "create" the hidden treasures of contemplation, we *can* prepare to receive them to the best of our ability, and she wants us to know that it's worth the effort. We don't have to be physically strong or achieve great things outwardly to "prepare"; the best preparation is to offer God our whole lives, whatever we have and whoever we are. Teresa describes this full surrender and the prayer of union, comparing the union to a wonderful death that somehow begins a new life in us. To help us understand how this prayer is different from what occurs in the fourth dwellings, Teresa goes on to talk about the sign and dynamics of an authentic prayer of union. The most telling sign, she says, is actually the gift of clear conviction: "God places Himself in the interior of that soul in such a way that when it returns to itself, it can in no way doubt that it was in God, and God was in it." Once again, this gift is not something we can "achieve" for ourselves; it is something God brings us to and does in us.

Chapter One (5.1)

THE HIDDEN TREASURES OF CONTEMPLATION

1. Oh sisters, how can I ever explain the riches, treasures, and delights found in the fifth dwelling places? I think it would be better to say nothing of the dwelling places I haven't yet described because no one *can* describe them. The intellect is incapable of understanding them, and no comparisons help in explaining them because earthly things are too coarse for this purpose. Send me light from heaven, my Lord, that I might be able to enlighten these your servants—some of whom You are pleased to give

these joys[91] to often—so that they may not be deceived when the adversary transfigures himself into an angel of light. For their only desire is to please you.

2. Although I said "some," there are really very *few* who fail to enter these dwelling places that I'm about to describe. Some get farther than others, but the majority do manage to get inside. Some of the things *in* this room I'm about to talk about are surely attained by very few, but if someone does no more than reach the door, God is showing them great mercy. For "many are called, few are chosen."[92]

I must say that, even though all of us wearing the sacred habit of the Carmel order are called to prayer and contemplation (because that was the first principle of our order), few of us prepare ourselves for the Lord to reveal these riches of contemplation to us. We are descendants in the line of those holy fathers from Mount Carmel who sought this treasure, this precious pearl we speak of, with such great solitude and with so much separation from the world.[93] So, as far as externals are concerned, we're on the right road to the essential virtues, but we still need to do a lot before we can arrive at this point, and we can't be careless in big or small things. Let's pause here, sisters: since it's possible, to some extent, for us to enjoy heaven on earth, let us beg the Lord that He will help us not to miss it by our own fault. May He show us the road and strengthen our souls to dig until we find this hidden treasure, because, truthfully, it's found within our very selves. I'd like to explain this if the Lord enables me.

FULL SURRENDER AND THE PRAYER OF UNION

3. I said "strengthen our souls" because you must understand that we don't need *bodily* strength if God doesn't give it to us. He doesn't make it impossible for anyone to buy His riches; as long as each gives what she has, He is content. Blessed be such a just God! But take note, daughters: for what we're talking about [union], He would have you hold nothing back.

91. The word here is *gozos*, a bit different from *gustos*, which is the word translated in this book as "spiritual delights."
92. Matthew 22:14: "For many are called, but few are chosen."
93. This is more literally "contempt" for the world, but, as Teresa herself has described, it's not necessarily the created world as a whole that is rejected but its values, priorities, distractions, and ways.

Whether little or great, He will have it all. In conformity to what you know yourself to have given, you will receive greater or smaller gifts.[94]

There's no better test than this of whether or not we've reached the prayer of union. Don't imagine it's a "dreamy" or sleepy state like I previously mentioned.[95] I say "dreamy" because the soul seems to be neither fully asleep nor awake. Here, we are *all* asleep to the things of the world, and to ourselves. In fact, for the short time that the condition lasts, the soul is left as though without its senses, unable to think even if it wanted to. There is no need for devising any method for suspending thoughts. Even in loving, if it is able to love, it can't understand how or who it loves, or what it wants.

Ultimately, it's like one who has died to the world in every respect so that it may live more fully than ever in God. Thus, it is a delicious death, an uprooting of the soul from all the activities that it can perform while in the body. Delicious and delightful because the soul seems to have left the body to abide more fully in God. This is so much the case that I don't know if it has enough life to be able to breathe. (I was just thinking about this, and I think it doesn't—or, at least, if it still breathes, it does so without realizing it.) The intellect would like to completely devote itself to understanding something of what is felt—but since the soul doesn't have the energy to do this, it becomes so stunned that even if there is any consciousness remaining, it can move neither hand nor foot. Like we say about someone who has fainted, it might be mistaken as dead.

Oh, the secrets of God! I would never tire of trying to explain them to you if I thought I could do so somewhat successfully. Thus, I will say a thousand foolish things so that I might even once succeed, and we may give great praise to the Lord.

4. As I said, this union is not some kind of dreamy state. In contrast, in the [fourth] dwelling place[96] that I've just described, the soul is doubtful about what has really happened until it's had a lot of experience. It wonders: Was the whole thing my imagination? Was I asleep? Was this a gift from

---

94. Gifts is *mercedes*—which, once again, can be translated as "favors" or "graces" as well.
95. She seems to be referring to the languid state mentioned in 4.3.11.
96. Peers notes that Teresa herself sometimes refers to dwelling places in the singular and other times in the plural; she is not always consistent. This is an instance where she uses the singular to name the fourth dwelling place.

God, or from the adversary transfigured into an angel of light? A thousand misgivings remain, as well they should, because (like I said) we *can* sometimes be deceived in this way, even by our own nature. Although there's less opportunity for the poisonous creatures to come in, a few little lizards are very agile and manage to hide themselves all over the place. Although they do no harm—especially if we don't pay attention to them—they are often quite bothersome, these little thoughts coming from our imagination. The lizards can't enter this dwelling place, though, even with all their agility. Here, our imagination, memory, or intellect can't be an obstacle to the blessings that are given. I will even venture to say that, if this is *truly* union with God, the adversary can't enter or do any harm. Because His Majesty is in such close contact and union with the essence of the soul, he won't dare approach. (He can't even understand this secret thing, obviously, because it's said that he doesn't understand our thoughts…and so he'll understand even less of a thing so secret that God doesn't even entrust our thoughts with it.) Oh, what a great blessing to be in this state, where the accursed one can't do us harm! What riches come to the soul when God works in such a way that neither we ourselves, nor anyone else, can hinder Him. What will He not give, who loves giving, and can give us all He wants to?

5. It seems I might confuse you by saying, "If this is *truly* union [with God]," and thus implying that there are other kinds of union. But of course there are! If we love vain things, the adversary can make us feel "transported" through them, but not in the way that God does: there isn't the same delight and satisfaction of the soul, or peace and joy. This joy is greater than all the joys on earth, greater than all its pleasures or consolations. These different consolations don't have a common origin, and they are felt very differently, too, as you will know by experience. Once, I said that it's like the difference between feeling something on the rough outer covering of the body versus in the very marrow of the bones. I think this was well put; I don't know how to explain it any better.

THE SIGN AND DYNAMICS OF AN AUTHENTIC PRAYER OF UNION

6. But I imagine that, even now, you won't be satisfied, because you'll still be thinking that you *might* be mistaken, and that these interior matters are very difficult to examine accurately. Although what has been said

will be enough for anyone who has experienced this union—because it's very different—I will give you a clear sign that will make it impossible for you to go wrong or to doubt if the union is from God. His Majesty brought it to my mind today, and it seems to me to be the true test. In difficult matters, even if I think I understand what I'm saying and that it's true, I use this phrase "it seems to me" because I'm very ready to listen to those who have more learning. For even if they haven't experienced these things themselves, very learned men have a certain something.[97] God uses them to give light to His church, and He helps them discern what is true so that it will be accepted. If they don't squander their talents, but are truly servants of God, they will never be surprised at His greatness. They'll know quite well that He is capable of doing more than they expect...and more. Anyway, if some of the inexplicable gifts are unfamiliar to them, they can read about others *like* them, showing that the former ones are possible.

7. I've had a lot of experience with such learned men. I've also had experience with fearful, half-learned men whose limitations have cost me dearly. At any rate, my own opinion is that anyone who doesn't believe that God can do much more than this—that He has been pleased and sometimes still *is* pleased to give His creatures such gifts—has closed the door shut to receiving them. Sisters, never let this be true of you. Instead, trust God more and more, and don't focus your attention on whether the individuals to whom He gives His gifts are bad or good. His Majesty knows all about this, as I've said. Meddling in assessing worthiness is quite unnecessary. Instead, we must serve His Majesty with humility and simplicity of heart, and praise Him for His works and wonders.

8. Now, turning to the sign that I say is the decisive one: here is this soul that God has made completely "foolish" in order to better impress with true wisdom—because during the time of this union, it can neither see, nor hear, nor understand. The state is always short, and seems to the soul even shorter than it really is. Yet God places Himself in the interior of that soul in such a way that when it returns to itself, it can in no way doubt that it was in God, and God was in it. This truth remains so firmly that even though God may not give this gift again for many years, the soul can't forget or doubt that it was in God, and God was in it. (I'm leaving aside for

97. "A certain something" in Spanish is similar to the French expression "*un je ne sais quoi.*"

now the *effects* that stay within the soul, which I'll talk about later.) This deep conviction carries the weight in the case.

9. But now you'll ask me: How did the soul see it and understand it if it couldn't see or understand anything? I'm not saying it saw the truth at the time, but that afterward, it sees the truth clearly. Not because of a vision but because of a certainty remaining in the soul that only God can put there. I know someone[98] who was unaware that God was in all things by presence, power, and essence. God gave her a gift of this kind, and it so firmly convinced her of this truth that even when she asked one of those half-learned men I was talking about *how* God was in us, and he told her that God was only in us by grace, she did not believe him—because she had the truth so firmly implanted within her. (This man knew as little of God's presence, power, and essence in all things as she did before God enlightened her.) She asked others about it who told her the truth, and this confirmation was a great comfort.

10. Don't make the mistake of thinking that this certainty has to do with a corporal or physical form, as in the case of the bodily presence of our Lord Jesus Christ in the Most Holy Sacrament [of Communion], unseen by us. It doesn't have anything to do with this—only with His divinity. How, you'll ask, can we be so convinced of what we have not seen? I don't know; it's the work of God. But I do know that I'm speaking the truth. If anyone doesn't have such certainty, I would say that what he has experienced is not union of the whole soul with God but only union of one of the faculties or one of the many other kinds of favors God gives. In all of these matters we need to stop searching with our reason for *how* they come about. Since our intellect can't understand this union, why try to perplex it? It's enough for us to know that He who caused it is almighty. Since it is God who does this, and we are completely incapable of achieving it ourselves no matter how hard we work, let's not yearn to understand it either.

11. As I was saying that we are completely incapable of achieving it ourselves, it brought to mind what the bride in the Songs says (as you've heard): "He brought me into the wine cellar" (or "*placed* me there," I think

98. This is also a reference to Teresa herself. She refers to this experience in her *Life*, chapter 18.

it says).[99] It doesn't say that she *went*. It says that she was wandering around in all directions, seeking her Beloved.[100] As I understand it, this is the cellar where the Lord is pleased to place us, when He wills and as He wills. But we can't enter by any of our own efforts; His Majesty must put us right into the center of our soul, and enter there Himself. In order to better demonstrate His wonders, it's His preference that our will—which has entirely surrendered itself to God—should have no part in this. He doesn't need the faculties and senses to be opened to Him, like a door; they are all asleep. He enters the center of the soul without a door, like He did when He came to His disciples and said, *Pax vobis* ("Peace be with you"),[101] or when He left the tomb without removing the stone. Later on, in the final dwellings, you'll see how His Majesty wants the soul to enjoy Him fully in its center, even more than here.

12. Daughters, how much we will see if we don't remain fixated on our own compromised nature, our deep faults and limitations,[102] *and* understand that we are not worthy to be the servants of such a great Lord, since we can't comprehend His mysteries. May He be praised forever. Amen.

---

99. A reference to Song of Solomon 2:4: "He brought me to the banqueting house, and his intention toward me [Hebrew, "banner above"] was love."
100. Song of Solomon 3:2: "'I will rise now and go about the city, in the streets and in the squares; I will seek him whom my soul loves.' I sought him but found him not."
101. John 20:19: "When it was evening on that day, the first day of the week, and the doors were locked where the disciples were, for fear of the Jews, Jesus came and stood among them and said, 'Peace be with you.'"
102. The Spanish phrase here is "*bajeza y miseria*," traditionally translated as "baseness and misery." But neither term is commonly used to refer to our sinful natures these days, even in the church.

Overview of Chapter Two

In this chapter, Teresa tries to explain what is happening in and through the prayer of union using an extended metaphor, one that she will use on off and on for the remainder of the book. She compares the soul to a silkworm that eats, labors, and grows until it reaches the point where it enters the cocoon. All of its activity before entering the cocoon might roughly be considered what's happening in the first four dwellings. But then, in the fifth dwellings, the silkworm is "hidden in Christ" and experiences a transformative death. All of this is a necessary prelude to the emergence of the soul as a white butterfly, which happens as a result of the prayer of union. After such a wondrous transformation, the soul has a certain kind of disorientation and restlessness. But, in that restlessness, it experiences a greater freedom and a greater ambition for God: "It's no longer bound up and entangled by relatives, friends, or wealth," she says. "Now it has wings: How can it be content with crawling along slowly when it has the ability to fly? Everything it can do for God seems trivial in comparison with what it *wants* to do." She continues to elaborate on this restlessness, as well as on the soul's further surrender to God—comparing the depth of complete surrender in and following this prayer to soft wax that is imprinted with God's seal: "God desires that the soul may go forth from this union impressed with His seal, without understanding how," she says, "so that this soul might know itself to be His."

Chapter Two (5.2)

1. It might seem to you like I've already described everything that might be seen in these dwellings, but there's actually much more—because, like I said, some receive more, and some less. Regarding the nature of union, I don't think I can say anything more. But when those receiving these gifts from God prepare themselves, there's a lot to be said about what the Lord then works in them. Some of these works, I'll describe now, along with

the soul's state. To better explain this, I'll use a suitable comparison. This metaphor will also show us how, even though this work is done by the Lord—and we can't do anything to make His Majesty give us this gift—we *can* do a lot to prepare ourselves for it.

THE IMAGE OF THE SOUL AS A SILKWORM

2. You've probably already heard about the wondrous way that silk is made, how it comes from a kind of seed that looks like tiny peppercorns—no one could invent such a thing but God. (I've never seen this myself, but only heard about it, so please don't blame me if I'm incorrect in any way.) When the warm weather comes, and mulberry trees begin to leaf, this seed begins to come to life. Until it has the leaves for food and sustenance, it seems almost dead. Then the silkworms feed on the mulberry leaves until they are full-grown, at which point people put down twigs by them. On the twigs, with their tiny mouths, they start spinning silk, making themselves very tight little cocoons in which they bury themselves. Then, finally, the large and ugly worm comes out of the cocoon—but now a beautiful white butterfly.

Now, if no one had ever seen this, and we were only told about it, as if we were hearing a story from long ago, who would believe it? What arguments could we find to support the idea that a non-reasoning creature like a worm or a bee would work with such diligence and skill in our service, so much so that the poor little worm loses its life in this work? Sisters, this image alone is sufficient for a brief meditation, enabling us to reflect upon the wonders and wisdom of our God. What if we knew the properties of all things? It's very beneficial for us to ponder these wonderful things of creation, and to rejoice in being the brides of such a great and powerful King.

3. Let's return to what I was saying. This silkworm starts to live when, through the energy coming from the Holy Spirit, it begins to make use of the general help God gives us all and the aids to growth that He left in His church: for example, frequent confessions, good books, and sermons. These are healing aids for a soul without life in its negligence and harmful ways, frequently overwhelmed by misdirected desires.[103] The soul begins to live and nourishes itself on this food, and on good meditations, until it

103. Literally: "a soul *dead* in negligences and sins and frequently falling into temptation" (emphasis added).

is fully grown. This is the stage that concerns me now—the rest doesn't matter so much at this point.

4. As I wrote at the beginning, when it is full-grown, the silkworm starts to spin its silk and build the house in which it will die. Here, this house might be understood as Christ. I read or heard somewhere that our life is hidden in Christ, or in God (which is the same thing), or that our life is Christ.[104] The exact words aren't important to what I'm trying to convey.

5. See here, daughters, what we can do through God's help: as He does in this prayer of union, His Majesty *Himself* becomes the dwelling place we build for ourselves. When I say He will be our dwelling place, and we can build it for ourselves and hide ourselves in it, it seems like I'm suggesting we can add to or subtract from God. But of course we can't do that! We can't subtract from or add to God, but we *can* subtract from and add to *ourselves*, just as the little silkworms do. And even before we've finished doing everything we can in this work, God will take our tiny achievement—which is practically nothing at all—and unite it with Himself, His greatness. He gives it such worth that its reward is the Lord Himself. Since He paid the highest price, His Majesty wants to join our little efforts with the great ones He suffered so that they might be joined as one.

6. Thus: courage, my daughters! Let's be quick to do this work and spin this cocoon by taking away our self-love and self-will, and our attachments to earthly things. Let's add acts of generosity,[105] prayer, fasting and self-control,[106] obedience, and all the other good works you know of. Let's do what we've been taught; we know what our duty is. Let the silkworm die—let it die, as it does and will when it has completed the work it was created to do! Then, we will see God, and we will be as completely hidden in His greatness as the little silkworm in its cocoon. Please note that when I say "see God," I'm referring to the way that He allows Himself to be known, or apprehended, in this kind of union.

104. Colossians 3:3: "For you have died, and your life is hidden with Christ in God"; Philippians 1:21: "For to me to live is Christ..." (KJV).
105. Again, literally, this is "penance," rendered as "acts of generosity" for a broader audience.
106. Literally: "mortification." The heart of "mortification" in monastic practice is any action that subdues bodily desires, especially inordinate desires that one feels have a "life of their own." Thus, for most modern and non-monastic readers, I think the concepts of fasting and self-control point to the same spiritual aim.

THE EMERGENCE OF THE SOUL AS A WHITE BUTTERFLY

7. Now let's see what this silkworm does, because that's the reason I've said everything else. When it's in this state of prayer, and quite dead to the world, it emerges as a little white butterfly. Oh, the greatness of God, that a soul comes out like this after being hidden in God and closely united with Him for so short a time—I think it's never even as long as half an hour! Truly, the soul doesn't recognize itself. Think about the difference between an ugly worm and a white butterfly; it's the same sort of contrast here. The soul can't think how it could have deserved so much good—or, rather, where this good might have come from, I mean, because it knows full well that it hasn't "earned" or deserved such goodness at all. The soul wants to praise the Lord, feels that it would gladly sacrifice itself and die a thousand deaths for His sake. It wants to suffer great trials for God, without being able to do otherwise. It passionately wants opportunities for sacrificial generosity,[107] for solitude, and for all to know God. And after this, when it sees God being offended, the soul is deeply pained. In the next dwelling place, I'll talk about this in greater detail, because even though the experiences of this dwelling place and the next are almost identical, their effects become more powerful. As I've said, after God comes to a soul here on earth, if it strives to progress even more, it will experience great things.

8. See, then, that the restlessness of this little butterfly—even though it's never been quieter or calmer in its life—is something to praise God for! It doesn't know where to settle and take its rest, when it has known *such* a resting place. Everything it sees on earth dissatisfies, especially when God has repeatedly given it this wine, bringing some new blessing almost every time. It's no longer impressed by the work it did as a worm—the slow, gradual weaving of the cocoon. Now it has wings: How can it be content with crawling along slowly when it has the ability to fly? Everything it can do for God seems trivial in comparison with what it *wants* to do. It's even less impressed with what the saints endured, knowing through experience how the Lord can help and transform a soul—so much so it seems no longer like itself. The weakness it used to have for sacrificial acts of generosity[108] it now finds its strength. It's no longer bound up and entangled by relatives, friends, or wealth. Whereas before, all of its acts of will, determinations,

107. Again: "penance."
108. "Penance."

and desires were powerless to loosen these entanglements and only seemed to bind them more, now, even their basic, rightful claims are a burden—the soul doesn't want these relationships to cause it to offend or betray God. Everything wearies it because it realizes that no true rest can be found in creatures.

RESTLESSNESS AND FURTHER SURRENDER TO GOD

9. It may seem like I've gone on at length about this, but I could say much more. Whoever has received this favor from God will realize that I've actually been very brief. It's not surprising that this little butterfly is seeking a new resting place, because it feels like a stranger to earthly things. Where can the poor little creature go? It can't "return to where it came from," because, as I've said, no matter how hard we try, it's not in our power to do that. We can't bring about this favor until God wants to give it again. Ah, Lord! What trials begin for this soul! Who would imagine that this would be the case after such a sublime gift? And yet, after all, we must bear crosses in one way or another for as long as we live. If anyone told me that, after reaching this state, he'd then enjoyed *continual* rest and joy, I would say that he hadn't reached it at all. (Maybe if he'd gotten as far as the previous dwellings, perhaps he experienced some kind of consolation. Possibly the effects of this consolation were enhanced by physical weakness, or maybe even the adversary, giving peace so as to afterward cause more destruction to him.)[109]

10. I don't mean to say that those who arrive in this dwelling don't have peace; they do have it, and it's very deep. Even their severe challenges are valuable and come from a worthwhile place, so they bring peace and contentment. The same discontent caused by the things of the world makes one want to leave it—the only source of comfort is the thought that life in this exile is God's will. And even this is not enough to really comfort the soul, because, despite all the progress made, it's not fully resigned to the will of God (in the way we'll see later). It doesn't fail to act in conformity to God's will, but it does so with a lot of tears and deep sorrow at not being able to do *more* because it doesn't have the capacity. In prayer, this regret and awareness of limitation is its pain. Maybe to some extent this grief is related to the great grief of noticing how often God is offended—and how

109. Literally: "wage a more severe war."

little respected—in this world: How many souls are lost, both heretics and Moors[110]...but those that cause the deepest sadness are Christians. It fears that many are being condemned, even though it knows God's mercy is so great that, however evil their lives have been, they can amend them and be saved.

11. Oh, the greatness of God! A few years ago—perhaps even days—this soul wasn't thinking of anything but itself. Who has plunged it into such deep concerns? Even if we tried to meditate for years, we couldn't feel this as keenly as the soul does now. God help me! If I could spend days, *years*, trying to comprehend how serious it is to offend God, how those who are condemned are His children (and my brothers), how good it would be for us to leave this dangerous and miserable life, it wouldn't be enough to create this depth. No, daughters—the grief I'm talking about here isn't like that resulting from such meditations. That kind of grief we could easily achieve, with the Lord's help, by thinking a lot about those things. But it doesn't reach into the depths of our being like this grief does. Without any effort on the soul's part—and sometimes without wanting it—this kind of pain seems to break and grind the soul to pieces. What, then, is this grief? Where does it come from? I'll tell you.

12. Haven't you heard it said of the bride that God brought her into the inner wine cellar and put love in her?[111] (I already mentioned it elsewhere, but not in this sense.) Well, that's the situation here. This soul has now delivered itself into His hands, and His great love causes such complete surrender that it doesn't know or want anything more than what He wants with her. (In my judgment, God will never give this favor except to a soul He takes as His very own.) God desires that the soul may go forth from this union impressed with His seal, without understanding how. Indeed, the soul doesn't do any more in this union than the wax when a seal is impressed upon it. The wax doesn't impress itself; it's only prepared for the imprint, by being soft. And it doesn't even soften itself in order to be

---

110. In Teresa's context, "heretics" included all the Protestant Reformers and those who had departed from the Roman Catholic Church; "Moors" is a reference to Muslims.
111. Again, a reference to Song of Solomon 2:4, paraphrased in Teresa's own words. The NRSV translates the verse from Hebrew thus: "He brought me to the banqueting house, and his intention toward me was love." However, the translation Teresa was most familiar with used the image of "wine cellar" rather than banqueting house, and the verb she uses (*ordenar*) is much stronger than "intention."

prepared; it merely remains still and gives its consent. Oh, goodness of God, that all of this is done at Your cost! You only want our will, and that there be no impediment in the wax.

13. You see here, sisters, what our God does in this union so that this soul might know itself to be His. He gives it something of His own, which is what His Son had in this life. He can't grant us a higher favor. Who could have wanted to depart from this life more than His Son did? As His Majesty said at the Last Supper: *I have earnestly desired.*[112]

"Well, Lord, didn't the painful death that You were about to die seem to be something devastating and horrible?" "No—because My great love, and My desire for souls to be saved, are incomparably more consequential than the suffering. And the greatest sorrows I've known since living in the world—and still suffer—are such that these other pains can't compare at all."

14. I've often thought about this, and it is true. I know a certain acquaintance[113] who has suffered torment—and suffers still—from seeing the Lord offended. The pain is so intolerable that she would rather die than endure it. And I've thought: if a soul that has so little love in comparison with Christ's that it might be said to be almost *nothing* beside His feels this to be so intolerable, how must our Lord Jesus Christ have felt? What kind of life must He have lived, if He saw everything and was constantly witnessing the great offenses being committed against His Father? I think this definitely must have caused Him much greater grief than the pains of His most sacred passion. There, at least He could see the end of His trials. That foresight, combined with the satisfaction of seeing our redemption achieved through His death, and proving His love for His Father by suffering so much for Him, would diminish His pain. It's like when those who have great strength of love perform great acts of sacrificial generosity:[114] they hardly feel it, and would like to do more and more. Everything they do seems small to them. What would His Majesty feel, then, when He was able to prove so fully to His Father both His obedience and His love for

---

112. Luke 22:15: "He said to them, 'I have eagerly desired to eat this Passover with you before I suffer.'"

113. Saint Teresa herself. See *Life*, chapter 8.14; and 32.9; *Way of Perfection*, chapter 1.3.

114. Literally: "great penances."

His neighbor? Oh, the great joy[115] of suffering in doing the will of God! But the constant sight of so many offenses against His Majesty and so many souls going to hell must have been so very painful to Him. If He'd been no more than a man, one day of that grief would have been enough to end not just one life, but many lives.

115. Literally: "delight"—in Spanish, *deleite*.

Overview of Chapter Three

Extending the metaphor of the little butterfly (sometimes referred to as a "little dove" instead), Teresa begins this chapter by talking about the benefit to others that comes from this gift of union. Even if the soul itself grows careless and goes astray—as happened with Teresa herself, she would say—there will be *some* benefit for others because "such a great gift isn't given in vain." Nevertheless, we are once again urged not to stray from God's will and God's ways, no matter what spiritual favors or graces we've experienced.

To that end, Teresa introduces another way that one might know "true union" with God, a way that she says is actually "the union I have desired all my life; it's this union that I continually ask of the Lord, and the one that is clearest and safest": the union of conformity to God's will, or "keeping our wills fixed on whatever is God's will." She notes that one can thus experience the union of the fifth dwellings without the previously described prayer, but we still need what might be called the death of our false self and the new life of freedom and even deeper surrender to God. Admitting that this is "harder work," because "death comes more easily when you can see yourself in such a new life," she assures us that "it is worth the effort."

Thankfully, Teresa also tells us here that such a union with God's will doesn't mean that we don't experience natural human griefs and losses and somehow become stoic and unfeeling as a measure of our "surrender." What really matters is that we live out love of God and love of neighbor to the fullest extent possible, with love of neighbor as the truest sign that we have achieved or experienced such union. She writes compellingly that humble, loving, and compassionate action is the essential fruit of all prayer and our love of God. With down-to-earth examples, she wisely observes that "we can't really know if we love God,...but we *can* know if we love our neighbor." This costly love for others is how we know and demonstrate true union.

Chapter Three (5.3)

THE BENEFIT TO OTHERS

1. Let's get back to our little dove, and consider what God gives her in this state. Always understand that she must strive to move forward in the service of our Lord and in self-knowledge. Because if she acts like she now has complete security and doesn't do anything beyond receiving this favor, growing careless with her life and abandoning the heavenly path (which consists of keeping the commandments), what happens to the creature that comes out of the silkworm will happen to her: it "gives the seed" for the creation of more silkworms and then dies forever. The reason I say it "gives the seed" is because I trust it's God's will that such a great gift isn't given in vain; even if the soul who receives it doesn't benefit from it, others will. Since this soul is left with these virtues and desires mentioned before, it will always help other souls as long as it leads a good life. They catch fire from its fire. Even after losing its own fire, the soul might still have an inclination to help others, and enjoy describing the gifts given by God to those who love and serve Him.

2. I know someone this happened to.[116] Even though she herself had gone far astray, she was happy for others to benefit from the gifts God had given her and show others the way of prayer who didn't understand it. She did them *a lot* of good. Later, the Lord again gave her light. It's true, though, that she hadn't yet experienced the effects mentioned. But how many are called by the Lord to be apostles, like Judas, and enjoy communion with Him—or are called to be kings, like Saul was—and afterward, through their own fault, are lost! Sisters, we might deduce from this that if we're going to continually gain more—and not be lost, like Saul and Judas[117]—our only possible security consists in obedience and not swerving away from God's law. I'm referring to those God gives such favors to, and actually...to everybody.

UNION OF CONFORMITY TO GOD'S WILL

3. This dwelling place seems a little obscure to me, despite all I've said about it. There's a lot to gain by entering it, and yet I want to avoid the

116. Once again, this is Teresa herself: see *Life*, chapter 7.

117. Judas Iscariot, the disciple who betrayed Jesus and handed him over to the authorities.

impression that there is no hope for those from whom the Lord withholds such supernatural gifts. For true union can be reached, with God's help, if we try to attain it by keeping our wills fixed on whatever is God's will. Oh, how many of us are there who *say* we do this and *think* we want nothing more, and would die for this truth, as I think I've said! Well, I tell you—and I'll repeat this often—that if this is really true, then you have *already* obtained this gift from God, and you don't need to care about the other gracious union that was mentioned. Because the most valuable thing about it actually *comes in and through this union* I'm now describing. We can't reach the heights I've talked about if the union in which we resign *our* wills to the will of *God* is uncertain.

Oh, this union is so desirable! Happy is the soul that has attained it; it will live peacefully both in this life and the next. Nothing that happens on earth—even sickness, poverty, or death—will be deeply distressing, except the danger of losing God, or seeing Him offended (or perhaps when someone dies who was needed by the church of God). For this soul sees clearly that God knows what He is doing better than the soul knows what it wants.

4. You must note that there are many kinds of sadness, or suffering. Some of them come to us suddenly, in natural ways, just as joys and pleasures do. They might even rise from love that makes us have compassion for our neighbors, as our Lord did when He raised Lazarus.[118] Being united with God's will doesn't take away these sorrows, but they also don't disturb the soul with a restless agitation that lasts a long time. They're griefs that pass quickly. Like I said about consolations in prayer, they don't seem to penetrate to the depth of the soul but only reach the senses and faculties. They are part of the previous dwelling places but don't enter the last dwelling (since the suspension of the faculties I've referred to is part of reaching these). Yet…how powerful is the Lord, able to enrich souls in *many* ways and bring them to these dwelling places by many other paths than by this "shortcut" mentioned.

5. But note carefully, daughters, that it is still necessary for the silkworm to die, and at greater cost to you. Because death comes more easily

---

118. See John 11:35: "Jesus began to weep."

when you can see yourself in such a new life;[119] here, [with the union that arises from conformity of will,] we must kill the silkworm ourselves while still living in this life. I confess that this will be harder work, but it is worth the effort, and the reward is precious if you are victorious. But you must not doubt the possibility of this true union with the will of God. This is the union I have desired all my life; it's this union that I continually ask of the Lord, and the one that is clearest and safest.

6. But alas! There must be so few of us who reach it, even when we take care not to offend the Lord and enter monastic religious life and think we have done everything! But oh—there are always a few little worms that we don't notice until they have gnawed through our virtues, like the worm that chewed through Jonah's shade-plant.[120] This happens with self-love, self-importance, judgments about our neighbors (even if only about small things), lack of compassion and care toward them, and failure to love them as we love ourselves. At the end of the day, we might have crawled along, fulfilling our obligations and avoiding sin, but not advancing very far in terms of what's needed for complete union with the will of God.

7. What do you think His will is, daughters? That we be completely perfect, one with Him and with the Father, as in His Majesty's prayer.[121] Just think about what a long way we are from reaching this! Trust me, it's painful for me to write about this, because I know how far I am from it myself—and completely through my own fault. For we don't need to receive great favors from God before we can achieve this. He's given us everything we need in giving us His Son to show us the way.

Yet, I don't want you to think this close conformity to God's will means that if something like the death of my father or brother happens, I shouldn't grieve at the loss. Or that if I have trials or illnesses, I must

119. Teresa seems to be referring to when one is granted the gift of the "infused" prayer of union she has talked about before, when the soul "knows that it is in God, and God is in it."
120. Jonah 4:6–7: "The Lord God appointed a bush, and made it come up over Jonah, to give shade over his head, to save him from his discomfort, so Jonah was very happy about the bush. But when dawn came up the next day, God appointed a worm that attacked the bush, so that it withered."
121. John 17:21–23: "As you, Father, are in me and I am in you, may they also be in us, so that the world may believe that you have sent me. The glory that you have given me I have given them, so that they may be one, as we are one, I in them and you in me, that they may become completely one, so that the world may know that you have sent me and have loved them even as you have loved me."

enjoy bearing them. (It's good if we can do this, and sometimes it's practical—when we can't change the situation, we make a virtue of necessity. Philosophers have often demonstrated or advised such acceptance, as have others with great wisdom.) Here, the Lord only asks two things of us: love of His Majesty and love of our neighbor. This is what we must work on. In keeping these commandments with perfection, we do His will and so shall be united with Him. But like I've said: how far we are from actually doing these two things as we should for such a great God! May His Majesty give us the grace to deserve to reach this state; it's in our hands, if we want it.

LOVE OF NEIGHBOR AS THE TRUEST SIGN

8. In my opinion, the most certain sign as to whether or not we are observing these two laws is whether we observe the love of neighbor well. We can't really know if we love God, even though we may have strong reasons for thinking that we do—but we *can* know if we love our neighbor. And, certainly, the more you advance in your love of neighbor, the greater your love will be for God. For His Majesty loves us so intensely that He will reward our love for our neighbors by increasing our love for Himself in a thousand ways. I can't doubt this.

9. It's very important to walk carefully in this matter, because if we have great perfection here, we've done everything. I don't think we could ever reach perfect love for our neighbor unless it were rooted in the love of God, since our nature is so twisted. Because this is so important, sisters, let's strive to know ourselves better and better, even in the smallest matters. Don't pay attention to all of the beautiful plans that crowd our minds when we're praying, imagining we'll carry them out for the good of our neighbors in the hope of saving just one soul. If our later *actions* don't match up with these plans, there's no reason to believe we will accomplish them. I say the same about humility, and all the virtues. The wiles of the adversary are terrible—he'll run around hell a thousand times if doing so will make us believe that we have a single virtue that we actually don't have. And he's right, because such notions are very harmful. When they come from this source, such imaginary virtues are always accompanied by shallow self-satisfaction[122]—just as real, God-given virtues are free from this, and pride.

---

122. Literally: "vainglory."

10. It's amusing to me how, when they are praying, some people think that they would like to be humiliated and publicly insulted for God's sake—and then they try to hide a very small failure. Oh, and if they're accused of anything that they haven't done!—God save us from having to listen to their protests! Anyone who can't stand such trials should take care *not* to pay much attention to the resolutions made while alone. Because they can't actually have been resolutions made by the will, but a work of the imagination (true determination coming from the will is another matter). The adversary uses the imagination to produce his illusions and deceptions,[123] and there are many that he can produce in women or uneducated people, because we don't understand the difference between the faculties and the imagination, and thousands of other things about the interior life. Oh, sisters! How *clearly* the true love of neighbor can be seen in some of you, and just as clearly the *lack* of such perfection in others! If you understood how important this virtue is for all of us, you wouldn't study or pursue anything else.

11. When I see souls very diligently trying to understand the prayer they have, and so completely and seriously wrapped up[124] in their prayers that they're afraid to move or indulge in a moment's thought (because they're afraid of losing even a touch of the tenderness and devotion they've been feeling), I realize how little they understand the road to attaining union. They think it's all about this [interior experience]. But no, sisters, no! The Lord wants *works*. If you see a sick woman you can help, never hesitate due to fear that your devotions or prayers will suffer: have compassion for her! If she's in pain, you should feel it, too. If needed, go without eating so that she may have your food, not so much for her sake as because you know this is what God wants. This is true union with His will. If you hear someone being praised, be happier than if they were praising you. This is easy if you have humility, in which case you won't like hearing yourself praised. To be truly glad when your sisters' virtues are celebrated is a great thing. And, on the other hand, when we see a

123. Literally: his "jumps and tricks"

124. The word here has a literal meaning involving being covered, muffled, or wrapped up—but it also has a connotation of sullenness or frowning.

fault in someone else, we should be sorry about it, and try to hide it as if it were our own.[125]

12. I have said a lot on this subject in other places,[126] sisters, because I know that if we fail in love of our neighbors, we are lost. May God not allow such failure, and never stop seeking after the union that has been described. Maybe you've had moments of devotion, gratifying experiences that make you think you've reached this stage. Perhaps you've enjoyed a brief period of suspension in the prayer of quiet, which some people think means they've accomplished everything. But if you find you are lacking in this love [of neighbor], you haven't yet reached union. Beg our Lord to give you this perfect love of neighbor, and then allow His Majesty to work. If you give your best effort and strive after this in every way you can, He will give you more than you know how to desire. Force your will to do your sisters' will in everything, even though this might mean you lose your own rights. Forget your own good in your concern for theirs, no matter how much your nature resists. If the opportunity comes up, try to accept work in order to relieve your neighbor of it. Don't think [this love] will cost you nothing, or that you'll find it all done for you. Think about the love our Spouse had for us, and how much it cost Him. He died that most painful death on the cross in order to free us from death.

125. For those not living in religious communities (or even households) and thinking about institutions, this advice can seem alarming. We know what serious and harmful consequences can come from hiding the sins of others or ourselves! But Teresa here seems to be referring to more minor faults in others that we often indulge in observing and commenting on, while trying to keep others from noticing similar faults in ourselves: "She's so greedy—she always takes the last piece of cake." While perhaps not referring to failings quite so frivolous, Teresa seems to be thinking along these general "character" lines and not speaking of serious sin.

126. For example, *Way of Perfection*, chapter 7.

Overview of Chapter Four

Here, in the final chapter of the fifth dwellings, we find ourselves in the place where Teresa returned to working on the manuscript after nearly a five-month break. It's almost as if she reenters the fifth dwelling places as a teacher with a fresh frame of mind, and this time she decides to describe what happens in union with God through the metaphor of engagement for marriage. Using the stages of engagement and marriage that were common at the time, she compares this stage to the initial meetings of the couple and the exchanging of gifts, both of which reveal to the soul who it is that they are dealing with. What follows, naturally, is the experience of falling in love and not wanting to do anything that might cause the soul to lose the Spouse. (All of this comes before the joining of hands, betrothal, and marriage, which she indicates happen in the sixth and seventh dwellings.) And yet, again, the soul should not think of itself as completely safe and secure because, from the adversary's perspective, there's much to be gained from the loss of such a beloved and devoted soul. In her section warning about the continued possibility of being misled, she describes how the temptations are much more subtle here: "Under the claim or illusion of doing good, [the adversary] begins confusing her in small ways, convincing the soul to get involved in things he makes her think are 'not bad.' Little by little, he darkens the understanding, weakens the will, causes self-love to increase, until, one way or another, he gradually withdraws it from the love of God and persuades it to follow its own desires." Yet, in closing with another encouragement to advance, Teresa notes that God does not leave us alone on this worthwhile journey. When we catch a glimpse of the gifts ahead, we might continue to strive and "run our course, enkindled in His love."

Chapter Four (5.4)

1. I imagine you want to know what this little dove is doing, and where it might rest, since you already understand that it can't rest either in

spiritual delights or in earthly consolations: its flight is higher. I can't fully satisfy this tension until we come to the final dwelling place. (God help me to remember it then, and give me a chance to write about it...because almost five months have passed since I started this book, and since my head is not in a state to read it over again, it might all be very convoluted. I might possibly say a few things twice. Since it's just for my sisters, it doesn't really matter.)

2. Still, I want to explain more about what I think this prayer of union is. I'll make the best comparison my wits will allow. Afterward, we'll talk more about this little butterfly, which never rests because it hasn't yet found its true repose—though it is continually fruitful in doing good for itself and for others.

THE METAPHOR OF ENGAGEMENT FOR MARRIAGE

3. You've often heard that God spiritually engages Himself to souls.[127] Blessed be God's mercy that wants so much to humble itself! I'm only making a rough comparison to the sacrament of marriage—though the two work differently, I can't find another metaphor that will better explain what I'm trying to say. In what we are dealing with here, there's never anything that is not spiritual. (Bodily union is a far-distant experience: the spiritual joys that the Lord gives and the pleasures that those who marry must have are a thousand leagues from each other.) Because it's all a union of love with love, and the actions of love are pure; so delicate and gentle that there's no way of describing them...but the Lord knows how to make them very clearly felt.

4. To me, it seems like this union hasn't yet reached the point of spiritual engagement, but is more like what happens when two people are *about* to get engaged. There's discussion about whether or not they are a well-suited match, whether they love each other, whether they might meet again to appreciate each other more deeply. It's like that here. The contract is written, and the soul clearly understands the goodness of her situation and is determined to do her Spouse's will in every way she can

127. This is one of those lines that boldly reminds us we live in a different context than Teresa! Very few of us in the twenty-first century hear much in church or Christian conversation about God getting "engaged" to souls; for Teresa, this language of "betrothal" (formal engagement) is a more common part of the landscape in the life of faith.

to bring Him happiness. His Majesty, who knows full well if this is the case, is happy with her. And so He grants her this mercy—wanting her to know Him better, and for them to meet together (as they say)—and joins her with Himself.[128] We can compare this kind of union to a meeting like this, because it's over very quickly. All giving and receiving of gifts has come to an end, and in a secret way the soul sees *who this Spouse is* that she's going to take. Using her faculties and senses, she couldn't understand in a thousand years what she now understands in the shortest period of time. But the Spouse, being who He is, leaves her after that one visit more worthy of the joining of hands (as they say). The soul is left so in love that she does everything she can to not mess up this divine engagement. If she's careless, though, and sets her affections elsewhere, she loses everything. That loss is as great as the favors He's been granting her, too great to convey.

5. So, Christian souls, if the Lord has brought you to this point, I ask you for His sake not to grow careless. Withdraw from occasions of sin. Even in this state, the soul is not strong enough to face them safely, as it will be in the sixth dwelling places (after the betrothal has been made). We might say this communication has been no more than one short meeting. The devil will take great pains to fight against and try to prevent this betrothal. Afterward, when he sees that the soul is completely surrendered to the Spouse, he doesn't dare. He's afraid of such a soul, and knows by experience that if he tries anything of the kind, he'll lose, and the soul will have a corresponding gain.

WARNINGS ABOUT THE CONTINUED POSSIBILITY OF BEING MISLED

6. Daughters, I tell you that I've known people of a very high degree of spirituality who have reached this state, and yet the adversary—with great subtlety and deceit—has won them back. To achieve this, he will call upon all the powers of hell, because if he wins a single such soul, he wins a whole crowd, as I've often said. The adversary has experience with this dynamic. Think about what a large number of people God draws to Himself through

128. Kavanaugh and Rodriguez's translation explains that Teresa seems to be alluding to stages that were followed in her day for engagement and marriage: (1) meetings between the couple; (2) exchanging gifts; (3) falling in love; (4) joining of hands; (5) betrothal; (6) marriage.

a single soul. God is to be praised for the thousands converted by the martyrs (for example, a young woman like Saint Ursula). And think of the souls the adversary must have lost through Saint Dominic, Saint Francis, and other founders of religious orders—and is losing now through Father Ignatius [of Loyola], who founded the Society [of Jesus]. All of these souls received similar favors from God, as we read. What would have happened if they hadn't made the effort not to lose this divine engagement by their own fault? Oh, my daughters, God is still so ready to grant us such gifts, just like He was then! In some ways, it's even more important that we want to receive them, because there are fewer people now who think about honoring God. We love ourselves so much, and are so careful not to lose any of our rights. Oh, what a big deception! May the Lord give us light so that, by His mercy, we don't fall into such darkness.

7. You're going to ask me, skeptically, about two things: First, if the soul is as ready to do the will of God as I said, then how can it be deceived—since it only wants to do His will in everything? Second, how can the adversary possibly come in and lead you so dangerously astray? You've so completely withdrawn from the world, and are so close to the sacraments, and we might say that you enjoy the company of angels—since, by God's goodness, you have no desire other than to serve and please the Lord in everything. You might say that it wouldn't be surprising for this backward turn to happen to those who are immersed in the cares of the world...[but to us?] You're right, God has been abundantly merciful to us. Yet, as I've said, when I read that Judas enjoyed the companionship of the apostles, and had continually talked to and listened to God Himself, then I realize that there's no security in this [good companionship].

8. To answer the first question: I'd say that if this soul were *always* attached to God's will, then clearly it would not go astray. But the adversary comes along with very skillful deceptions, and under the claim or illusion of doing good, begins confusing her in small ways, convincing the soul to get involved in things he makes her think are "not bad." Little by little, he darkens the understanding, weakens the will, causes self-love to increase, until, one way or another, he gradually withdraws it from the love of God and persuades it to follow its own desires. And this is also the answer to the second question: there's no enclosure so strictly guarded that he can't enter, no desert so solitary that he can't visit. And I'd add one more thing:

the reason the Lord allows this is so He might see the response of the soul that He wants to set up as a light for others. Because if it's going to be a failure, then it's better for this to happen at the beginning than when the fall can harm a lot of people.

9. To my mind, the following ways of being diligent are the most effective: First, we need to continually ask God in prayer to hold us in His hand, keeping in mind that if He leaves us, we'll soon sink to the depths, as is the case. So, we must never trust in ourselves—that would be foolish. But most of all, we must walk with special care and attention, taking note of what kind of progress we make in practicing the virtues: Are we improving or going backward, especially in our love for one another, in our desire to be thought the least of all the sisters, and in doing ordinary tasks? If we reflect on this, and earnestly ask the Lord to give us light, we will quickly discern either the gain or the loss. Don't think that when God has brought a soul so far that He leaves it like easy prey in His hand, or that the adversary has an easy task. His Majesty would be so sorry to see this soul lost that He gives it a thousand interior warnings of many kinds, and so it can't fail to detect the danger.

ENCOURAGEMENT TO ADVANCE

10. In conclusion: we must always strive to advance. And if we aren't advancing, we should walk with great fear, because, without a doubt, the adversary wants to work his deceptions. It is unthinkable that a soul that has come so far should stop growing: love is never idle, so such failure to move forward would be a bad sign. A soul that has tried to be the bride of God Himself, has already become intimate with His Majesty, and has reached the point described must not go to sleep.

And let's begin to talk about the sixth dwelling places, daughters, so that you may see how our Lord treats those whom He makes His brides. You'll see how small our part is: the ways we can serve Him, the suffering we might experience for Him, the preparation we make for such *great* gifts. It could be that the Lord ordained that I should be ordered to write this so that we might forget our little earthly satisfactions when we set our eyes on the reward and on His greatness; seeing His boundless mercy—how He desires to reveal Himself to and commune with some of us worms—we might then run our course, enkindled in His love.

11. I pray that He might enable me to explain some of these difficult things; I know it will be impossible unless His Majesty and the Holy Spirit guide my pen. If it weren't for your benefit, I would ask Him to keep me from explaining any of it. For, as His Majesty knows—as far as I can judge—my only desire is that His name be praised, and that we make every effort to serve Him. He gives us *such* a reward here below, giving us some *idea* of what He'll give us in heaven (without the delays, trials, and dangers of this stormy sea). If there wasn't the possibility of losing Him and offending Him, it would be easy to live until the end of the world, so that we could [continue to] work for such a great God, Lord, and Spouse. May it please His Majesty to make us worthy of His service, without as many faults as we always have, even in good works. Amen.

Questions for Reflection

1. Teresa's most basic criterion and description of the prayer of union is this: "God places Himself in the interior of that soul in such a way that when it returns to itself, it can in no way doubt that it was in God, and God was in it." Based on this definition, would you say you have known the prayer of union? If so, in what ways was it similar to Teresa's further explanations? How was it different?

2. How does the metaphor of the silkworm, its cocoon, and the emergence of a white butterfly speak to your own spiritual life, past or present? Where do you see echoes of these images in Scripture?

3. Whether or not we are given the prayer of union, Teresa says we can achieve the most meaningful aspect of union through a process of death and new life that leads to the "union of conformity to God's will." She leans on the greatest commandments (love of God and love of neighbor) in directing this conformity and surrender. On a day-to-day and week-to-week level, how do you seek to align your life with God's will? What are the teachings, tools, concepts, or warning signs that help you to notice if you are "on" or "off" track?

4. How do you respond to the metaphor of engagement and marriage? Is it helpful or off-putting for you? What are the benefits of this scriptural image? What challenges does it carry for you? How is this concept affected by cultural norms and ideas of marriage that may not be particularly holy or helpful?

SIXTH DWELLINGS

Overview of Chapter One

Just as the reader might think the spiritual journey is all roses and gifts and experiences of love, Teresa opens her longest section of the book with a partial catalog of the trials and suffering we can expect if we tread this path. In the first of the eleven chapters that make up the sixth dwellings, she addresses trials of reputation, drawing from her own experience. People will talk, she promises, and much of what they say will be cruel, gossipy, and mocking. There's a reason that Teresa of Ávila is the patron saint of people ridiculed for their religious faith! Even though we might assume that this is the worst kind of "social" trial we can endure, Teresa surprises our sensibilities by insisting that trials of praise are actually more difficult because the soul knows that if there's any good in it, this is purely a gift of God. Still, she offers a path for safely accepting praise without letting it distort one's sense of self or essential humility.

Next, she turns her attention to physical trials, including the severe pain and illnesses that were part of her own story. Finally, she focuses on *interior trials*, a topic she addresses at length. She centers her discussion on the torment of potential deception and what might be called general "spiritual storms." In these times of inner turmoil, self-doubt, agitation about being potentially deceived, and spiritual dryness, we might find it difficult to pray. Teresa admits that she doesn't know of "anything that *removes* the trouble," but she says that "the best medicine to help the soul endure it is to occupy oneself with external tasks and works of love for others—and to hope in God's mercy." Ultimately, it is God who will lift this burden from the soul, and it will seem then "like it has never been clouded over."

Chapter One (6.1)

1. Now, with the help of the Holy Spirit, let's talk about the sixth dwelling places, where the soul has been wounded with love for the Spouse.

It looks for more opportunity to be alone, trying as much as possible to renounce everything that disturbs this solitude. That sight of Him was so deeply impressing; its whole desire is to enjoy this sight again. I must repeat that nothing is *seen* in this state of prayer that one might say is "really seen," even by our imagination—I use the word "sight" within the comparison [to engagement] I made before.

TRIALS AND SUFFERING

The soul is now completely determined to take no other spouse. But the Spouse disregards its yearnings for the completion of the engagement, wanting the desire to deepen even more, and wanting this greatest of all blessings to be won by the soul at some cost to itself. And even though everything is insignificant compared to this exceptional benefit, trust me, daughters—if the soul is going to bear its trials, it will need nothing less than the sign or token of the engagement that it currently holds. Oh, my God, these trials the soul will suffer before entering the seventh dwelling place are great, both within and without!

2. Honestly, when I think about them, I sometimes fear that if we comprehended their intensity beforehand, it would be very hard to gather enough determination to endure them. We are naturally weak, so our resolution still might not be enough to get us through to the seventh dwelling place (where there is nothing more to be feared, and the soul will dive deep into suffering for God's sake. This is possible because the soul is almost continuously near His Majesty, and such closeness brings strength.) Still, I think it will be helpful if I tell you about *some* of the things that I know will happen here. Now, perhaps not all souls will be led along this [painful] path, though I sincerely doubt that souls that truly have a taste of heavenly things—even from time to time—can live in freedom from earthly trials, in one way or another.

TRIALS OF REPUTATION

3. Even though I didn't intend to talk about these trials, it has occurred to me that a soul who finds itself in this state might be really comforted [through this writing] if it knew what happens to those to whom God has given such gifts, especially at a time when everything seems to be lost. I won't write about these experiences in the order they happen, but as they

come to my memory. I'll begin with the smallest trials. People around her make an uproar—acquaintances, and even those she would never in her life have imagined giving a thought to her. "How *holy* she's getting!" they cry, or "She's trying to act like a saint," or "She's only going to these extremes to deceive the world and to make other people look bad, when they are actually better Christians than she is without this outward show!" (By the way, take note that she's not really indulging in an "outward show" at all—she's only trying to fulfill her vocation and state in life well.) Then people she had thought were her friends abandon her. They say the worst things of all, expressing deep sorrow that (as they put it) she's "gone astray" and is "obviously deluded"; that "this is the devil's work," and she's going the way of others who "ruined their own lives and dragged good people down with them," and that she's deceived her spiritual mentors and confidants.[129] (They actually go to her confessors and say this, giving examples of those who have been lost in this way.) There are a thousand kinds of ridicule and things said like those above.

4. I know a person who was terribly afraid that nobody would be willing to hear her confession because she was the target of such gossip.[130] There's so much more that I could say about this, but I won't stop to get into it here. The worst of it is that these things don't pass quickly—they last for a person's whole life, including the warning not to have anything to do with such a person.

TRIALS OF PRAISE

You'll say that there are also those who speak well of such an individual. But oh, daughters, how few there are who believe the good things in comparison with the many who dislike us! And anyway, to be spoken *well* of is only another trial—and worse than what we've been talking about. Because the soul sees quite clearly that if there's any good in her, this is a gift of God, and not due to herself. Only a short time ago, she saw herself to be very poor and surrounded by sin. So, such praise is intolerable, at least

129. This is "confessors"—I seek to broaden the application here.
130. Teresa herself; see *Life*, chapter 28. Through 6.1.4 and 6.1.5, I have changed the non-gendered "soul" used by Teresa in the original text with various references to "it" to the feminine pronoun, not because this refers only to Teresa herself, but because the passage was more difficult to understand otherwise. I kept references to "the soul" as subject to remind readers of Teresa's broad aim.

at the beginning. Afterward, it is less so, for a few reasons. First: experience clearly shows how people will speak well of others as readily as they will speak poorly of them, and so she takes no more notice of the praise than of the harsh gossip. Second: the Lord has enlightened her to see that no good thing comes from herself, but is rather given by His Majesty. So, the soul turns her praise to God, forgetting she had any part to play, as if seeing the gift at work in another person. Third, the soul sees that others have benefitted from observing the gifts God has given her, and thinks perhaps His Majesty wants them to think of her as good (though, in fact, she isn't), so they might be strengthened in some way. Fourth, the soul now prizes the honor and glory of God more than her own; the beginning sense of danger (that these praises would destroy her, as she's seen happen with others) is removed. Dishonor matters little to this soul if, in exchange, God might be praised even once—afterward, come what may.

5. These developments and other considerations mitigate the great distress caused by praise, though some distress is almost always felt (except when one ignores such things completely). But to find oneself publicly and undeservingly described as good is incomparably harder than the negative gossip mentioned. Once the soul has learned to pay little attention to praise, it cares even less about disapproval. On the contrary, it now sounds like sweet music and brings rejoicing. This is true! The soul is strengthened rather than diminished by severe disapproval, because experience has shown what great benefits it can bring. It then seems one's persecutors are not offending God, but that His Majesty allows this for the benefit to the soul. Being quite clear about this, the soul develops a special and tender love for her persecutors. She thinks of them as truer and more advantageous friends than those who speak well of her.

PHYSICAL TRIALS

6. The Lord is also in the habit of sending the most severe illnesses. This is a much greater trial [than gossip or praise], especially if the pain is severe. In some ways, when pains are very acute, I think they are the greatest earthly trial that exists—the greatest exterior trial, I mean. Again, I'm only referring to very strong pain. For they affect a person both outwardly and inwardly, until the soul becomes so oppressed that it doesn't know what to do with itself; it would rather suffer any martyrdom than these

pains. Still, at the very worst, they don't last long—no longer, generally, than other bad illnesses. After all, God gives us no more than we can bear, and He gives patience first.

7. I know someone who can't truthfully say that since the Lord began—forty years ago—to give her this merciful gift mentioned that she has spent a day without pains and other kinds of suffering.[131] I mean specifically because of her poor physical health, to say nothing of other trials. It's true that she had been very messed up,[132] and everything seemed small compared to the hell that she deserved. Others, who have not offended our Lord so greatly, will be led by Him along another path. But I would always choose the way of suffering, if only to imitate our Lord Jesus Christ, and even if there were no other benefit to it—and there always are, many. But oh! Wait until we come to interior sufferings! If these could adequately be described, they would make all physical sufferings seem trivial, but it's impossible to describe them well.

INTERIOR TRIALS: POTENTIAL DECEPTION AND SPIRITUAL STORMS

8. Let's start with the torment of having a confessor who is so scrupulous, careful, and inexperienced that he thinks *nothing* is safe: he's afraid of everything, and doubtful about everything, as soon as he sees that he's dealing with anything out of the ordinary. This is especially true if he sees any imperfections in the soul undergoing these experiences. He thinks that people God gives these gifts to must be angels. And since this is impossible while we're still in the body, he attributes the whole thing to mental illness or to the adversary.[133] The world is so full of mental illness that this certainly doesn't surprise me; there's so much of it right now, and the adversary uses it so often to do harm. Confessors have good reason to be wary of it and to watch for it carefully. But when a poor

131. This, too, is almost undoubtedly Teresa herself; at the time when she wrote this text, it had been almost exactly forty years since she entered monastic life.

132. Again, the Spanish word here is *ruin*—sometimes translated as "wretched," "wicked," "vile," or "mean." It is difficult to find a word that modern Christians of any denomination use regularly to describe themselves at their worst. Here, I try "messed up," while, in other places, I have used "pathetic."

133. The term rendered here as "mental illness" is *melancholia*, often translated as "melancholy" but used historically to account for a broad swath of what we would now call mental illness, including but not limited to, depression.

soul—wary of the same possibility—goes to the confessor as a judge of what's going on, and he condemns her, she can't help but be upset and tortured by what he says. Only a person who's gone through such a trial will know how terrible it is. This is another trial of these souls, especially if they've gone far astray in the past[134] to think that, because of their sins, God will allow them to be deceived. Although, [as was mentioned,] they *do* feel secure when His Majesty gives them this gift and simply cannot believe that it comes from any other spirit than a spirit of God, remember that it's a state that passes quickly. Then, since the soul is ever mindful of its sins and sees its own faults (which are never lacking), it begins to suffer this torture [of potential deception]. When a confessor is reassuring, the soul calms down, though eventually it gets troubled again. But when all the confessor can do is make the soul *more* fearful, it becomes almost intolerable. This is especially the case when, on top of everything else, there come seasons of spiritual dryness in prayer, during which the soul feels like it's never known God and will never know Him; to hear people talk about His Majesty is like hearing about a person who is far, far away.

9. All of this would amount to nothing if it wasn't immediately followed by the feeling that she can't be rightly describing her case to her confessor and has somehow deceived him. Nevertheless, when she reflects on it, she's sure that she hasn't kept back anything, even the first movements of her mind. Still, it's no use. Her understanding is dim and incapable of seeing the truth, believing what the imagination (which is now driving her understanding) presents. [She struggles] with the nonsense the adversary tries to present, when our Lord allows him to test her soul—even making her think she is cast off by God. There are so many things assaulting her soul; an interior oppression is felt so keenly, and is so intolerable, that I don't know what to compare it to except the torment of those in hell. In this spiritual storm, no consolation is possible.

If she decides to talk with her confessor about this, it seems like the devils are helping him torture her soul even more. A certain confessor, dealing after the fact with someone who had been in this tormented state, thought the oppression was a dangerous kind, since it involved so many

134. This is another use of *ruines*, and an alternate attempt at a modern translation of the same word.

trials. Thus, he told her to report to him whenever she was in this state. But this made her so much worse that he realized there was nothing he could do for her. Because, even though she could read, in such times she found that if she took up a book written in her own language, she couldn't understand it any more than if she didn't even know the alphabet; her intellect wasn't capable of taking it in.

10. In sum, there's no solution for this storm but to wait for the mercy of God. Suddenly, at the most unexpected hour, God lifts this whole burden from the soul with a single word or chance happening: it seems like it has never been clouded over, and it is now full of sunshine and far happier than before. Then, like someone who's escaped from a dangerous battle and emerged victorious, the soul praises our Lord, knowing it is He who fought and enabled the win. It knows full well that it didn't do the fighting itself. It saw that all its own defensive weapons were in the hands of the enemy, was clearly aware of its extreme poverty and powerlessness,[135] and realized how little we can do if the Lord forsakes us.

11. In this state, we don't need [intentional] reflection to understand this. The soul's experience of enduring it, and finding itself completely powerless, has made it realize how utterly helpless we are—impoverished creatures. Because, although the soul can't be lacking *all* grace (despite all this torment, it doesn't offend God and wouldn't do so for anything on earth), this grace is buried so deeply that the soul doesn't seem to feel the smallest spark of any love for God. It doesn't feel that it ever has. If the soul has done anything good, or His Majesty has given it any gift, the whole thing seems like a dream or work of imagination; all it knows for certain is that it has sinned.

12. Oh, Jesus! What a sad thing it is to see this kind of forsaken soul. How little it can gain from any earthly consolation! So, if you ever find yourselves in this condition, sisters, don't imagine that people who are wealthy, or free to do as they like, have any better remedy for this kind of season. No, no—offering them earthly satisfactions would be like telling a criminal sentenced to death about all the joys in the world. Not only would this fail to comfort them, but it would actually *increase* their

135. The word *miseria* is often translated as *misery*, but it's not just suffering that Teresa is referring to—it's also our awareness of lack of resources and power to fight. *Miseria*, in this sense, can also connote destitute poverty.

torment. Comfort must come from above, because earthly things have no value for them anymore. Our great God wants us to know our own poverty as creatures and understand that He is King—this is very important for what's ahead.

13. Now, what is this poor soul to do when such torment goes on for many days?[136] If she prays, it's as if she might as well not be praying, in terms of the comfort it brings her. Because she is incapable of receiving any interior comfort, and even when her prayer is spoken, she can't understand what she is saying. Mental prayer is certainly impossible—her mind is not capable of it. Solitude is even worse, though it's also torturous to be in anyone's company, or have anyone talk to her. Thus, despite all her efforts to hide what's happening, she becomes very noticeably upset and despondent. Is it even possible that she'll be able to say what's the matter? It's inexpressible; this distress and oppression are spiritual troubles and can't be given a name. I don't know of anything that *removes* the trouble, but the best medicine to help the soul endure it is to occupy oneself with external tasks and works of love for others—and to hope in God's mercy, which never fails those who place their hope in Him. May He be forever blessed. Amen.

14. Other exterior trials caused by devils must be quite unusual, and not nearly as serious, so there's no reason to talk about them. Because whatever these devils do, in my opinion they can't go as far as inhibiting the functioning of the faculties or disturbing the soul in this way just described. After all, the soul rightly thinks that they can't do any more than the Lord allows, and so as long as it is not lost, nothing matters much compared to the above.

15. We'll deal next with other interior sufferings in these dwelling places, addressing different kinds of prayer and gifts[137] from the Lord. Although there are a *few* sufferings harder to bear than what's been referred to (as seen by the effects they leave on the body), they don't deserve the

136. Peers translates "many days" as "for a long time," noting that Teresa often uses the "many days" phrase quite vaguely. Kavanaugh and Rodriguez keep the literal translation. Because the state at issue seems quite extreme, I'm inclined toward the more literal sense.

137. Still, the word is *mercedes*—"gifts," "mercies," or "favors." Again, I prefer the word "gifts" to "favors" when possible because it has less connotation of unsavory and sometimes shallow transactions, though the benefit of "favor" over "gift" is the (correct) implication of a power imbalance between giver and receiver.

name “trial.” It wouldn’t be right to give them such a term, because they are such great gifts of God, far beyond deserving, and the soul understands them as such. This severe suffering, along with many others, comes just before the souls enters the seventh dwelling place. I’ll only describe a few of them, since it would be impossible to address them all, or explain their nature. They’re of a different, much higher, sort than the sufferings already mentioned—and if I haven’t been able to explain myself in great detail with these lower kinds, I’ll be able to do so even less with these others. May the Lord give me His help in everything I do, through the merits of His Son. Amen.

Overview of Chapter Two

In this chapter, Teresa focuses on one topic: the experience or gift of God-given impulses that awaken love and increase desire. Although she doesn't always use the word *impulses* to describe them, this term helps us distinguish this unexpected action of God from spiritual delights (which happen in prayer). This movement can occur at any time, and Teresa says that when it does, the soul is "awakened by His Majesty—as if by a streaming comet or a clap of thunder. Although no sound is heard, the soul is very well aware that it has been called by God." This paradox of being *called* and simultaneously *knowing* that God is very near is at the heart of this experience, as is the blend of pleasure and painful yearning. To explain this paradox, Teresa uses the image of God's presence as a fire from which "a spark flies out and touches the soul. It can feel the burning heat, but the fire is not hot enough to set the soul on fire, and the experience is so delectable that the soul is left with that pain." She knows that this sounds pretty fantastical, which is why she keeps appealing to those who have had this experience ("They know what I'm talking about!" she essentially says) and repeatedly explaining that, for those to whom this is happening, "It's perfectly clear that the source of this movement is the Lord...not an imaginative fiction." Like so many other gifts of God, even if we *try* to experience this, we can't fake it. As with other gifts, we can only respond with praise, thanks, and faithful action.

Chapter Two (6.2)

GOD-GIVEN IMPULSES THAT AWAKEN LOVE AND INCREASE DESIRE

1. It seems we have left the little dove a long way back, but we haven't really. These trials enable it to fly higher. So, now let's begin to address the way the Spouse deals with it. We'll see how, before it's completely one with

Him, He fills it with a strong desire. This happens in ways so delicate that the soul itself doesn't understand the means. (I don't think I'll be able to describe them in an understandable way, except for those who have experienced this.) These impulses are so refined and subtle, coming from very deep within the soul; I don't know of a comparison I can make that will fit.

2. All of this is very different from what we can achieve or acquire ourselves on earth, and even from the spiritual delights previously described. Because, often, when a person is quite unprepared and isn't even thinking about God, he's awakened by His Majesty—as if by a streaming comet or a clap of thunder. Although no sound is heard, the soul is very well aware that it has been called by God. [The call is so clear] that sometimes he begins to tremble and complain, even though he doesn't feel anything that causes pain. The soul feels it has been wounded in a wonderful way, but it doesn't understand how, or by whom. It *is* certain that this is a precious experience and would be happy if the wound never healed. It complains to its Spouse with loving words, even out loud (not being able to refrain from doing so). It realizes that He is present yet will not manifest Himself in a way that allows the soul to enjoy Him. This is painful, although also delightful and sweet. Even if the soul didn't want to suffer this wound, it wouldn't have a choice—but anyway, it wouldn't want to refuse. It's much more satisfying to a soul than the delightful and painless absorption that happens in the prayer of quiet.

3. I'm struggling with all my might, sisters, to explain this act of love to you, yet I don't know how. For it seems contradictory to say that the Beloved is making it very clear that He *is* with the soul and yet [at the same time] is giving it such a clear, undoubtable sign that He's *calling*; that the call is so penetrating that the soul can't fail to hear it. The Spouse, who is in the seventh dwelling place, seems to be calling the soul with unspoken words, and none of the inhabitants of the other dwelling places (the senses, the imagination, the faculties) dares to stir. Oh, my powerful God—how great are Your secrets, and how different spiritual things are from what can be seen or understood here below! There's no way to describe this gift, even though it's small compared with the very great ones you work in souls.

4. He performs such a powerful action on her that she dissolves with desire and doesn't know what to ask for, because it clearly seems to her that

God is [already] with her.[138] [You might say to her,] "Tell me: If you know this, what do you want, or what pains you? What greater good do you want?!" I don't know. I know that this pain seems to reach her entrails—her very depths—and that when the One who wounds her takes the arrow out of them, it truly seems that He draws out these inmost depths after Him, following the deep feeling of love.[139]

I've just been wondering if my God might be described as the fire in a lighted firepit; it's as though a spark flies out and touches the soul. It can feel the burning heat, but the fire is not hot enough to set the soul on fire, and the experience is so delectable[140] that the soul is left with that pain; the spark merely touching the soul creates this effect. This seems the best comparison that I've been able to find, because this delectable pain—which isn't really pain—isn't continuous. Sometimes it lasts for a long time, and sometimes it suddenly comes to an end, according to how the Lord wants to give it, because it's something that can't be procured or obtained in any human way. Even though sometimes it's felt for a long while, it comes and goes. In short, it's never permanent. So, it never completely sets the soul on fire; just as the soul is about to ignite, the spark dies, leaving the soul yearning again to suffer the loving pain.

5. There are no grounds for thinking this experience comes from any natural cause, or is caused by mental illness, or that it's an illusion of the adversary or the imagination. It's perfectly clear that the source of this movement is the Lord, who is unchanging. Its effects are not like those in other feelings of devotion, where an intense sense of absorption in a spiritual delight can make us doubt their reality. Here, all the senses and faculties remain alert, without absorption, wondering and watching what

138. This is a time when Teresa does not speak of "the soul" as a non-gendered "it." In the original manuscript, she uses the feminine pronoun here. Previous translations (Peers, Kavanaugh and Rodriguez, Stanbrook) all change this word to "the soul" or "spirit."

139. Previous translations of this section seem uncomfortable with (or at least shy away from) the direct language Teresa is using. I have chosen to keep the feminine pronouns as well as "entrails," the literal word Teresa uses here, while also trying to provide a broader sense. When she speaks about what is "drawn out," it is a reference to "her entrails," a word and image that has so many connotations: literally, intestines or internal organs, one's "bowels," but also internal parts, innermost workings, interior depths.

140. The Spanish word here is *sabroso,* which has the same connotations as the English word *delectable,* —those of being good, pleasant, and satisfying, but also being associated with the pleasures of eating food, like something being "yummy."

is happening. As far as I can see, they don't cause any disturbance—they can't increase this delectable pain or remove it.

Anyone to whom our Lord has given this gift will recognize it upon reading this. He must give Him heartfelt thanks, and not fear that it might be a deception. Instead, let his greatest fear be that he shows ingratitude for such a great gift, and let him strive to serve God and to improve throughout his whole life. He will see the results of this, and receive more and more. One person who was granted this favor spent several years enjoying it, and it satisfied her so completely that, even if she had served the Lord for many years by suffering through great trials, she would have felt well-rewarded. May He be blessed for ever and ever. Amen.

6. You might wonder why there is greater security in this experience than in other things. I think it's for the following reasons: First, because the adversary can't give delectable pain like this. He can give pleasure and delight that seem to be spiritual, but it's beyond his power to unite pain—and so much—with tranquility and joy in the soul. All his powers are in the external arena, on the outside, and when he causes pain, it's never delectable or peaceful, but restless and combative. Second, the delectable storm comes from a region other than where he has authority. Third, this gift brings wonderful benefits to the soul. As a general rule, the soul is filled with a determination to suffer for God's sake, wanting to have many trials to endure, and becoming more resolute about withdrawing from the satisfactions and entanglements of this world.

7. It's very clear that this gift is not an imaginative fiction [brought on by our own craving].[141] Even if we try to experience it at other times, we are unable to counterfeit it. And it is such a conspicuous and obvious thing that there's no way it can be created by our imagination: one simply can't *think* it's there when it's not—and when it *is* there, there's no doubt about it. (If any doubt remains, if the soul wonders whether he had this or not, then it can be sure that these are not genuine impulses.) It's felt as clearly as we hear a loud voice with our ears. And there's no possible way that it

141. The word *antojo* has often been translated as "fancy" (i.e., "That this is no fancy is very evident"), but this term, while recognizable to many, has almost completely fallen out of common use. The term also has the implication of desire within it.

can be due to depression or mental illness,[142] because the illusions created by mental illness only exist in the imagination, and this comes from the interior part of the soul. It's possible I am mistaken. But until I hear arguments to the contrary from someone who understands this experience, I'll always hold this opinion. For example, I know of a person who was terribly anxious about being deceived in prayer, and yet never had any fears about this kind of prayer.

8. Our Lord has other ways of awakening the soul, too: quite unexpectedly, when it is praying aloud and not thinking of anything interior, it suddenly seems to catch fire in a wonderful way. It's as if a fragrance were suddenly to become so powerful that it spreads through all the senses, only in order to convey to the soul an awareness that the Spouse is there. (I'm not saying it *is* a fragrance; it's only a comparison.) The soul is moved by a delectable desire to enjoy Him, and thus the soul is prepared to do great acts and make praises to our Lord. The source of this gift is the one already referred to, but in this case there's nothing that causes pain, and the soul's desires to enjoy God aren't painful in any way—this is actually how the soul *usually* experiences it. For many of the reasons already mentioned, I don't think there's much cause for fear here; one should try to receive this gift with gratitude and give thanks for it.

142. Again, *melancholia*, often rendered as "melancholy" but with a broader history of being associated with depression and other mental illnesses.

Overview of Chapter Three

In this chapter, Teresa addresses another way that God awakens the soul—one that we are a *bit* more comfortable discussing in our current context: when words or phrases come to us as a communication from God. The technical term for this is a "locution." In her day, as much as our own, just because someone says they are "hearing from God" doesn't mean they actually are. Thus, Teresa initially talks about how we should respond (especially in religious communities) with compassion and common sense to suspected false communications from God—to those who say God is speaking to them when there are good reasons to believe it's not true. Then she turns her attention to how we distinguish between different words and phrases we hear: How do we know what is a product of our own imagination, what is of the adversary, and what is of God? She wants to take such divine communications seriously even while downplaying their importance in terms of our ego, noting that Jesus talked a lot to the Pharisees! She gives three signs that words are of divine origin: (1) the power and authority of the words; (2) a resulting sense of peace and desire to praise God; and (3) their lasting imprint on the memory. As a community safeguard, she directs those who believe God is asking them to do something specific to check in with a trusted mentor, among other helpful and pragmatic advice for response and discernment.

What Teresa speaks of next is not a "vision" in the way that we typically think of visions (we'll hear more about them later) but a "contact" that "takes place so far down in the soul's depths, in such secret, and the words spoken by the Lord seem to be heard so clearly with the ears of the soul." These are "intellectual visions" that include communications from God. How can we tell whether *these* experiences aren't just products of our imagination? Teresa outlines five ways, and then reminds us that even if the adversary could "fake" this kind of communication, he can't produce the *effects* of peace and praise that accompany a genuine communication of

God. Finally, she notes that it's impossible to ignore the communications of God even if we wanted to.

Chapter Three (6.3)

1. God awakens the soul in another way, one that *seems* a greater gift than the others in some respects—but may also be more perilous. For this reason, I'll spend some time describing it. The soul is awakened by words or phrases[143] that come in many ways: some seem to come from outside, others from the very interior of the soul, others from its higher part, others so completely outside the soul that they are heard with the ears and seem to be from an actual voice.

RESPONDING TO FALSE COMMUNICATIONS FROM GOD

Sometimes—in fact, often—this might be a figment of our imagination, especially in people with true mental illness, or who have weak and impressionable imaginations.

2. From my perspective, with these two kinds of people, we shouldn't pay serious attention [to the words they say they hear from God], even if they say they see or hear or have been given understanding about certain things—but we also shouldn't upset them by telling them their experiences are from the adversary. One should listen to them, as one would to any sick person. The prioress, or the confessor, or whatever person she confides in should advise her not to pay attention to these communications, because they aren't essential to serving God (and many people have been deceived by the adversary in this way, though perhaps this might not be the case for her). One should respond in such a way that doesn't distress her further. If she is told she is suffering from mental illness, there won't be any end to it. She'll simply swear she sees and hears things, and she really believes that she does.

3. It's necessary to be firm about giving her less time for prayer, and to insist strongly that she doesn't attach great importance to what she hears.

143. Although this word is often translated as "locutions"—and there are benefits to having a specific word with theological layering and history—Teresa's word here is not technical; it is simply *hablas*, referring to speech, words, phrases, and talking.

For the adversary is likely to take advantage of the sickness of these souls, to the detriment of others (if not to their own as well). Both with sick and healthy souls, there are always reasons for misgivings and uncertainty about these things, at least until we understand the spirit at work. I say it's always better to push aside such things at first. Because if they *are* of God, doing so will help us to advance (when put to the test, they'll tend to increase). This is true, but it doesn't press or disturb the soul too much, because truly it can't control these experiences.

DISTINGUISHING BETWEEN DIFFERENT WORDS OR PHRASES WE HEAR

4. Getting back to what I was saying about words or phrases: these may come from God, in any of the ways I've mentioned, or they may equally well come from the adversary or our own imagination. With the Lord's help, I'll try to describe the different signs for these different experiences, and when they are dangerous. Since there are many prayerful people who experience them, this is my aim, sisters: I don't want you to think you are wrong when you *don't* give them credit or weight, or when you *do* give them weight when they are directed at you (either as a nice consolation or a notice of your faults), no matter where they come from, or if they are only imaginary. But I'll warn you about one thing: even if you hear words or phrases from God, don't think that you are somehow superior to others. After all, He talked a great deal with the Pharisees. Any benefit depends on how you respond to what you hear. And unless it agrees strictly with the Scriptures, don't pay any more attention to it than you would if the words came from the adversary himself. Such words might actually only be coming from your weak imagination, but they must be seen as a temptation against matters of faith, and always resisted. They'll then fade away because they have little effect on you.

5. Getting back to our first point: whether the words come from within, above, or outside the soul has nothing to do with discerning whether or not they are from God. The surest signs that one can have [of their divine source] are as follows:

The first and truest sign is the sense of power and authority they carry with them, both in themselves and in the actions that follow. I'll explain more. Consider a soul experiencing all the interior tumult and hardships that have been described, and all the spiritual dryness and darkened understanding. A single word of this kind [from God]—just a "Don't be troubled"—is enough to calm him. No other word needs to be spoken; a great light comes, and all his trouble is lifted—even though he had been thinking that if the whole world and all the smartest people in the world were to come together to give reasons why he should not be troubled, they couldn't bring relief, no matter how hard they tried. Or consider a soul distressed because its confessor and others have told her that she has a spirit sent by the devil, and she's full of fear. Yet that single word she hears, "It is I; don't be afraid,"[144] takes all the fear away. She is wonderfully comforted and trusts that no one will ever be able to make her feel otherwise. Or consider a soul really worked up because of some important piece of business, and he has no idea how it can possibly work out. He's then given to understand that he should be calm, and everything will turn out all right. He is left confident, and free from anxiety. This is the way it goes in many other cases.

6. The second sign is that a great quiet is left in the soul, along with a devout and peaceful sense of recollection, and a readiness to sing praises to God. They say that in this dwelling place, at least, such words are uttered by an angel, not the Lord Himself. Oh, Lord! If there's so much power in a word sent by one of Your messengers, what power will You leave in the soul that is bound to You, and You to it, by love?

7. The third sign is that these words stay in the memory for a very long time. Indeed, some are never forgotten. Those we hear on earth—I mean from people, however important and wise they might be—are not so deeply engraved in our memories. And if they refer to the future, we don't give weight to them in the same way we do these [divine] words, which impress us with *such* certainty: though they sometimes seem impossible to fulfill (and we can't help wondering if they will come true, and our mind hesitates to believe it), within the soul itself there's a certainty that cannot be overcome. It might seem that everything is moving in the opposite direction than we had been led to expect...and yet, even after many years, the belief is never lost that even though God may use ways and paths we humans can't comprehend, in the end, what He said will come true; as, in fact, it

144. Both stories have resonance with Luke 24:36: "While they were talking about this, Jesus himself stood among them and said to them, 'Peace be with you.'"

does. Nevertheless, the soul is still distressed when it sees things going badly astray, because some time has passed since it heard the words (and the effects and certainty present about them being from God have passed, too). So, these doubts rise up, and the soul wonders if the whole thing came from the adversary, or might have been a figment of the imagination. Yet, at the time, it had no such doubts, and would have died in defense of their truth. But, I'd say these [doubtful] imaginings must be put in our minds by the adversary to distress us and intimidate us. This is especially the case if obeying the words presents considerable difficulties, and yet will bring many blessings to others, or produce good works that align with the honor and service of God. What will the devil not do in such a case to encourage misgivings? At the very least, he'll weaken the soul's faith, because it does great harm to not trust that God can do things beyond our understanding.

8. Despite all these struggles, despite the people—I mean confessors—who say that these words are pure nonsense, and despite the many unfortunate events that might persuade the soul that they can't come true, there *still* remains a living spark of conviction that they *will* come true. (Where this comes from, I can't say.) Though all other hopes may be dead, this spark of certainty cannot die, even if the soul wanted it to. And in the end, as I've said, the Lord's word is fulfilled, and the soul is so comforted and happy that it wants nothing more than to praise His Majesty forever. This is more because what He had told was fulfilled than because of what actually happens, no matter how important the work is to the person.

9. I don't know why the soul is so anxious for these words to turn out to be true. If the same person were caught in the act of lying, I don't think she would feel nearly as upset and sorry. And yet there's nothing else she can do except repeat what's said to her! In such a case, a certain person was frequently reminded of the prophet Jonah, when he feared that Nineveh would *not* be destroyed.[145] Of course, since the words come from the Spirit of God, it's right we would have this trust in Him, and not want Him to ever be thought of as false; He is supreme truth. Thus, there's great joy for the one who sees His word come true, after a thousand ups and downs

145. See Jonah, chapters 1 and 4. Jonah is anxious about God's integrity or reliability because he is told to proclaim that the city will be destroyed—and then, when the people repent and change their ways, God does not do it. He is upset (by God's mercy, and perhaps—implicitly—the experience of saying words that didn't turn out as expected, on the surface), but God reminds Jonah that his concern is for the *people*.

and in the most difficult circumstances. Such a person might have to suffer great challenges in the course of this fulfillment, but she would much rather have these trials than have what the Lord told her would happen *not* happen. Perhaps not everybody will have this weakness—if it really is a weakness, because I can't really condemn it as wrong.

10. If the words or phrases come from the imagination, there are none of these signs: not certainty, peace, or interior consolation. It might happen that when a person is deeply absorbed in the prayer of quiet and in a spiritual sleep, they think the words come to them in a kind of dream, seeing things and thinking they are of God. The effects of these words are like those of a dream. (I know a few people this has happened to. For some people get so entirely carried out of themselves in deep recollection that they are unconscious of everything external, and all their senses are in such slumber that it's *like* they are sleeping. This happens because of the weakness of their constitution or imagination, or other reasons.) It may also happen that, when such a person is begging our Lord for something with great love, they imagine that the voices are telling him what he wants to hear; this does in fact sometimes happen. But I don't think anyone who has a lot of experience with words coming from God will be deceived in this way by the imagination.

11. With words from the adversary, there's more to fear. But if the words are accompanied by the signs already described, we may be very confident they're of God. However, this confidence is not extreme: if what is said is of great importance and involves the hearer taking action, or includes matters affecting someone else, we shouldn't do anything about it—or consider doing anything—without taking the advice of a wise mentor,[146] a person of clear insight and a servant of God. [This should be done] even when one discerns the words better and better, and it might seem evident that they're of God. This [accountability with another] is His Majesty's will, so by doing this we aren't failing to obey. He has told us to put our confessor in His place, even when it can't be doubted that the words are His. If it's a difficult matter, this [affirmation from a confessor] will help to give us courage, and if our Lord wants to, He will speak to the confessor and make him recognize the work of His spirit. If He doesn't do this, we are no longer under any obligation. To do something other than what [the

146. Literally: the advice of a "learned confessor, a man."

mentor or confessor] has said and follow nobody's opinion but your own is a very dangerous thing, I think. And so, sisters, on behalf of our Lord, never let this happen to you.

INTELLECTUAL VISIONS THAT INCLUDE COMMUNICATIONS FROM GOD

12. There's another way the Lord speaks to the soul: with a kind of intellectual vision. I hold that it is very definitely from Him, and I'll explain its nature further.[147] This contact takes place so far down in the soul's depths, in such secret, and the words spoken by the Lord seem to be heard so clearly with the ears of the soul: the very way in which they are heard, combined with the effects of the vision, convinces and assures the person that the adversary has no part to play in this. The wonderful effects produced are enough to make us trust this, or at least we can be sure that such words and phrases don't come from our imagination. With reflection, we can always be sure of this distinction, for the following reasons:

First, some communications are much clearer than others.[148] A genuine communication is so clear that even if a single syllable is missing from what the person heard, or if it was said in one style or another, he remembers—even if it's a whole sentence. In communications created by the imagination, the voice will be less clear and the words less distinct, like something heard in a half-dream.

13. Second, often the soul hasn't been thinking of what it hears—I mean the voice comes unexpectedly, sometimes even during a conversation. Often, it does refer to something that was passing through one's mind, or what one was thinking of before. But it often refers to things that one never thought would or could happen, in such a way that the imagination couldn't have invented them. The soul can't be deceived about things it hasn't desired, wished for, or even thought about.

14. Third, in a genuine communication, it's like the soul is *hearing* something. In those from the imagination, it's like someone *composing* bit by bit what she wants to hear.

---

147. She also speaks of intellectual visions in 6.5.8–9, 6.8, and 6.10.

148. In this section, what other translators have rendered as "locutions" is updated to "communication."

15. Fourth, there's a big difference within the words themselves: with a single word one understands so much—a depth of meaning our intellect could not compose so quickly.

16. Fifth, in a way I don't know how to explain, these communications often give us much more to understand than is implied by the words themselves—without further explanations. I'll talk more about this understanding in another place; it's something very subtle that should bring praises to our Lord.

Some people have been very doubtful about this way of understanding communications and the differences between them—especially one person that they've happened to.[149] Thus, there are no doubt others who did not quite understand. I know this person has thought it all over very carefully because the Lord has granted her this gift many times. The greatest doubt she had in the beginning was whether or not she was *imagining* the whole thing. It's easier to recognize when communications come from the adversary (although he's so wily that he can imitate the spirit of light quite well). From my perspective, he'll do this by speaking clearly, so that—just as if they were being spoken by the spirit of truth—there's no doubt about their being understood. But he won't be able to fake, imitate, or counterfeit the *effects* that have been described, or leave peace and light in the soul. What is left is only restlessness and turmoil. He can't do much harm, or any, if the soul is humble and follows what I've said—that is, doesn't act on what is heard.[150]

17. If the communications are gifts and favors[151] from the Lord, the soul should carefully consider whether, because of them, she thinks she is better than others. If, as the words of gift and favor grow more intense, and she is not somewhat confused, I believe it's not the spirit of God. Because it's quite clear that when the spirit is from God, then the greater the favor given, the less the soul thinks of itself; the more it is mindful of its sins, the more it is forgetful of its own interest, the more it passionately strives

149. In the following, Teresa is referring to herself, her suspicions and careful attention to not being misled.

150. Teresa seems to be referring to not acting without talking to a confessor first, not acting independently or hastily; based on other sections, she's not eliminating responsive action at all.

151. Here the word is not *merced*, but actually *favores* ("favors"), along with the most basic word for gifts: *regalos*.

to seek nothing but the honor of God instead of its own profit, and the greater is its fear of departing even in the smallest ways from the will of God. (The certainty that it has never deserved these favors, but only hell, is greater too.) When these are the results of all the experiences and gifts that come in prayer, the soul doesn't need to be afraid. She can walk confidently, trusting in the mercy of the faithful Lord, who won't allow the adversary to deceive her…though it's always good to walk with some fear.

Those whom the Lord does not lead by this road might think that people don't *need* to listen to the words addressed to them. They might imagine that if they're *interior* words, they should simply turn their attention elsewhere, so they don't hear them—and then they won't run the risks of these dangers. My response: that's impossible. Now, I'm not referring to words and phrases conjured by our imaginations; a solution there *is* to be less anxious about certain things and to try not to pay attention to our imaginings. But when the communications come from God, there's no such solution. For the Spirit Himself, as He speaks, inhibits all other thought and compels our attention to what He says. So, I truly think that it would be easier for someone with excellent hearing not to hear a person speaking with a very loud voice…because he *might* simply not pay attention, and occupy his thoughts with something else. In what we're talking about, though, that's impossible. We don't have ears that we can plug or the power to refrain from thoughtful attention; we can only think of what's being said. For He who was able to make the sun stand still at the request of Joshua[152] (I think it was him) can still the faculties and all the interior parts of the soul. It happens in such a way that the soul becomes fully aware that another Lord, greater than itself, is ruling that castle. This brings great devotion and humility. So there's no "solution"—the soul can't do anything but listen. May His Divine Majesty give us the solution of fixing our eyes on pleasing Him and forgetting ourselves, as I've said. Amen. May He grant that I might have successfully explained what I was trying to, and that I might have given some help to anyone who's experienced such communications.

---

152. Joshua 10:12–13: "On the day when the Lord gave the Amorites over to the Israelites, Joshua spoke to the Lord; and he said in the sight of Israel, 'Sun, stand still at Gibeon, and Moon, in the valley of Aijalon.' And the sun stood still, and the moon stopped, until the nation took vengeance on their enemies."

Overview of Chapter Four

The fourth chapter contains Teresa's treatment of some of the more "extraordinary gifts" given by God: the suspension of the soul in prayer through rapture, ecstasy, or transport—which, in her own introduction to the chapter, she indicates are different terms for the same thing—and intellectual visions. There are different kinds of rapture, all of which "draw the soul out of its senses." Secondary to this concept of rapture is her teaching on imaginative and intellectual visions, which take place when the Lord wants to reveal to or share some sacred mysteries with the soul. She struggles a bit to find a suitable metaphor, especially because the person often doesn't remember the details of what has been "seen" or revealed, and eventually compares it to being shown a room with an overwhelming number of ornate things. We can see Teresa get worked up with enthusiasm over the wonder of these gifts as she spontaneously writes an interlude of encouragement to persevere. Finally, she returns to her original train of thought, sharing the effects of rapture. Here she describes the physical, spiritual, and social effects, alluding to the troubles that her "public" raptures gave her in community life and indicating that it's much simpler if no one witnesses this extraordinary gift at work, should we receive it.

Chapter Four (6.4)

1. In the middle of these trials and other things I've described, what kind of rest can this poor little butterfly have? All these sufferings serve to increase her desire to enjoy the Spouse. His Majesty, knowing well our weakness, strengthens her through these challenges and others so that she might have the courage for union with such a great Lord and take Him as her Spouse.

2. You'll laugh at my saying this, and think it's ridiculous. You'll all think that courage is unnecessary—that there's no woman, however lowly,

who wouldn't be brave enough to be married to the King. This would be the case with an earthly king, I think, but for a marriage with the King of Heaven, I have to warn you that courage is more necessary than you imagine. Our nature is very timid and lowly when it comes to something so great, and I'm certain that unless God gives us strength, no matter how much we might see that the gift is good for us, it would be impossible to receive.

SUSPENSION OF THE SOUL THROUGH RAPTURE, ECSTASY, OR TRANSPORT

Now, you're going to see what His Majesty does to conclude this engagement, which, as I understand it, happens when He gives raptures that draw the soul out of its senses. Because if the soul saw that it was so close to such great majesty while still in possession of its senses, it might die. You must understand that I'm talking about genuine raptures, not women's weaknesses, in which it's imagined that everything is rapture and ecstasy. As I've said, there are some people who have such weak constitutions that one experience of the prayer of quiet kills them.

Here, I want to list some different kinds of rapture that I've learned about through conversations with spiritual people. I'm not sure if I will be able to successfully describe them and other things that occur in this dwelling place, any more than when I wrote about this before.[153] For various reasons, it seems worthwhile to discuss all of this again, regardless of whether I repeat myself, if for no other reason than to have all that might be said about each dwelling put down together in one place.

3. One kind of rapture: the soul, even though not engaged in prayer, is touched by some word it remembers or hears from God. It seems that His Majesty, from the interior of the soul, makes the spark mentioned grow. He's moved with compassion at having seen the soul suffer so long in her yearning for Him. The spark catches fire; she is burned and renewed, like a phoenix. One can piously believe that her faults are forgiven.[154] After the soul is purified in this way, God unites it with Himself in a way that no one here can understand but the two of them. Not even the soul itself understands in a

153. *Life*, chapter 20; *Spiritual Testimonies* 59, no. 9.

154. In the margin, Teresa adds here, in Peers' translation: "Assuming that it is in the proper disposition and has used the means of grace, as the Church teaches."

way that it can describe afterward, even though it's not deprived of its interior senses. It's *not* like someone who suffers a fainting spell or other fit, in which there is no understanding or consciousness, internally or physically.

4. What I do understand in this case is that the soul has never been more awake to the things of God, or had such enlightenment and knowledge of His Majesty. This might seem impossible, because if the faculties and senses are so completely absorbed that they almost might be described as dead, how can we say the soul understands this mystery? I can't say—maybe no creature can. Maybe only the Creator Himself can say what happens in this state. (I mean these [final] two dwelling places, since this and the last one might be thought of as one, because there's no closed door separating one from the other. Since there are a couple of things in the last dwelling place that aren't yet shown to those who haven't reached it, though, I thought it best to separate them.)

IMAGINATIVE AND INTELLECTUAL VISIONS

5. When the soul is in this suspension, the Lord sees fit to reveal some mysteries, things about heaven, and imaginative visions. Afterward, the soul is able to describe them because they're so deeply impressed into the memory that they can't ever be forgotten. But when they are *intellectual* visions, they can't be described like this. These kinds of visions are so sublime that those who live on earth aren't fit to understand them well enough to describe them. Nevertheless, after regaining possession of their senses, they can describe *some* of these intellectual visions.

Maybe some of you don't understand what I mean by "a vision," especially an "intellectual vision." I'll explain this, as I've been told to by those with authority over me. Even though it might seem irrelevant, there might be souls who will find it helpful.

6. "But wait," you'll say, "if the soul isn't going to remember these sublime gifts that the Lord gives in this state, how can this be beneficial?" Oh, daughters, the benefit is so enormous that it can't be exaggerated. Because even though one can't *describe* these gifts, they are still clearly imprinted in the very depths of the soul, and never forgotten. "But wait," you'll say next, "if the soul doesn't keep any image of them, and the faculties are unable to understand them, how can they be *remembered*?" This is beyond my

understanding, too. Yet I know that certain truths about the greatness of God remain firmly in the soul—so much so that, even if before this the soul didn't have enough faith to say who God is, or didn't believe Him to be God, from that moment on, the soul *would* adore Him as God, just like Jacob did when he saw the ladder.[155] Jacob must have "understood" other mysteries that he didn't know how to explain. For if there hadn't been deeper interior enlightenment, he wouldn't have understood such great mysteries just by seeing a ladder with angels going up and down it. (I don't know if I'm right in what I'm saying here, because even though I've heard of this story, I'm not sure I remember it correctly.)

7. Moses also didn't know how to describe everything that he saw in the [burning] bush, but only as much as God wanted him to.[156] Yet if God hadn't revealed mysteries to his soul in such a way that he became *sure* of their truth—recognizing and trusting Him to be God indeed—he wouldn't have taken up so many works, and such difficult ones! Amid the thorns of that bush, he *must* have understood profound truths, things that gave him the courage to do what he did for the people of Israel. Therefore, sisters, we shouldn't look for reasons to understand the mysteries of God. Instead, trusting in His great power, we should realize that it's impossible for limited worms like ourselves to understand God's greatness. Let us give Him heartfelt praise that we are even allowed to understand some part of it.

8. I wish I could find a comparison or metaphor that would explain what I'm talking about, but I can't think of any that fit. Let me put it like this, though: You go into a private apartment in the palace of a king, a place I think they call a "treasure room." There's an infinite variety of glassware, pottery, all kinds of things displayed in such a way that you can see almost everything as you enter. I was once taken into a room like this in the Duchess of Alba's house, where I was ordered by my superiors to stay for two days while on a journey, due to the Duchess's insistence. When I went in, I was amazed, and yet wondered what good could come from such a collection of things. I saw that one might be led to praise

155. Genesis 28:12: "And he dreamed that there was a ladder set up on the earth, the top of it reaching to heaven; and the angels of God were ascending and descending on it."
156. Exodus 3:2: "There the angel of the Lord appeared to him in a flame of fire out of a bush; he looked, and the bush was blazing, yet it was not consumed."

the Lord in response to seeing such a vast array, and now I'm laughing to myself as I realize how useful the experience was for this explanation. Because even though I was there for some time, there was so much to see that I couldn't remember it all. I could no more recall what was in those rooms [specifically] than if I'd never seen them. I couldn't say what the things were made of; I only remember seeing them as a whole. It's just like that here. The soul, while made one with God, is brought into this heavenly room that we must have in our depths. Clearly, the soul has some of these dwelling places within, since God abides within it. And even though the Lord doesn't want the soul to see these mysteries every time it's in ecstasy—the soul can be so absorbed in enjoying Him that this sublime good is enough—sometimes He wants the soul to come out from its absorption enough to see what is in this room. After it returns to itself, the soul will remember a general representation of the wonders it saw, but it won't be able to describe them; our nature doesn't grasp any more of the supernatural than God wants us to see.

9. You might therefore object, saying I admit that the soul has *seen* something—so this is an imaginative vision. But I don't mean that at all; I'm talking about intellectual visions, not imaginative ones. It's just that I have no education and am too dull to explain anything clearly. It *is* clear to me that if what I've said about this prayer so far is any good, it was not I who said it. My own belief is that if the soul in raptures never understands any of these secrets, they are not raptures given by God at all, but are caused by some natural weakness. This can affect people with weak constitutions, such as women. But any spiritual force will overcome their natures and cause them to remain in a state of absorption, as I think I said when dealing with the prayer of quiet. These experiences don't have anything to do with raptures. When a person is enraptured, believe me, God carries off for Himself the entire soul. As with someone who is His own and His Spouse, He is showing the soul some little part of the kingdom that was gained by this marriage. This might only be a small part, but everything that is within this great God is magnificent. And He doesn't want us to be disturbed by anything, including the faculties or the senses; He immediately commands that all the doors of these dwelling places shall be shut, and *only* the door of the dwelling place where He dwells remains open, so that we might go inside. Blessed be such great mercy! Those who

have not wanted to benefit by it, and thus give up on the presence of their Lord, will rightly be called accursed.

ENCOURAGEMENT TO PERSEVERE (INTERLUDE)

10. Oh, my sisters, what *nothingness* is everything we've given up, and all that we're doing or could ever do, for a God who desires to share Himself[157] in this way—with a worm! If we might hope to enjoy this blessing while we are still alive, what are we doing about it? Why are we waiting? What reason could possibly be sufficient for delaying even a short time instead of seeking this Lord, just as the bride [in the Song of Solomon did], through the streets and squares?[158] Everything in the world is a cruel joke if it doesn't lead us and help us on the way toward this goal—and this would be the case even if all the worldly comforts, riches, and joys that we can imagine lasted forever! Because everything is disgusting and worthless compared to the treasures that will be enjoyed eternally. And even these treasures are nothing compared to having the Lord of all treasures, and of heaven and earth, as our own.

11. Oh, the blindness of humanity! How long, how long before this dust is removed from our eyes? Even though it doesn't seem bad enough to blind us altogether (at least among ourselves), I do see specks and tiny pebbles. If we allow them to increase, they'll be enough to do us great harm. For the love of God, sisters, let us benefit from these faults, learning from them what pathetic creatures we are, and may they somehow give us clearer sight, like the clay on the eyes of the blind man who was healed by our Spouse.[159] Realizing our own imperfections, we might ask Him more and more earnestly to bring good out of our weakness, so that we might please His Majesty in everything.

12. I've gotten way off track without realizing it. Forgive me, sisters. It's just that now that I've come to writing about these great things of God, I can't help but feel the deep sadness of it when I see how much we are losing,

---

157. The literal phrase or word here is "communicate Himself," which implies added layers of sharing but is also not commonly used as a verb anymore.

158. Song of Solomon 3:2: "'I will rise now and go about the city, in the streets and in the squares, I will seek him whom my soul loves.' I sought him, but found him not."

159. John 9:6–7: "When he had said this, he spat on the ground and made mud with the saliva and spread the mud on the man's eyes, saying to him, 'Go, wash in the pool of Siloam' (which means Sent). Then he went and washed and came back able to see."

and all through our own fault. Because even though it's true that these are things that the Lord gives to whomever He wants, He would give them to *all* of us if we loved Him as He loves us. For He wants nothing else but to have someone to whom He might give His gifts; His riches do not diminish when He gives them away.

THE EFFECTS OF RAPTURE

13. Getting back to what I was saying: the Spouse commands that the doors of the dwelling places be closed, including those of the castle and the outer wall. In wanting to carry off this soul [in rapture], He takes away its breath so that even if the other senses last a little longer sometimes, it can't possibly speak. Other times, it loses all its powers at once, and the hands and body get so cold that the person doesn't seem to have any life—sometimes it's doubtful if he is even breathing. This lasts only for a short period of time in its intensity. For when this extreme suspension lifts a little, the body seems to return to itself again somewhat, only to be encouraged to die once more, giving fuller life to the soul. Such great ecstasy doesn't last long.

14. But even though the extreme ecstasy ends, for as long as a day, or even several days, the experience leaves the will so absorbed and the intellect so withdrawn that the soul seems incapable of grasping anything that doesn't awaken the will to love. In terms of the will to love, it is wide awake; it's asleep in terms of attachment to any creature.

15. Oh, what confusion the soul feels when it returns completely to itself! How intense is its desire to be used for God in any and every way that He might want to employ it! Since this effect has been described as a result of *previous* forms of prayer, what can I say about [this effect from] a gift this great? Such a soul would happily have a thousand lives so as to use them all for God, and wishes everything on earth would somehow be a tongue, to help in praising Him. The desire for sacrificial generosity[160] is incredibly strong. Yet whatever acts of sacrifice and generosity are offered, it doesn't seem that helpful, because the great strength of love makes the soul feel like everything it does doesn't amount to much. The soul sees clearly that it wasn't such a great matter for the martyrs to suffer all their torments because, with the help of our Lord, such a thing becomes easy.

160. Again, this is literally "penance."

And so these souls complain to our Majesty when He doesn't offer them ways of suffering.

16. When this gift is granted privately, they value it highly. When it's given in the presence of others, their shame and embarrassment are so strong that the angst and worry about what those who have seen it will think decreases the soul's enjoyable absorption, at least somewhat. For they know the malice of the world, and realize that their experience might not be seen for what it is (a reason to glorify the Lord) and instead might be the target of criticism. This pain and embarrassment aren't within the soul's power to control, and yet they seem to me to signal a lack of humility. For if such a person really wants to be treated with disdain, how can she then mind when she is? One person who was troubled in this way heard the Lord say to her, "Don't be distressed, because they will either praise Me or criticize you, and either way you benefit."[161] Later, I learned that these words were very helpful and comforting; I share them here for the sake of anyone who finds themselves in this predicament. It seems that our Lord wants everyone to realize that this person's soul is now His, and no one should touch it. It's fine if people attack her body, honor, or possessions—because any of these attacks might still bring honor to His Majesty. But her soul, they may not touch. As long as the soul itself doesn't withdraw from its Spouse with blameworthy boldness, He'll protect it from the whole world, and all of hell.

17. I don't know if I've managed to convey anything about the nature of rapture. Explaining it is completely impossible, as I've said. But I don't think there's been any harm in my trying, so that *some* of its nature might be understood—especially because the effects of fake raptures are so different. (I don't use the word "fake" because those who experience them want to deceive others, but because they themselves are deceived.) Since the signs and effects of these fake raptures don't match this [true] great blessing, true raptures are discredited, and those to whom the Lord then gives this gift aren't believed. May He be blessed and praised forever. Amen. Amen.

---

161. *Life*, chapter 31.

Overview of Chapter Five

For those of us reading about raptures for the first time, we might not realize that what Teresa is describing in chapter five is not another experience entirely, but rather a *kind* of rapture. She essentially continues her teaching on raptures but focuses on one subset, an experience she calls the "flight of the spirit." Most basically, this is when "suddenly, the soul feels a movement that is so fast it seems the spirit is being carried away—and at a scary speed, especially in the beginning." To make things even more intense, "this happens without the soul knowing where it's going, who's taking it, or how, because when this movement begins, the soul is not certain the rapture is from God." Teresa tries to explain and describe this phenomenon using a number of images and metaphors. We can clearly see why she insists that "courage is necessary" to receive many of God's gifts in prayer, but then she turns her attention to an ancillary need for courage: we also need courage and continued self-knowledge, amid such wondrous gifts, to continue to face the reality of our own smallness and limitations. This is spurred, in part, by a strong sense of obligation to repay God's goodness through service and action; one quickly realizes that such "repayment" by one's own power or will is impossible. The humility and deeper self-knowledge that result are helpful.

After this interlude, Teresa returns to the chapter's initial topic in order to describe more fully the dynamics of the flight of the spirit. She tries to further illuminate what this fearsome experience is like and its effects: "When the soul is outside herself—at least as far as she can understand—great things are shown to her. When the soul returns to herself, she has greatly benefitted.... Compared to what she has seen, she takes no stock in earthly things." All of this "seeing" of wonderful things is with the eyes of the soul, in what Teresa calls an intellectual vision, a term she began to discuss earlier in the sixth dwellings. Returning briefly to the engagement metaphor, she refers to such experiences as "jewels" that the

Spouse gives, acknowledging the reality that the soul may feel fear during these experiences—and citing the need for courage—but indicating that the richness of what is seen is well worth it.

Chapter Five (6.5)

FLIGHT OF THE SPIRIT

1. There is another kind of rapture that is *substantially* the same, but *experienced* within the soul in a very different way: I call it flight of the spirit. Sometimes, suddenly, the soul feels a movement that is so fast it seems the spirit is being carried away—and at a scary speed, especially in the beginning. This is why I told you that great courage is needed for anyone in whom God works these graces, in addition to faith and confidence and great surrender, so that our Lord may do what He wills with the soul. Do you think it's "no big deal" to a person in complete possession of her senses to see her soul carried off? (We've even read from some authors that, in some cases, the body is transported, too.) And this happens without the soul knowing where it's going, who's taking it, or how, because when this movement begins, the soul is not certain the rapture is from God.

2. Are there any ways to resist this experience? None at all. In fact, it's just the opposite—resistance makes things worse. I know this from a certain person.[162] It seemed to her that God wants the soul to understand that, in and of itself, it doesn't have a part to play anymore—having so often, so unconditionally, and with complete willingness offered everything to Him. And thus the soul is carried off with a noticeably more impetuous movement. This person then decided not to offer any more resistance than a piece of straw does when [attracted to and] lifted up by amber, if you've ever seen this.[163] Seeing that the safest thing to do is to make a virtue of necessity, she decided to abandon herself into the hands of the One who is all powerful. And, speaking of straw, it's a fact that a powerful man can't carry away a piece of straw any more easily than this great and powerful Giant of ours carries away the spirit.

162. Teresa herself; see *Life*, chapter 20, 5–6.
163. When friction is applied, amber becomes negatively charged and attracts lightweight particles, such as pieces of straw, fluff, or dried leaves.

3. It seems to me that the basin of water we talked about in the fourth dwelling place was filling at that stage quietly and gently, without movement. (I don't remember *exactly* where this was.) But now, this great God, who holds back the springs of water and doesn't let the sea move beyond its limits, lets the springs loose that fill the basin.[164] With tremendous force, a wave rises up powerfully, lifting the little ship of our soul. When the waves crash upon a ship and toss it around, the ship can't do anything about it, and neither can the captain or the crew. The interior part of the soul is even *less* capable of staying where it wants, or of making the senses and faculties do anything other than what they are commanded. The exterior senses are quite useless here.

4. Really, sisters, just writing about this makes me amazed as I reflect on how the enormous power of this great King and Emperor is shown here. Imagine, then, the feelings of anyone who experiences it! From my perspective, I think that if His Majesty were to reveal Himself to those who travel through the world, lost, in the ways He does to these souls, then they wouldn't dare to offend Him (out of great fear, though maybe not out of love). How great, then, are the obligations of these souls who have been warned in such a *wondrous* way to strive with all their power not to offend this Lord. For His sake, sisters, I beg you to remember: anyone to whom His Majesty has given these gifts, or others like them, must not simply receive them and then grow careless; anyone who owes a lot must pay a lot.[165]

COURAGE AND CONTINUED SELF-KNOWLEDGE

5. This is another reason why great courage is necessary, because the [sense of obligation] is extremely daunting. If our Lord didn't give such courage, the soul would constantly be distressed. When she reflects on what His Majesty is doing with her, and then turns to reflect on herself, she sees how little she's doing to fulfill her obligations, and how weak the small things she does are, and how full she is of faults and failures and laziness.

164. An allusion to Proverbs 8:29: "when he assigned to the sea its limit, so that the waters might not transgress his command, when he marked out the foundations of the earth."
165. Potentially an allusion to Luke 12:48: "But the one who did not know and did what deserved a beating will receive a light beating. From everyone to whom much has been given, much will be required, and from one to whom much has been entrusted, even more will be demanded."

So that she doesn't dwell on remembering how imperfectly she's done some work—if she has—she strives to forget her works, keep her mind on her sins, and bring them to the mercy of God. Since she doesn't have anything with which to "pay," she begs for the compassion and mercy God has always had toward sinners.

6. He might respond the same way He answered someone who was really distressed about this, looking up at a crucifix and thinking about how she never had anything to give to God, or to give up for Him. The Crucified Himself comforted her, saying He had given her all the pains and trials He'd suffered in the passion so that she could have them for her own to offer to His Father.[166] This soul was so comforted and enriched by this experience that she can never forget it; whenever she feels miserable, she remembers this moment, and it comforts and encourages her.

There are a lot of other points on this subject I could add—because I've known so many saintly and prayerful people, I know of a lot of cases like this—but I don't want you to think that I'm referring to myself, so I'll pass them over. This incident I've described seems like a very helpful one for understanding how glad our Lord is when we truly get to know ourselves, continually try to see our poverty and pathetic capacities, and recognize that we have absolutely nothing that we haven't been *given*. My sisters, courage is necessary for this [self-knowledge], and for many other graces given to a soul brought to this state. To my thinking, if the soul is humble, this [knowledge of one's own nature] requires more courage than almost anything. May the Lord give us this humility out of His own bounty.

DYNAMICS OF THE FLIGHT OF THE SPIRIT

7. Returning to this quick rapture of the spirit: It might be said of this kind of rapture that the soul really seems to leave the body. Yet, on the other hand, it's clear that the person is not dead, even though for a few minutes even he can't be sure if his soul is in the body or not. He feels like he's been in another world, very different from this one where we live, and been shown a different kind of light. It's a light so unlike anything found in this life that even if he'd been trying to imagine it, and other wonders seen, for his whole life, he couldn't have possibly succeeded. In an instant, his mind learns so many things at once that if the imagination and intellect

166. Her own experience, spoken of in *Spiritual Testimonies*, 46.

spent years striving to systematize it all, it wouldn't be able to, not even with one part of a thousand of them. This is an imaginary vision, not an intellectual one. It's "seen" with the eyes of the soul much more clearly than we can see things with the eyes of our body. Some of the revelations are communicated without words. For example, if he sees any of the saints, he knows them well, as if he'd spent a lot of time with them.

8. Sometimes, in addition to what he sees in an intellectual vision (with the eyes of the soul), other things are perceived, particularly a host of angels with their Lord. Even though he doesn't see anything with the eyes of the body *or* soul, this and many other indescribable things are revealed by some wonderful intuition that I can't explain. Maybe those who have experienced this and have more ability than I do could describe it, though it seems to me an extremely difficult task. I can't say if the soul is in the body or not while all of this is happening. I wouldn't swear either way myself.

9. I've often thought that if the sun can stay in the sky, and yet its rays are so strong that they can immediately reach us here on earth (even though the sun doesn't move at all), it must be possible for the soul and the spirit to act in the same way. Because they are as much the same thing as the sun and its rays; through the power of the heat that comes to them from the true Sun of Justice, some higher part of them could rise above itself [like the rays]. Frankly, I don't really know what I'm saying. But I *do* know that, just as quickly as a bullet leaves a gun when the trigger is pulled, this is the speed of the interior flight experienced. This soundless "flight of the soul" (I don't know what else to call it) is so clearly a movement that it can't possibly be due to the imagination. When the soul is outside herself—at least as far as she can understand—great things are shown to her. When the soul returns to herself, she has greatly benefitted from the experience. Compared to what she has seen, she takes no stock in earthly things—they seem like filth. From here on out, living on earth is a difficult challenge for her. If she sees the things that used to give her pleasure, she no longer cares for them. It seems the Lord wanted to show her something of the place she's traveling to, so that she can endure the trials of this trying road, just like the Israelites who brought back tokens of the promised land [to those still traveling].[167] She knows where she must go to get her final rest. Although you might be thinking that something that happens so quickly

167. See Numbers 13:18–24.

can't really be that beneficial, the blessings for this soul are so great that only someone else with the experience can truly understand their value.

10. On this note, the experience is obviously *not* from the adversary. It would be impossible for the imagination or the evil one to represent things that leave so much peace, calm, improvement, and good fruit in the soul. In particular, there are three things it enjoys to a very high degree: First, knowledge of God's greatness. We are more deeply conscious of this the more we see it. Second, self-knowledge and humility. We see how creatures as lowly as we are in comparison with the Creator of such wonders have nevertheless dared to offend Him and even dared to raise our eyes to Him. Third, very little value for earthly things, except those that can be used in the service of such a great God.

11. These are the jewels the Spouse begins to give His spouse; they are of such great value that the soul won't be reckless or careless with them. These meetings with the Spouse are so deeply engraved in the memory that I think it's impossible for the soul to forget them until it's living their reality forever.[168] If it did forget them, it would suffer greatly. But the Spouse who gives them to the soul also has the power to give enough grace so that they aren't lost.

12. Getting back to the courage that is necessary: Does it seem to you that this is such a trivial thing after all? Because the soul really feels that it is separated from the body as it loses its senses, and doesn't understand why. So, He who gives everything else needs to give courage, too. You might say that this fear is well-rewarded; so do I. May He who can give so much be praised forever. And may it please His Majesty to grant that we are worthy to serve Him. Amen.

168. Here Teresa continues the metaphorical language of meetings and jewels first introduced in 5.4.3.

Overview of Chapter Six

Chapter six continues the theme of the previous two chapters by discussing more generally the emotional effects of raptures—in particular, the restless longing for God. This can be a challenge to our modern sensibilities because Teresa says quite clearly that the soul is longing for death. It's an echo of the longing or sense of separation that Saint Paul describes in 2 Corinthians 5:6 ("While we are at home in the body we are away from the Lord") and Philippians 1:23 ("I am hard pressed between the two: my desire is to depart and be with Christ, for that is far better"). In many ways, such a longing makes perfect sense. Who wouldn't feel restless on earth after being shown glimpses of the glories of heaven? This first section is one of the more plainly autobiographical of the book, even though Teresa still tries to keep the writing generic. In section four, in particular, we see her frustration about the limitations imposed on her due to her being a woman, and her passionate longing to transcend these earthly limitations with God's help. Beyond herself, however, Teresa plainly says that a passion for doing "great things for God" is a typical effect of such marvelous gifts like the flight of the spirit.

After this, she moves to a few cautions about excessive longing for God, encouraging readers to accept God's will that we continue to live and serve on earth. She also notes that tears of longing aren't virtuous in and of themselves. We catch an amusing glimpse into Teresa's personality here: apparently, she wasn't one who cried very easily herself! She closes by discussing a very different sort of spiritual state: the prayer and praises of overwhelming joy. These are times when we might be considered "fools for Christ" due to being filled with a jubilation that cannot be contained. This is a "valuable and beautiful" gift not only for the recipient, but also for those in his or her community, because then others might be moved to join the jubilant soul in praise.

Chapter Six (6.6)

EFFECTS OF RAPTURES: RESTLESS LONGING FOR GOD

1. As a result of these wonderful gifts, the soul is so full of longings to *completely* enjoy the One who gave them that life becomes sheer, though delectable, torture. Such a soul longs for death, frequently and tearfully asking God to take her out of this exile, where everything she sees wearies her. Only solitude brings some relief, for a little while, but soon the grief returns. When this pain is absent, something seems to be missing, and she hardly knows herself without it. In sum: this little butterfly can't find any lasting rest. Indeed, her love is so tender that any situation that serves to strengthen this fire causes the soul to take flight. Thus, in this dwelling place, raptures happen very frequently, and they can't be resisted, even in public. As a result: persecutions and criticisms. And even though she wants to be fearless about this, it's not entirely possible because there are many people who lay fears *on* her, especially confessors.

2. On the one hand, this soul seems to feel great interior security, especially when she's alone with God. Yet, on the other hand, she's in deep distress because she's afraid the adversary might somehow trick her into offending the One she loves so much. She doesn't care much what people say about her, except when her own confessor blames her (as if she could prevent having these raptures). She asks everyone to pray for her, and asks His Majesty to lead her by another road since this one is very dangerous (just as she's been advised to do). At the same time, she's gained so much from these gifts that she can't help but see that this path is leading her on the way to heaven, based on what she reads, hears, and knows of God's commandments. So, though she really tries, she can't abandon it entirely, and simply leaves herself in God's hands. And even this inability [to willfully stop the raptures] is distressing to her, because she thinks she's not obeying her confessor—and she believes that the only way to avoid deception and offending God comes through obedience. Since she feels that she would rather be cut in pieces than intentionally commit even a small sin, it's very distressing to find that she can't avoid committing a great many, unknowingly.

3. God gives these souls the strongest desire not to displease Him in any way, however small; they want to avoid every imperfection, if possible. If for no other reason than this, the soul wants to flee from other people, envying those who live in deserts. On the other hand, it wants to plunge right into the heart of the world to see if it might be able to help one soul praise God more. A woman in this state will be frustrated that she can't do this because she's female, and be very envious of those who are free to cry aloud and proclaim all over the world who is this great God of hosts.

4. Oh, poor little butterfly, tied up with so many chains that prevent you from flying wherever you would like! Have pity on her, my God! Ordain and arrange her path so that she might be able to accomplish some of her desires for Your honor and glory! Don't take into account how undeserving she is or her lowly nature. You have the power, Lord, to make the vast ocean pull back, and the Jordan river open wide, to allow the children of Israel to pass through. And yet—You don't need to take pity on her. Because, with the help of Your strength, she *is* capable of enduring many challenging works; she's determined to do so and wants to suffer through them. Stretch out Your mighty arm, O Lord, and don't let her life be spent in such lowly things! Let Your greatness appear in her, feminine and base though she may be, so that the world might understand that none of it comes from *her*, and might give *You* praise. No matter what it costs, this is what she wants. She would give a thousand lives, if she had them, so one soul might praise You a little more. She would consider them well spent, because she truly understands that she doesn't deserve to suffer even a very small trial for You, let alone die for You.

5. I don't know what my aim was in saying this, sisters, or why I said it; I didn't plan it. You should know that such desires, without a doubt, are the remaining effects of these suspensions or ecstasies. The desires are not fleeting, but permanent. When one has the opportunity to act on them, it becomes clear that the experience wasn't fake.

You might ask why I say the effects are "permanent," since sometimes the soul *does* feel timid, and is so afraid and lacking in courage that it seems impossible to be courageous enough to do anything, even the most insignificant work. But this, I think, happens when the Lord leaves the soul to its own nature. It's an extremely good experience—the soul realizes any usefulness it may have had was only a gift from His Majesty. This is seen with a clarity that annihilates any self-satisfaction, and fills the soul with a fuller knowledge of God's greatness and mercy (which He nevertheless wanted to show to something so lowly). But *usually*, the soul's state is more like the [courageously desiring to work and sacrifice mentality] we've just mentioned.

CAUTIONS ABOUT EXCESSIVE LONGING FOR GOD

6. One thing to note, sisters, about these great desires to see our Lord: sometimes they will be so oppressive that you must avoid encouraging them and distract yourself from them—if you can. (For there are other desires I'll write about later that can't be dealt with in this way, as you'll see.) The ones I'm talking about now, it *is* possible to distance yourself from, since your reason is still free to resign itself to God's will. In this way, you can echo the words of Saint Martin.[169] A person can reflect on this sentiment if the desires are very oppressive. Since these longings are generally found in very advanced souls, the adversary might encourage them in us so that we *think* we're advanced, too. It's always good to proceed with caution. But I don't believe the evil one could cause the calm and peace given by this yearning pain; the feelings he stirs up are more likely to be the uneasy, passionate ones like those we experience when we're troubled by a worldly concern. Anyone who hasn't had experience in *both* kinds of sorrow won't understand the difference. Then, thinking such yearning pain to be a great thing, the person will encourage and stoke the feeling as much as possible—which is damaging to one's health, since these longings are incessant, or at least very frequent.

7. Also note that this kind of distress is likely to be caused by a weak constitution, especially in the case of emotional people who weep over every little thing. Again and again, they think they're crying for godly reasons, but this isn't the case. Sometimes they shed floods of tears—and can't keep from doing so—*whenever* they think of God or hear Him mentioned.

169. Peers notes that in the office of Saint Martin, the church recalls these words: "Lord, if I am still necessary to Thy people, I do not refuse to toil: Thy will be done."

The cause of these tears might be an emotional imbalance and distortion[170] rather than a deep love of God. It seems as if they'll never stop crying; because they've come to believe that tears are good, they don't try at all to control them. In fact, they wouldn't stop even if they could, and they try their best to induce tears. In such cases, the adversary does his best to weaken them: then they are unable to practice prayer or keep their Rule of life.

8. I can imagine you asking me what on earth you *should* do, since I mark "danger!" everywhere. If I think there can be deception in something as good as tears, you might be wondering if maybe *I'm* the one who is deceived! Yes, of course—I might be. But, trust me, I'm not talking about this without having actually seen it in others. I've never been like this myself, because I'm not the least bit emotional. On the contrary, my hardness of heart sometimes worries me. Nevertheless, when the fire within my soul is strong, it distills, [purifies, and transforms] the heart like an alembic, no matter how hard it may be. You'll easily recognize when tears arise from *this* source, because they are comforting and calming instead of disturbing, and rarely do any harm. The good thing about false tears is that, although they may harm the body, they cannot harm a humble soul. If the soul is not humble, it won't hurt to remain suspicious about tears.

9. Let's not think that everything is accomplished through much weeping, but instead set our hands to working hard and practicing the virtues. This is what we need the most. Let the tears come when God wants to send them; we shouldn't try to induce them ourselves. These tears [from God] leave our dry grounds well-watered and will help us produce fruit, but the less attention we pay to them, the more they'll do, since they are water that falls from heaven. The water we draw ourselves, digging and tiring ourselves out to get tears, is not the same; we can wear ourselves out without coming upon even a puddle of water, let alone a flowing stream. For this reason, sisters, our best plan is to place ourselves in the Lord's presence, meditate on His mercy and grace (as well as our own lowliness), and leave Him to give us what He wills, whether water or dryness. He knows what

170. Teresa literally uses the phrase "humor affecting the heart," which refers to the ancient medicinal theory of four types of humors in the body that were either in balance (in health) or out of balance (in various kinds of sickness).

is best for us; in this way, we'll walk in peace, and the adversary will have less opportunity to fool us.

THE PRAYER AND PRAISES OF OVERWHELMING JOY

10. Together with these experiences that are simultaneously painful and delectable, our Lord sometimes gives the soul some feelings of jubilation, and a strange prayer it doesn't understand. I write about it here so that if He gives you this gift, you might enthusiastically praise Him, knowing that such a thing really does happen. I think it's a great union of the faculties, but our Lord leaves both the faculties and the senses free to enjoy this exultant joy, even as they don't understand what they're enjoying or how they're enjoying it. This sounds kind of crazy, but it definitely happens this way. The joy of the soul is so excessive that it doesn't want to rejoice in God alone but wants to share its joy with everyone so they might help praise our Lord. It directs all its activity and energy toward this praise. Oh, what elaborate festivals and demonstrations such a soul would organize, if possible, so that all might understand her joy! For it seems to her she has found herself, and so, like the father of the Prodigal Son,[171] she wants to have a great party and invite everybody because she sees herself in an undoubtedly safe place, at least for now. I think this is for good reason because such interior joy in the depths of one's being, with such peace, and all this happiness stirring praises of God—this can't possibly come from the adversary.

11. While living with this great energy of joy, it's a lot to remain quiet and hide it, and no small pain. This must have been Saint Francis' state of mind when robbers met him as he was running through the fields, yelling about how he was the herald of the great King. Other saints retreat to desert places so that they can similarly proclaim the praises of their God. I knew one such saint, Fray Peter of Alcantara. (Judging from the life he led, I certainly think he's a saint, yet those who heard him sometimes called him crazy.) Oh, what a *blessed* madness, sisters! If only God would give it to everyone! And how good He's been to you, putting you in a place where you would receive encouragement—and not the criticism you'd receive in the world—if God does give you this gift, and you show signs of it, too.

171. See Luke 15:11–32, especially verses 23–24: "'And get the fatted calf and kill it, and let us eat and celebrate; for this son of mine was dead and is alive again; he was lost and is found!' And they began to celebrate."

12. Oh, we live in times that are so unfortunate and miserable; happy are those who have the good fortune to remain apart from the world! Sometimes it's a particular joy for me when we're all together, and I see sisters almost competing with each other in praising our Lord for bringing each of them to the convent; it's obvious that these praises come from the inner depths of the soul. I would like you to praise Him often, sisters, because when one of you begins, she inspires the rest. When you're together, how can your tongues be better put to use than in the praises of God? We have so many reasons for offering Him praise.

13. May His Majesty be pleased to give us this prayer often, because it's so safe and so beneficial. It's entirely supernatural; we can't possibly acquire it. It might last for a whole day, and the soul will then be like someone who has had a lot to drink—but not like a person so drunk as to be senseless... or like someone with a mental illness who is not entirely out of his mind but also can't get free of something in his imagination (and no one else can coax this release, either). These are very rough comparisons to represent something so valuable and beautiful, but I'm not clever enough to think of others. The real truth is that this joy makes the soul so forgetful of itself, and everything else, that it isn't aware of or able to speak about anything that isn't the *source* of its joy—in other words, the praises of God. So let's all join this soul, my daughters. Why would we want to be more *sensible*? What could give us greater happiness? And may *all* the creatures join with us, forever and ever. Amen, amen, amen.

Overview of Chapter Seven

In this chapter, Teresa addresses two erroneous ideas that seem to have been floating around the contemplative life of prayer. The first is the notion that those enjoying such marvelous graces from God surely wouldn't feel bad about themselves anymore; that is, they wouldn't feel sorrow or grief over their sins. In response, Teresa says no, on the contrary, they feel continual sorrow over their sins, and might feel even *more* sad than others about all the grief they've given God over the years! In symbolic language, she says, "It's as if a mighty river were running through the soul, and from time to time, the water brings these graces with it. But the soul's sins are like the river's slimy bottom; they are always fresh in the memory, and this is a heavy cross."

Most of this chapter, however, is dedicated to the necessity of meditating on the humanity of Christ. Then, as now, there were some teachers who indicated that once you had advanced along this spiritual road, you could forget about Jesus and the gritty details of his life and death. Why not spend all of one's time and energy pursuing the sublime encounters of the *spirit* that one has tasted? Among other answers to this notion, Teresa says this: "Because, although angelic spirits—freed from everything physical—might stay permanently enkindled in love, this isn't possible for those of us who live in a mortal body. We *need* to engage with, and think about, and be accompanied by those who did such great things for God while having a mortal body."

She acknowledges certain challenges to meditation on Christ's life and death (especially the detailed intellectual sort) but nevertheless outlines the many benefits of such efforts, especially when we feel a bit aimless or lackluster. She reminds us that when we look at the particulars of Christ's life and self-offering on the cross, "then the will is awakened, maybe not with tender emotions but with a desire to somehow serve in response to this great mercy." Toward the end of the chapter, she again references her own past false steps in this regard, and reiterates and expands upon all the ways that keeping our eyes fixed on Jesus helps us on this road of prayer, no matter how "far" along we may have traveled.

Chapter Seven (6.7)

CONTINUAL SORROW OVER SINS

1. Sisters, you'll probably think that these souls—with whom the Lord communicates Himself in this unusual way—will be so sure of enjoying Him forever that they don't have any reason to fear, or weep for their sins. (I'm talking in particular to those who *haven't* had these gifts, because if they *have* been granted enjoyment of such gifts from God, they'll know what I'm about to say.) This assumption would be a big mistake; for the more they receive from our God, the *more* their sorrow for sin grows. I myself believe that this never leaves us until we reach that place where nothing can cause us pain.

2. It's true that this sorrow is more oppressive at some times than others, and there are also different kinds. For the soul doesn't now think about the pain that it's bound to suffer because of its sins, but only of how ungrateful it has been to Him to whom so much is owed, and who so greatly deserves our service. For through these expressions of His grandeur that He shares with the soul, one understands much more of God: the soul is horrified at having been so daring; it weeps for its lack of respect; its past foolish mistakes seem *so* stupid that it never stops feeling sorry about them, remembering that it abandoned such a great Majesty for such base things. It thinks about this much more than about the gifts it receives, even if they are great (like the ones I've already described, and the ones we'll explore later). It's as if a mighty river were running through the soul, and from time to time, the water brings these graces with it. But the soul's sins are like the river's slimy bottom; they are always fresh in the memory, and this is a heavy cross.

3. I know a person[172] who stopped wanting to die so that she might see God, but then wanted to die so she wouldn't feel the continual pain of how

172. Again, this "person" is Teresa: see *Life*, chapters 26 and 34; *Spiritual Testimonies* 1, 48, and 59.

ungrateful she'd been to the One to whom she owed so much. It seemed that nobody's wickedness was as bad as hers, because she thought there was no one else [quite like her]: she'd made God put up with so much, and He'd given her so many favors.

In terms of a fear of hell, these souls don't have any. They are sometimes deeply distressed by the thought that they might lose God, but this rarely happens. Their only fear is that God might let them out of His hand, and that they might then offend Him and find themselves in a miserable state, like before. They don't have anxiety about their own pain or glory. If they don't want to stay a long time in purgatory, it's less about the pain they'd have to suffer than the fact that, while there, they'd be apart from God.

4. However favored[173] by God a soul might be, I wouldn't consider it safe for the soul to forget the miserable state it once saw itself in. Even though such remembrance might be painful, it's often profitable. Maybe it's because I myself have been so terrible that I feel like this and always keep it in mind; those who have been good won't have anything to grieve over—although, as long as we live in our mortal body, we'll always have failures. There's no relief from reflecting that our Lord has forgiven and forgotten our sins; in fact, the thought of so much goodness and such gracious gifts given to one who only deserves hell makes the distress greater. I think this must have been a regular anguish[174] for Saint Peter and [Mary] Magdalene. Because their love was so great, and they'd received so many gracious gifts,[175] and understood the greatness and majesty of God, such remembrance [of their past sins] must have been very hard to endure, and moved them deeply.

THE NECESSITY OF MEDITATING ON THE HUMANITY OF CHRIST

5. It will probably also seem to you that anyone who enjoys such lofty things will no longer meditate on the mysteries of the most sacred humanity of our Lord Jesus Christ, because such a person would now be entirely

173. Here Teresa is not using the word *merced* but actually *favorecida,* simply "favored."
174. Teresa uses the word *martirio,* or "martyrdom," here, but since most people rarely use this term today (except, perhaps, sarcastically), I offer a broader description of pain.
175. Here we return to the term *mercedes.*

engaged in love. This is something I wrote a lot about elsewhere. I've been told by some, "Because these are the paths along which our Lord leads us, when we've passed through the first stages, it's better to stay focused on things concerning the Godhead and stay away from *all* physical or earthly things"...but they definitely will *not* make me concede that this is a good way, even though I've been challenged, and confronted, and told that I don't understand it. I might be wrong, and we all might be *meaning* the same thing, but it was clear to me that the adversary was trying to deceive me in this way. Thus, I've learned my lesson from experience, and I'm going to speak to you about it again—even though I've talked about this often[176]—so that you might walk very carefully. Take note: I'm even going so far as to advise you not to believe anyone who tells you something else. I'll try to explain myself better than I did before. (If, by chance, a certain person has written about it—as he said he would—I hope it was explained more fully. To write about it generally or vaguely to those of us who are not very intelligent could be harmful.)[177]

6. It will also seem to some souls that they can't think about the passion [of Christ], or even less about the Blessed Virgin and the lives of the saints; yet the remembrance of both of these is so helpful and encouraging. I can't imagine what they're thinking. Because, although angelic spirits—freed from everything physical—might stay permanently enkindled in love, this isn't possible for those of us who live in a mortal body. We *need* to engage with, and think about, and be accompanied by those who did such great things for God while having a mortal body. It's even more essential not to move away on purpose from our greatest help and blessing, which is the most sacred humanity of our Lord Jesus Christ. I can't believe that people really do this; but they just don't understand, and they bring harm to themselves and to others. At any rate, I can assure you that they won't enter these last two dwelling places: if they lose their guide, the good Jesus, they won't be able to find their way. It would be impressive if they're able to remain safely in the other dwelling places. For the Lord Himself says that He is the Way, the light;[178] that "the one who sees Me

---

176. *Life,* chapters 22–24.
177. Kavanaugh and Rodriguez note that this "person" Teresa alludes to is unknown.
178. John 14:6: "Jesus said to him, 'I am the way, and the truth, and the life. No one comes to the Father except through me.'"

sees My Father";[179] and that no one can come to the Father except through Him. It might be said that these words have another meaning. I don't know other meanings; I've gotten on very well with this one, which my soul always feels to be true.

CHALLENGES TO AND BENEFITS OF MEDITATION ON CHRIST'S LIFE AND DEATH

7. There are some people—brought by our Lord to "perfect contemplation"—who would like to *always* be in that prayer; many have talked to me about this. That's impossible. Yet this gracious gift of the Lord remains with them in such a way that, afterward, they can't reflect on the mysteries of the passion and the life of Christ as before. I don't know why this is, but it's quite a common experience for the intellect to become less capable of meditation. I think it must be because the whole aim of meditation is to seek God, and once He is found, the soul gets used to seeking Him again by means of the *will*. It has no desire to wear itself out with intellectual work. It also seems that since the will is now on fire, this generous power doesn't want to take advantage of the other [the intellect] if it can avoid doing so. It's not a *bad* or harmful approach, but [such setting aside of the intellect entirely] will be impossible, especially until the soul reaches these last dwelling places. And it will only lose time by trying [to jettison the intellect], because we often *need* the help of the intellect in order to ignite the will.

8. Take note of this point, sisters. It's important, so I want to explain it even more. The soul wants to be completely occupied in love, and doesn't want to be engaged with anything else. But this can't be, even if the soul wants it to be so. For [imagine this], even though the will is not dead, the fire that usually kindles and reignites it *is* gone; someone needs to blow on it if it's going to produce heat. Would it be good for the soul to stay in this state of dryness, waiting for fire to come down from heaven like our father Elijah did,[180] burning this sacrifice it's making of itself to God? No,

179. John 14:9: "Jesus said to him, 'Have I been with you all this time, Philip, and you still do not know me? Whoever has seen me has seen the Father. How can you say, "Show us the Father"?'"

180. See 1 Kings 18:30–39, especially verses 37–38: "'Answer me, O Lord, answer me, so that this people may know that you, O Lord, are God, and that you have turned their hearts back.' Then the fire of the Lord fell and consumed the burnt offering, the wood, the stones, and the dust, and even licked up the water that was in the trench."

certainly not; it's not right to expect miracles. The Lord will perform them for this soul when *He* sees fit to do so, as I've said and will say again. But His Majesty wants us to consider ourselves undeserving of them because of our ordinariness,[181] and to do everything we possibly can to help ourselves. I myself believe that such an attitude is necessary until we die, no matter how sublime our prayer might be.

9. It's true that anyone the Lord places in the *seventh* dwelling place rarely, or almost never, needs to make this active effort. (I'll give the reason, if I remember, when I come to that dwelling place. There, in a wonderful way, the soul never stops walking with Christ our Lord but is always accompanied by both His divine and human nature.) But here, when the fire of the will mentioned before[182] is not lit, and the presence of God is not felt, it's necessary that we seek it—like the bride did in the Song of Solomon.[183] This is His Majesty's desire. He wants us to ask the creatures who it is that made them—as Saint Augustine says he did in his *Meditations* or *Confessions*[184]—and not stupidly waste time by waiting to receive what was given to us once already. At first, it might be that the Lord will not again give it to us for as long as a year, or even many years. His Majesty knows why; we shouldn't want to know, nor is there any reason that we should. Since we know the path to pleasing God—through the commandments and guidance [given]—let's be diligent about walking in this way, meditating on His life and death and all that we owe Him. The rest comes when the Lord wants.

10. At this point, some people might reply that they *can't* stop and meditate on these things, and they're right in a certain way—because of what was already said. You know that reasoning with the intellect is one thing, and having truths represented to the intellect through the memory is quite another. You might say that you can't understand me, and truly I might not understand it well enough to explain it, but I'll put it the best I can. By "meditation," I mean extensive *reasoning* with the intellect, like this: We start off by thinking about the mercy God offered us in giving us

181. This word is again *ruines*, which is often translated as "wickedness" but has other possible layers of meaning that approach the deep humility Teresa is referring to.
182. In 6.7.7.
183. Song of Solomon 3:3: "The sentinels found me, as they went about in the city. 'Have you seen him whom my soul loves?'"
184. See *The Confessions of St. Augustine*, X, chapter 6, nos. 9–10.

His only Son, and we don't stop there—we continue on to the mysteries of His entire glorious life. Or, we begin with the prayer in the garden and don't stop the intellect [from reviewing all the events] up until He's placed on the cross; or we take one part of the passion—let's say His arrest—and walk slowly through this mystery, considering in great detail the things that we need to think about Him and what to feel, through the betrayal of Judas, the flight of the apostles, and all the rest. This is a wonderful and very worthwhile kind of prayer.

11. Yet this is the prayer those whom God has brought to supernatural things and to perfect contemplation rightfully claim they can't practice. As I've said, I don't know why this should be, but ordinarily they can't. But I would also say that it's not right for such people to claim they don't dwell on these mysteries, or often have them on their mind, especially when they are being celebrated by the Catholic Church. It isn't possible for a soul that has received so much from God to forget all these valuable signs of His love—they are living sparks that will ignite the fire of the soul more and more in its love for our Lord.

But these mysteries are not *understood* [with the reasoning intellect]; the soul understands them in a more perfect way. The intellect depicts or shows them, and they're stamped in the memory—so that just seeing the Lord, fallen down with that horrible sweat in the garden, [for example], is enough, not just for an hour, but for many days. We simply gaze, considering who He is and how ungrateful we have been to the One who bore such pain for us. Then the will is awakened, maybe not with tender emotions but with a desire to somehow serve in response to this great mercy, and to suffer something for One who has suffered so much Himself. It's like this with other similar things that the memory and intellect dwell on. I believe this is why the soul can't go on to *reason* further about the passion, and that's why it seems we can't "think" about it.

12. If you don't already do this [prayerful meditation on the mysteries of Christ's life], it would be good for you to try to practice this. Because I know that it won't be an obstacle to sublime prayer, and I think it's a mistake not to engage in this sort of exercise often. If, from this practice, the Lord should suspend the soul, well and good; in that case, He'll make it stop such meditations even if the soul doesn't want to abandon them. I'm

quite certain that this method of prayer isn't a hindrance to the soul but really helpful for every good. The hindrance would be if the soul forcefully exerted itself in the meditative intellectual reasoning described at the beginning—in fact, I think such work is impossible for someone who has reached more [in prayer]. (This might not be the case for everyone, since God leads souls in many different paths.[185]) On the one hand, don't condemn such souls who are unable to walk the [reasoned reflection] road, but also don't judge them as disqualified from enjoying the great benefits held in the mysteries of our good, Jesus Christ. No matter how spiritual the person, no one will persuade me that [neglecting to contemplate Christ's life] will go well.

KEEPING OUR EYES FIXED ON JESUS

13. Some souls follow prayer principles and methods where the thinking goes that when you begin to experience the prayer of quiet, and enjoy the gifts and spiritual delights given by the Lord there, it would be a very good thing to *always* be enjoying them. Well now, let them believe me when I say they shouldn't be so absorbed, as I've said.[186] For life is long; there are many trials in it, and we *need* to look at Christ, our paragon and pattern, and His apostles and saints, reflecting on how they endured these trials, so that we might also bear them perfectly. The good Jesus is too good company for us to abandon Him and His most sacred mother. It pleases Him when we mourn over His sorrows, even though we leave our consolations and spiritual delights sometimes to do so. On that note, though, daughters: consolations in prayer aren't so frequent and ordinary that there isn't time for everything. If someone told me that she experienced them continuously—so much that she couldn't do what was mentioned [basic meditation on the mysteries of Christ]—I would be suspicious. And so: try to get out of that deception; strive to free yourself from this error with all your strength. If your efforts to do so aren't enough, tell the prioress, so that she can give you work that will keep you so engaged that this danger [of excessive absorption] goes away. For if it lasts a long time, it really is dangerous—at least for the brain and the head.

---

185. There is the same multilayered meaning in Spanish as in English with this term. Teresa says God leads souls in many different *caminos*, which means "road," "path," and "way" alike.
186. *Foundations*, chapter 6.

14. I think I've explained what is really good for you to know: no matter how spiritual you are, be careful not to turn away from "physical" things so completely that you think even the most sacred humanity causes harm. Sometimes people bring up that the Lord said to His disciples that it was good for them that He should go away.[187] I can't allow that as an argument. He didn't say this to His most sacred mother, because she was firm in her faith, and knew that He was God and man; and even though she loved Him more than they did, her love was so perfect that His presence on earth was actually a help to her. At that time, the apostles couldn't have been as firm in their faith as they later were, and as we have reason to be now. I'm telling you, daughters—this is a dangerous road, and if we take it, the adversary might even make us lose our devotion to the most holy sacrament.[188]

15. The mistake I used to make myself wasn't quite this extreme: it was just that I didn't enjoy thinking about our Lord Jesus Christ as much as I used to, and I would go along in that state of absorption, waiting to receive some gift. And I saw clearly that it was going poorly. Since it was impossible to constantly have consolations, my thoughts wandered from here to there. It seemed my soul was like a fluttering bird that couldn't find a place to stop—wasting a lot of time, without making progress in the virtues or thriving in prayer. I couldn't understand *why*—and I don't think I ever would have understood it, because I thought I was on the right road—until one day I was discussing my prayer methods with a servant of God, and he gave me some advice. I then saw clearly how wrong I'd been, and I've never stopped regretting that there was a time when I failed to realize that such a great loss couldn't possibly result in a gain. Even if I *could* have it, I want nothing good except that which I get through Him from whom all good comes to us. May He be praised forever. Amen.

---

187. John 16:7: "Nevertheless, I tell you the truth: it is to your advantage that I go away, for if I do not go away, the Advocate will not come to you; but if I go, I will send him to you."
188. This would be a logical extension of rejecting *all* things *corporeal* (which is the world translated as "physical" in this section)—to lose interest, devotion, or appreciation for the elements of Holy Communion, the body and blood of Christ.

Overview of Chapter Eight

Although, in chapter seven, Teresa wrote about staying close to Jesus in an attentive or meditative sense—efforts that we can control—in chapters eight and nine, she turns to the ways in which Jesus might come close to *us* through intellectual and imaginative visions. Intellectual visions are those that we do not "see"; they are truths that we see only with the eyes of the soul. An imaginative vision is one that does contain an image. In chapter eight, Teresa writes only about a certain kind of intellectual vision, the gift of Christ's company. This happens when a soul feels "our Lord Jesus Christ near, though it can't see Him with the eyes of the body or soul." Teresa is writing here about her own experience of this gift and its effects, in a way that allows the reader to both imagine what she lived and to potentially identify this gift in their own lives. In addressing the responses to this gift, she identifies the blessings and benefits of such an experience, but she also urges caution in how and who we might talk to about it. If, as she would put it, we are "led by the Lord along this path," we must be judicious about sharing, minimally. And, as always, she urges humility, noting that receiving this gift—like any other gift—doesn't mean the recipient is somehow better than anyone else: "The Lord leads each of us as He sees we need," and it might even be a sign of weakness to receive such remarkable help.

Chapter Eight (6.8)

1. Sisters, in order for you to see that what I've been saying to you is true—that the further a soul advances, the *closer* it is accompanied by the good Jesus—we'll consider how sometimes (when His Majesty wills it) we can't help but walk with Him constantly. This is clear from the ways and means that His Majesty communicates Himself to us, revealing His

love for us through wonderful visitations and visions.[189] So that you aren't afraid if the Lord gives you any of the gifts I mention, I'll describe some of them (if the Lord gives me the ability to do so). Even though He might not give these gifts to us, we should still greatly praise Him for the fact that He—of such great majesty and power—would nonetheless be happy to commune in this way with a creature.

THE GIFT OF CHRIST'S COMPANY

2. It might happen this way: while the soul is not in the least expecting this gift, and even though it's never even *thought* that it deserved such a thing, it will feel our Lord Jesus Christ near, though it can't see Him with the eyes of the body or soul. This is called an intellectual vision; I don't know why. I saw the person God had given this gift to, along with others I'll describe later.[190] At first, she was very worried, because she couldn't *see* anything and so she couldn't understand what the vision was. She understood with such certainty that it was Jesus Christ our Lord who had somehow revealed Himself to her, and in a way that she couldn't doubt that the vision was there. But she was very confused about whether or not it was from God—even though its remarkable *effects* suggested it came from Him. She'd never heard of an intellectual vision, or knew there was such a thing. Yet she understood quite clearly that this was the Lord, who often spoke to her in the way I described.[191] Although she understood the words, she never knew who was speaking to her until He granted her this gift I'm now talking about.

3. Since she was afraid about this vision, she went to her confessor, very worried. (This isn't like an imaginary vision that quickly passes; it can last for many days and sometimes even more than a year.) "If you don't see anything," he asked her, "then how do you know it's our Lord?"[192] Then he told her to tell him what His face looked like. She replied that she didn't know: she hadn't seen a face, and she couldn't tell him any more than she already

---

189. The literal words here are "apparitions and visions" (*aparecimientos y visiones*), but "apparitions" is no longer a word with much common understanding. "Visitations" is not perfect but does include the element that Teresa goes on to emphasize, which is a sense of Christ's *presence*.

190. Teresa herself: see *Life*, chapter 27, nos. 2–5.

191. In 6.3, the section on communications and "hearing" from God.

192. See *Life*, chapter 27, no. 3.

had. What she *did* know was that it was He who'd been speaking to her, and that it wasn't in her imagination. And even though people stirred up serious doubts in her about it, she felt again and again that she couldn't doubt it was genuine, especially when He said to her, "Don't be afraid; it is I."[193] These words had such power that when she heard them, she couldn't doubt—and was deeply strengthened by and happy about such good company. For she clearly saw that it was very helpful to be in regular and constant awareness of God wherever she went, and to be extra careful not to do anything that would displease Him (since she felt that He was always looking at her). Whenever she wanted to come close to His Majesty in prayer or at other times, she felt He was so close that He couldn't fail to hear her. She *wasn't* able to hear Him speaking to her whenever she wanted to, but only unexpectedly, when the words were necessary.

She was aware that He was walking at her right hand, but this consciousness came in a subtle way that's indescribable—it didn't come from the senses that tell us when another person is near. It's just as unmistakable, though, and creates a feeling of equal certainty, or even more. Other things of the kind might be attributed to make-believe, but not this: it comes with great gains and interior effects that couldn't exist if it were only an aspect of mental illness. The adversary would not do so much good [if it were his work]: the soul wouldn't then walk with such peace, with such continuous desires to please God, and with such scorn for everything that doesn't lead to Him. Later, she understood clearly that it wasn't the adversary, because it became more and more obvious.

4. Still, I know that sometimes she felt intensely afraid and deeply confused, because she didn't know why so much good had come to her.[194] (She and I were so close that nothing happened in her soul that I didn't know about. Thus, I'm a reliable witness, and you can be sure that everything I say about it is true.) This gift of the Lord brings with it both the greatest confusion [about why one has been given such a gift] and humility.

If it came from the adversary, the reverse would be true. And as it's something clearly recognizable as a gift from God (no human effort could produce such feelings), in no way should anyone who has this think of it as their *own* good, but only as a gift from the hand of God. And even

193. This assurance is seen elsewhere: *Life*, chapter 25, no. 18; *Interior Castle*, 6.3.5.
194. See *Life*, chapter 27.

though I think some of the other experiences I've described are greater gifts than this one, it still brings with it a particular awareness of God; from this constant companionship, a very tender love toward His Majesty is born. It brings yearnings to give oneself up to His service completely (even deeper than those already described), along with a great purity of conscience (because the presence at its side makes the soul pay attention to everything). For although we already know that God is present in all we do, it's our nature to lose sight of that fact. But when this gift is given, a soul can't do this because the Lord, near at hand, awakens it. Even the gifts mentioned before happen much more commonly, since the soul is walking almost continuously with an in-the-moment love for the One it sees and knows to be by its side.

5. In summary, we see the greatness and the precious value of this gift in what the soul gains. The soul thanks the Lord, who has given it what it could never earn or deserve, and would never trade for any earthly treasure or pleasure. And so, when it's the Lord's will to withdraw, the soul is left with great loneliness. All possible efforts that it might make to again have His company do very little; the Lord gives this when He wants, and it can't be acquired.

Sometimes, too, the company is that of a saint, and this is also a great help.

6. You might ask how the soul knows that it's Christ, or a saint, or His most glorious mother, if nothing is seen. The soul won't know how to explain this—it can't understand how it knows—but it *does* know, with the greatest certainty. When it's the Lord, and He speaks, it seems easier [to understand how the recognition comes]; but what's more amazing is when it's a saint who doesn't speak, yet seems to have been put there by the Lord to be a help and companion. There are other spiritual things, impossible to describe, through which we understand how inadequate our natural capacities are for understanding the great wonders of God. For we *can't* understand, but can only marvel at them, and praise His Majesty for giving them to us. So, let's give particular thanks for them. Since this isn't a gift that's given to all, it's one that should be highly valued: and she [who receives it] must try to do greater works, because God helps her to do so in so many ways.

RESPONSES TO THIS GIFT

From this point comes the fact that such a soul *doesn't* consider herself better than others because of this gift. It seems to her that she's the *least* useful to God of everyone on earth, because she seems to have a greater obligation to Him. Thus, any fault she commits pierces her to the core,[195] and with good reason.

7. Any one of you whom the Lord leads by this road can recognize these described *effects* of such visions; this is how you can know that the vision isn't a deception or illusion. Because, as I've said, if the visions are from the adversary, I don't think they can possibly last so long, do the soul so much good, or bring it such inward peace. Typically, one who is evil doesn't do such good; he couldn't, in fact, even if he wanted to. If he tried this [vision in a deceptive way], the soul would quickly become clouded over with the mist of self-importance, and start to think of itself as better than others. And yet, the soul's continual walking with a sense of attachment to God, always thinking of Him, would make the evil one so angry that he probably wouldn't try it again. And God is so faithful that He won't allow the adversary to have *too* much of a hand over a soul whose only aim is to please Him and spend its whole life for His honor and glory; He will order the soul freed from such an illusion.

8. My point is and will continue to be that if the soul benefits from these divine gifts through the effects described here, His Majesty will make sure that the soul will be the one to gain: even if He ever allows the adversary to tempt it, the evil one will end up on the run. Therefore, daughters, if any of you do travel along this path, don't be alarmed. It *is* good for us to have reservations and walk with great care; upon receiving such gifts, you shouldn't become overly confident and careless. Because if you don't find they are producing in you the results described, it's a sign that they're not of God. It's good, especially initially, to share what's happening [with this vision] in confession to a very educated man—the kind we seek out for illumination. Or, talk with a very spiritual person. If your confessor is not very spiritual, someone with learning is better; best yet if you can find someone who is both spiritual and educated. If he tells you that it's just a figment of your imagination, don't let that bother you—because such

195. Interestingly, this is again the word that is literally "entrails" in Spanish.

figments can't affect your soul much, either for good or for evil. Simply entrust yourself to the Divine Majesty, and pray that He won't allow you to be deceived. If the confessor tells you that it's the adversary, this will be harder for you (though no truly educated man would say such a thing if you've experienced the *effects* described). But, if he does say it, I know that the Lord Himself will console you and reassure you—He who is walking at your side. The Lord will continue to enlighten your confessor so that he might in turn give light to you.

9. If this person you confide in has not been led by the Lord along this path (even though he practices prayer), he'll immediately be alarmed and condemn it. This is why I advise you to go to a confessor who combines spirituality and broad learning, if possible. Your prioress should give you permission to seek such a person out. Because even though she might think your soul is safe (since she observes you leading a good life), she's bound to allow you to consult with someone for your own safety, and hers too.

And, after such consultation(s), calm yourself down and don't go around reporting this experience anymore. Sometimes, when there's no reason to fear, the adversary places such strong fears in the soul that the person won't feel content with one consultation. Then, especially if the confessor is inexperienced, and notices her fear, he might urge her to go and communicate and consult with others. This only leads to what should have been a very secret matter being published, and her persecution and torment. She finds that what she thought was private has now become public, and this leads to many difficult trials, which—given the way things currently are[196]—might affect her religious order. Thus, I strongly urge great caution here, and recommend that prioresses take careful notice.

10. Don't think that because a sister has had such experiences, she's any better than the others. The Lord leads each of us as He sees we need. Such experiences, rightly used, prepare us to be better servants of God. But sometimes, God leads the weakest by this road; there's nothing here to either approve or condemn. We only need to look at the virtues, and who serves the Lord with the most self-denial, humility, and purity of conscience: this is the holiest one. However, we can't know much about

196. Probably a reference to the Inquisition.

this with any certainty here—until the true Judge gives each one what he or she deserves. There [in heaven], we'll be amazed to see how different His judgment is from what we understand here. May He be forever praised. Amen.

Overview of Chapter Nine

In the ninth chapter, Teresa writes about the kind of visions that most people think of when they hear the term: a communication from God in the form of an image, something that is "seen" with the inner eye and then remains stamped in our memory for good. She refers to these as imaginative visions. One notable distinction of such visions is that the image is not like a still-life painting; what is seen is full of light and life. Typically, she says, such a gift comes and goes quickly, and it happens when the soul is already in a rapture—because we can't handle it otherwise. Knowing this is an area of the spiritual life that is rife with confusion and self-deception—because we can easily start to think that anything we see in our imagination is a "vision" from God—Teresa spends some time trying to distinguish between true visions and false visions, as well as how to interact with and respond to doubtful confessors. She counsels always being open and truthful with our confessors or spiritual mentors, but she also addresses a particularly bad piece of advice she was given that she *doesn't* want others to follow: making an offensive gesture at any vision of Christ, just in case it is a trick of the adversary. Although there are "great benefits" to the soul from the gift of a vision, such as the comfort of remembering the Lord's face, Teresa seems almost reluctant to talk much about them and certainly doesn't want to encourage the pursuit of this seemingly popular and desirable gift in any way. In fact, she closes this chapter with a detailed outline of six reasons not to desire such visions. This list includes the possibility that if we want such a thing so badly, our imaginations will begin playing tricks on us. Teresa also reminds her readers that such gifts will no doubt be accompanied by heavy work and trials.

Chapter Nine (6.9)

IMAGINATIVE VISIONS

1. Let's now consider imaginative visions. They say the adversary interferes more often in these than the ones already described, and this is probably true. It seems to me that when they do come from our Lord, they are in some ways more beneficial, because they're a better fit for our nature. (I'm not including in this comparison the visions the Lord gives in the final dwelling place; with these, no others can compare.)

2. Well, let's look now at how, as I told you in the last chapter, the Lord is present. It's as if we had a gold vessel, and inside was hidden a precious stone of the highest value and curative qualities. We know for sure that the stone is there, even though we've never *seen* it. And the virtues of the stone continually bring us advantages if we carry it with us. So, although we've never seen it, this doesn't make it any less precious: through experience, we've found that it has cured us of certain illnesses (for which it's the appropriate remedy). But we don't dare to look at it, or open the vessel. We can't, because only the jewel's owner knows how to—and though he's lent the stone to us for our benefit, he's kept the key. As it still belongs to him, he'll open it when he wants to show it to us, and he'll take it back when he sees fit, as he does.

3. Well, let's now say that he *wants* to open the vessel suddenly sometime, for the benefit of the person to whom he's loaned it. Obviously, this person will be much happier afterward, when he can remember the wonderful brilliance of the stone, and it will stay more deeply engraved in his memory. This is what happens here: when our Lord is pleased to give more to this soul, He clearly shows it His most sacred humanity in the way that He wants—as He was when He walked in the world, or after the resurrection. And although He does this so quickly that we might compare it with a flash of lightning, it leaves this most glorious image so engraved in the imagination that I think it would be impossible to leave behind—until the soul sees the same where it can be enjoyed forever [in eternity].

4. Although I say "image," you must understand that it's not "painted" according to the one who sees it, but truly alive. And sometimes it's even

speaking with the soul, and revealing great secrets. But you have to understand that, even though the soul is arrested by this sight for a certain length of time, you can't keep staring at this any more than you can keep staring at the sun. So the vision always passes very quickly. This is *not* because its brilliance hurts the interior sight—which sees all this—like the sun does. (When it's with the exterior vision, I wouldn't know how to say anything about it, because this person that I've been talking about—whom I can speak about so particularly—hasn't experienced this, and we can hardly talk with certainty where there's no experience.) The brilliance of this vision is like an infused light or like a sun covered with something as thin and transparent as a diamond, if such a thing could be made; the garment looks like the finest Dutch linen. Almost every time that God grants this gift to the soul, it remains in rapture, because its lowly nature can't endure such a frightening[197] sight.

5. I say "frightening" because, although the sight *is* the most beautiful and delightful imaginable—even if someone lived and labored for a thousand years thinking about it, they couldn't picture it, because it's beyond the limits of our imagination and intellect—this presence carries such extraordinary majesty that it causes the soul great fright. It's unnecessary at this point to ask how they would know who it is without being told, because He reveals Himself quite clearly as the Lord of heaven and earth. Earthly kings won't do this: on their own, they aren't much, without their couriers or staff with them, or heralds proclaiming their greatness.

6. O Lord, how little we Christians know You! What will it be like on that day when You come to judge us? O daughters, if the sight of Him causes such fear when He comes here in such a *friendly* way to speak with His bride, what will it be like when He says with such a severe voice, "Depart, you accursed of My Father!"[198]?

---

197. The Spanish word here is *espantosa*, which is usually translated as "frightening" or even "terrible." Based on the next paragraph, Teresa is aware that this word has some negative connotations that we wouldn't normally associate with a vision of Jesus, and so I chose to keep this "scary" word rather than making it more blandly theological (as with a word like "fearsome" or "awesome").

198. A reference to the judgment scene in Matthew 25:41: "Then he will say to those at his left hand, 'You that are accursed, depart from me into the eternal fire prepared for the devil and his angels.'"

7. Let's keep the above in mind when we remember this gift given by God, for it will be no small blessing. Even Saint Jerome—holy as he was—didn't push this thought away. If we keep this [day of judgment] in mind, we won't care at all about all that we've suffered by strictly keeping the practices of our religious order. For, no matter how long this takes us, the time is short compared with eternity. I can truly say that—wicked as I am—I've never feared the torments of hell, for that seems like nothing compared with the thought of the damned seeing anger in the beautiful, meek, and benign eyes of the Lord. I don't think my heart could bear to see that, and I've felt like this my whole life. How much greater the fear for those to whom He's revealed Himself in this way—and given *such* a consciousness of His presence that it makes them unconscious![199] This must be the reason that the soul stays suspended; the Lord helps it in its weakness—a weakness He unites to His greatness in this elevated communication with God.

TRUE VISIONS, FALSE VISIONS, AND DOUBTFUL CONFESSORS

8. When the soul can stay a long while looking at the Lord, I don't think it can be a vision. Instead, it must be a striking or intense idea creating a picture in the imagination—but this will be like something dead when compared with a vision.

9. Some people become so absorbed in their imagination that *everything* they think about seems to be clearly "seen." I know this is true, because they have talked with me about it—and not three or four people, but many. Maybe it's that their imagination is so weak, or their intellect so overactive... I don't know what the cause is, really. If they'd ever seen a true vision, they would realize their mistake, beyond the possibility of a doubt. Little by little, they compose the picture they see in their imagination, but this doesn't have any effect on them, and they are left cold—even more than if they were to see a devotional image. It's wise not to pay attention to such a thing; what was seen is much more easily forgotten than a dream.

---

199. Peers rightly points out that although this sentence sounds a bit forced in English, it is a great example of Teresa's fondness for wordplay, and a time when it's possible to translate such wordplay from Spanish to English.

10. The experience of a [true] vision described above is different. While the soul is nowhere near an expectation of seeing anything, or even having the thought of such "seeing" cross its mind, suddenly the whole vision is revealed to it. All of the faculties and senses are thrown into a great fear and commotion, in order to *later* put them in that happy peace. Just like how a storm and commotion came from heaven when Saint Paul was thrown to the ground, in this interior world there's a great commotion. And then everything grows calm all at once, and the soul is left so well-instructed about so many great truths that it doesn't need another master. Without any effort on its own part, true wisdom has overcome its dullness and dimness: for a while, it enjoys complete certainty that this gift comes from God. No matter how often this soul might be told that this isn't so, it can't be led into fear that it was mistaken. Later, when the confessor insinuates the same possibility of deception, God allows the soul to *start* to hesitate a bit, wondering whether He could possibly give this gift to such a sinner. But it doesn't believe this. Because, as I've said in other cases when talking about temptations in matters of faith, the adversary can *disturb* the soul, but he can't stop the soul from being firm in its belief. Yet, the more he attacks, the more certain this soul becomes that the adversary could never leave her with so many blessings [like she received from the vision]. And this is true, because he can't do much in the interior of the soul: he might be able to show or reveal something, but not with this kind of truth, majesty, or results.

11. Since confessors can't see this vision—and possibly those God gives this gift to don't know how to describe it—they fear, and rightly so. They'll need to proceed with caution, and even wait for a while, to see the *results* of these visions or visitations: observing how much humility they leave in the soul, how much its virtues are strengthened. If [the visions] come from the adversary, there will soon be a sign; he will be caught in a thousand lies. If it's an experienced confessor, and he has been given such visions himself, it won't take long before he's able to make a judgment. From the account given, he'll see whether the vision is from God, the imagination, or the adversary, especially if His Majesty has given him the gift of discerning spirits. If he has this gift and is a learned man, he'll know very well what's going on, even though he might not have [personal] experience.

12. What's essential, sisters, is that you go in very openly and truthfully with your confessor. Here, I'm not talking about when you're confessing your sins, because of course you'll do so then, but when you're describing your experiences in prayer. Because unless you do this, I can't reassure you that you're progressing well, or that it's God who is teaching you. He's very fond of our speaking to those who are in His place with truth and clarity, and wants them to be acquainted with all our thoughts, and even more our actions, however trivial these may be. If you do this, you don't need to be disturbed or anxious, because even if something [in prayer] is not of God, it won't do you any harm if you are humble and have a good conscience. His Majesty can bring good out of evil, and through the road the adversary hoped might bring you to destruction, you can still benefit. Because, since you'll assume that it's God who is giving you these gifts, you'll strive to please Him more fully, and keep His image in your mind.

A very learned man used to say that the adversary is a very skillful artist, and so if he were to show him an absolutely lifelike picture of the Lord, it wouldn't worry the man—because such an image would heighten his devotion to God, and so he would be using the evil one's own twisted weapons to wage war back. Even though a painter might be very bad, that doesn't mean we shouldn't reverence the *image* he makes, if it's of the One who is all our good.

13. Some people advise "giving the fig" [as a sign of rejection] whenever a vision is seen, but this seemed like a terrible idea to that same learned man.[200] For, he said, wherever we see our King painted, we have to revere Him. I think he's right, because even here on earth we feel this way. If a person loves another, and yet knew that the beloved friend made similar insults to his portrait, he wouldn't like it at all. Well, how much more reasonable, then, to always be respectful when we see a crucifix or any portrait of our Emperor?

Even though I've written about this elsewhere, I'm happy to put it down again here because I knew someone who was greatly distressed over

200. To "give the fig" (*dar higas*) means to make a mildly obscene hand gesture that uses the thumb wedged between the pointer and middle fingers; it's been in use since at least the Roman Age in southern Europe, including Spain. It has connotations of warding off or rejecting evil spirits, and presumably the instinct behind the advice was to "reject" any vision at all because its origins were unknown. The theologian (or "very learned man") Teresa refers to here is Padre Bañez (*Life*, chapter 29; *Foundations*, chapter 8).

being ordered to use this "remedy." I don't know who would have invented such advice—such a torment to someone who couldn't help but obey it, if the confessor gave her this advice (because it seemed to her then that she would be lost if she didn't do it). My *own* advice is that, even if someone tells you to do this, don't take their word. With all humility, tell them this reasoning I've given you. I'm extremely appreciative of the good reasoning of the person who advised me in this case.

14. There's a great benefit to the soul from this gift [of a vision] from the Lord: it's that when it thinks of Him, or His life and passion, it remembers His most gentle and beautiful face, which is a great comfort. I'm telling you, such a rich memory gives a lot of comfort and strength. It also brings many other blessings, but since so much has already been said about the effects of this (and there's still more to come), I won't tire myself—or you—by adding more now. I'll only warn you that when you learn, or hear, that God is giving some souls these gifts, you must never ask or want Him to lead you along this road.

REASONS NOT TO DESIRE SUCH VISIONS

15. Even though it might seem like a very good path, one to be highly prized and revered, desiring it is not appropriate for a few reasons: First, it shows a lack of humility to want what you've never earned or deserved, so I think anyone who wants this can't be very humble. For just as a lowly laborer's desires are far from being a king—because it's seemingly impossible, and because he doesn't deserve it—that's how it is for the humble with similar things. I think they'll never be given to a person lacking humility, because before the Lord does these graces in a soul, He gives it a deep self-knowledge. And how can someone who has such thoughts understand that, truly, He is doing a very great favor not to have her in hell? Second, such a person will quite certainly be deceived, or be in great danger of deception, because the adversary only needs to see a *slight* opening in a door to enter and play a thousand tricks on us. Third, the imagination itself makes a person *think* she sees or hears what she wants to, when the desire for something is great. It's like how people who go around desiring something all day begin to dream about it at night because they think about it so much. Fourth, it's very bold for me to want to choose

my path, not knowing which one is best for me.[201] Instead, it should be left to the Lord who knows me to lead me by the path that's best, so that in everything His will be done. Fifth, do you think the works and trials suffered by those in whom the Lord does these graces are small ones? No; they're extremely big, and of many kinds. How do you know you would be able to bear them? Sixth, it might be that the very thing you *think* will help you gain will bring you loss, just like Saul did in becoming the king.[202]

16. In the end, sisters, there are lots of reasons besides these, and believe me, the safest thing is to not want anything but what God wants. He knows us better than we know ourselves, and He loves us. Let's put ourselves in His hands so that His will might be done in us. We can't go wrong if we remain in this posture with a determined will.

And you must note that you won't deserve any more glory for having received a lot of these gifts; rather, those who do are more obliged to *serve* more because they've received more. The Lord doesn't take from us [any choice or action] that's actually more commendable, because those are up to us—in our own hands. So, there are many holy people who have never known what it's like to receive a gift like these, and there are others who *have* received them but aren't holy. And again, don't think that they happen continually; for each time the Lord does them, it also brings many works—and so the soul isn't thinking about receiving more, but only how to serve in response.

17. It's true that it must be a huge help in having greater virtue, with higher perfection. But anyone who has done this through his own labor is deserving of much more credit. I know a person to whom the Lord had given some of these gifts—actually, two people; one was a man. Both of them wanted to serve His Majesty at their own expense, and without being given any of these great gifts. And they were so anxious to suffer that they complained to our Lord because He gave them some [gifts]—and if it would have been possible not to receive them, they would have passed. I'm talking here about gifts that the Lord gives in contemplation,

201. Teresa doesn't often drop into the first-person "me/I" when not in a "teaching voice," but this is one such place.
202. First Samuel 15:10–11: "The word of the LORD came to Samuel: 'I regret that I made Saul king, for he has turned back from following me, and has not carried out my commands.' Samuel was angry; and he cried out to the LORD all night."

not these visions (which, in the end, bring great benefits and are to be greatly valued).

18. It's also true, in my opinion, that these are supernatural desires and characteristic of souls very much in love—those who would want the Lord to see that they don't serve Him for pay. And so, as I've said, they never think of receiving glory as a motive for making the effort to serve more. Instead, they serve for the satisfaction of their love, and it's natural to express and act out love in a thousand ways. If it could, the soul would invent ways to be consumed in Him. And if it were necessary to remain annihilated forever for the greater honor of God, it would do so very willingly. May He be praised forever, amen. He stoops to communicate with such miserable creatures, wanting to show His greatness.

Overview of Chapter Ten

After addressing very specific gifts at some length, in chapter ten, Teresa seems to be looking for a place to put a couple of miscellaneous experiences that don't fit anywhere else. Her own brief introduction to the chapter is just a vague declaration that this section "speaks about other favors God grants the soul, in a different way from those already mentioned, and of the great profit they bring." Nevertheless, the two intellectual visions she describes here are beautiful and worth our consideration: the first is a deepened understanding of God holding all that is: an experience of the theological and biblical idea that it is in God that "we live and move and have our being."[203] Understandably, such an experience leads to an even greater desire to avoid sin, since all that we do takes place "within God." The other intellectual vision she describes results in a deepened awareness of God as truth and the need to walk with as much truth, integrity, and lack of deception in our lives as possible.

Chapter Ten (6.10)

1. There are many ways the Lord communicates Himself to the soul through these visions or visitations.[204] Some of them come when the soul is troubled; others when a great trial or work is on the way; others so that His Majesty might enjoy the soul, and also share His enjoyment with it.[205] There's no need to specifically address each of these. My intention, sisters,

---

203. Acts 17:28.

204. Once again, the word here is literally "apparitions" (*apariciones* in Spanish), but this is no longer a common word or concept. To my mind, something between a "vision" and a "visitation" is what Teresa is describing.

205. This is a very interesting verb and claim: using a reflexive verb, *regalarse*, most literally Teresa says that sometimes God simply wants to "gift Himself" and also "be gifted." This has been translated in the following way by Peers: "His Majesty may take His delight in it and at the same time may comfort it"; by Kavanaugh and Rodriguez as: "Might take his delight in the soul and give delight to it"; and by Stanbrook as: "for the sake of the mutual delight of Himself and His beloved." In all cases, the image of mutual delight and gifting is clear.

is simply to explain the different kinds of experiences that there are on this road (as far as I understand them) and the effects that they leave. Yet I don't want it to seem to you that *everything* you imagine is a vision...but also so that, when it *is* a vision, you don't go around agitated or distressed. The adversary wins when this is the case, and he loves to see a soul distressed and restless, because he knows this keeps the soul from occupying its whole self in loving and praising God.

His Majesty also communicates Himself in other ways that are even more sublime and less dangerous, because I don't believe the adversary has the power to fake them. But they're very difficult to describe because they're very obscure and mysterious things; the imaginative visions are easier to explain.

GOD HOLDING ALL

2. When the Lord wills, this might happen: while the soul is in prayer, and fully in possession of its senses, it suddenly experiences a suspension in which the Lord leads it to understand great secrets—which it seems are seen *in* God Himself. These aren't visions of the most sacred humanity. Even though I say "sees," nothing is "seen," because it's not an imaginary vision, but rather an intellectual one. In this, the soul discovers how all things are seen in God, and how He contains all things within Himself. This is of great benefit because, even though it only lasts a moment, it remains engraved upon the soul. And it also causes great confusion in showing us more clearly the wrongness of offending God, because it's *in* God Himself—I mean, while dwelling within Him—that we do all this wrong. I want to make a comparison, if I can, to explain this. Because even though this is the case, and we've heard it a lot of times, we either don't pay attention to this truth or refuse to understand it. It doesn't seem possible that we would be so bold, if we really understood how this is.

3. Let's suppose that God is like a very large and beautiful dwelling, or palace. I'm saying this palace is God Himself. Now, can the sinner leave this palace and go away to do wrong? No, clearly not; the abominations and dishonesties and all the wrongdoing that we sinners do take place *inside* this same palace, within God. Oh, this is a scary thought—worthy of deep consideration and very beneficial for those of us who are ignorant and unable to understand these truths, so that we wouldn't possibly be so

stupidly daring! Let's consider, sisters, the great mercy and long-suffering patience of God in not throwing us straight into the depths; let's offer Him the deepest thanks and be ashamed about any resentments we have when things are done or said against *us*. It's the worst thing in the world to see that God our creator should suffer so much from His creatures within Himself, while we are so sensitive to *one word* that someone says behind our backs, maybe even when there aren't any bad intentions behind it.

4. Oh, human misery! How long, daughters, until we imitate this great God in any way? Oh! Let's not pretend that we're doing anything by putting up with insults. Instead, let us willingly go through everything and *love* those who offend us, because this great God hasn't stopped loving us, even though we've offended Him greatly. Thus, He has good reason for wanting everyone to forgive those who wrong us. I'm telling you, daughters, that even though this vision passes very quickly, it is a great gift and grace that our Lord does for those who receive it. If they want to really profit from it, they must try to keep it habitually in mind.

GOD AS TRUTH

5. Very suddenly, and in a way that can't be described, it also might happen that God will show a truth within Himself. It's shown in a way that it seems to leave in shadowy darkness all "truths" there are in creatures, and it's very clearly understood that God alone is truth, unable to lie. It gives a good understanding of what David is saying in one of the psalms, that every man is a liar.[206] Although we've heard it many times, it was never understood like this, and it's a truth that won't fail us. I'm reminded of Pilate, who questioned our Lord so much, asking during His passion, "What is truth?"[207] How little we understand down here [on earth] about this supreme Truth.

6. I would like to be able to give more understanding here, but there's nothing more I can say. Let's learn from this, sisters: in order to become more like our God and Spouse, it's good for us to seriously study at all times how to walk in this truth. I don't simply mean that we shouldn't tell lies, for as far as that goes—glory be to God—I see that in our convents you are very careful never to lie for any reason. I mean that we must *walk* in

206. Psalm 116:11: "I said in my consternation, 'Everyone is a liar.'"
207. John 18:38.

truth, in the presence of God and people, in as many ways as we can. We should especially not want to be considered any better than what we are, and in all our works we should attribute to God what is His and to us what is ours. We should try to draw out the truth in everything. Thus, we'll have little care for this world, which is all lie and falsehood. As such, it will not endure.

7. Once, I was wondering why our Lord so loved this virtue of humility, and all of a sudden—it seemed to me without really considering it, quickly—this thought came to me: it's because God is total truth, and to be humble is to walk in truth, because it's a very deep truth that we have no good thing about us, only misery and nothingness. Whoever doesn't understand this walks around in falsehood. Those who understand it more please the highest Truth, because then they are walking in truth. May it please God, sisters, to give us the mercy of never departing from this self-knowledge. Amen.

8. Our Lord gives the soul gifts like this because, just as with a true wife—one who is already determined to do His will in everything—He wants to give her some knowledge of what she has to do, and of His greatness. There's no need to say more; I've said these two things because they seem so helpful to me. There's no reason to be afraid of these experiences; instead, praise the Lord because He gives them. It seems to me that there's little room for the adversary or even one's own imagination here, and so the soul is left with deep satisfaction.

Overview of Chapter Eleven

In the final chapter of the sixth dwellings, Teresa describes an experience that she places at the threshold of the seventh dwellings. She says it may happen to a soul after they have spent many years desiring to know and serve God more fully—although, as always, she refuses to limit or place timelines on how God will act. There is really only one topic in this chapter, summarized somewhat shockingly by Teresa in her introduction as "the desires to enjoy God that He gives the soul, which are so great and impetuous that you're put in danger of losing your life." Of course, she is also attentive to the "profit" or benefit of receiving such fearsome graces, and this chapter is no exception. Because the topics of "desire unto death" and "precious pain" are so evocative and historically loaded, here the reader will benefit from paying close attention to what Teresa does (and does not) say. Her use of images is minimal. In describing these powerful desires and interior suffering, she says it comes like an "arrow of fire," while making sure that we don't take her literally on this. Like so many extraordinary gifts before it, this is clearly an action that comes from outside of our nature, and yet, paradoxically, it is born of our own desire for God, too. It seems to be an intense pain of longing, and yet Teresa is clear that it is a precious pain, one that the soul wouldn't trade for anything—and not just because of its effects. And indeed, following this great pain, "the soul is left with wonderful effects, losing at once its fear of any trials that might happen to it. For, compared to the feelings of deep anguish that its soul has felt, they seem to be nothing." Additionally, there's even greater detachment from the world and greater care not to offend God. These are consistent themes of genuine effects that we have seen repeatedly through these dwellings, and they remain steadfast even in the most "controversial" places of these dwellings.

Chapter Eleven (6.11)

1. Have all these gifts given by the Spouse to the soul been enough to satisfy the little dove or butterfly (don't think I have forgotten her!) so that she might find rest in the place where she'll die? Definitely not; she's in an even worse state than before. Because even though she might have been receiving these gifts for years, she's always moaning and walking around with sorrow, because each of them leaves her with more pain. The reason for this is that the more she learns about the greatness of her God, while still finding herself so far from Him and unable to fully enjoy Him, the more her desire grows. After all, the more one discovers how much this great God and Lord *deserves* to be loved, the more love also grows. And over these years, little by little, this desire has grown in such a way that it finally comes to a point of suffering, as I'll now explain. (I'm saying "years" here to line up with the experiences of the particular person I'm speaking about. But I understand very well that we can't put limits on God, and that, in one moment, He could bring a soul to the highest point described here. His Majesty has the power to do all that He wants to do, and He's eager to do a lot for us.)

POWERFUL DESIRES AND INTERIOR SUFFERING: THE "ARROW OF FIRE"

2. Well, there come times when something else will happen to a soul with these anxieties, tears, sighs, and great yearning desires mentioned. All of these *existing* effects seem to have come from our love, and they come with their own deep emotions, but they are nothing in comparison with this other experience: they are like a smoldering fire, with quite bearable heat, even if it hurts. While the soul is walking in this way, burning on the inside, it often happens that, because of a very fleeting thought, or some word heard pointing to how long it will take to die, a blow comes, as if arriving like an arrow of fire—it's not known from where it comes, or how. I'm not saying that it actually is an arrow—but whatever it is, it clearly couldn't have come from our own nature. Nor is it actually a blow, even though I use that word; it hurts more sharply, and not where pain is felt here [on earth], I think, but in the very deep and intimate part of the soul. Where this quickly passing lighting strikes, everything it finds of our earthly nature, it brings to dust. During the time that it lasts, it's

impossible to remember anything except our Lord: all at once, it binds the faculties in such a way that they don't have freedom for anything, except what will increase this pain.

3. I wouldn't want this to seem like an exaggeration, because I'm actually beginning to see as I go on that my words fall short: it's indescribable. It's an enrapturing of the senses and faculties, except, as I've said, in ways that help us feel this affliction. For the intellect is very alive to understanding *why* the soul feels absent from God; at this time, His Majesty helps it with a lively knowledge of Himself, in such a way that it causes the pain to grow to such a degree that the one who has it begins to cry aloud. No matter how long-suffering she might be, and however used to suffering great pains, she can't help but do this—because the feeling is not in the body, as I've said, but deep within the interior of the soul. This is how this person discovered how much more sensitive the soul is than the body. It was revealed to her that those who suffer in purgatory are like this: not having a body doesn't prevent them from suffering much more than all those who still have a body on earth do.

4. I once saw a person like that; I really thought she was dying, and this was not very surprising, because there is in fact a great danger of death. Although it only lasts for a short time, it leaves the body very out of joint, and while it continues, the pulse is as weak as if the soul were about to give itself up to God. This is no exaggeration: because while the natural heat of the body is lacking, the soul is burning so fiercely that, with only a little more intensity, God would have fulfilled its desires. The danger is not because it feels any bodily pain. (Notwithstanding, the body *is* disjointed, as I've said, in such a way that, for two or three days afterward, it's unable to find the strength to write and is in great pain...and it always seems to me that the body remains weaker than before.) It must not feel any pain because the inner feeling of the soul is so much more intense that it pays no attention to the body. It's like when we have a very acute pain in one spot; although we might have many other pains, we barely feel them. I've experienced this and proven it well. In this case, the body feels neither a little nor a lot, and I don't think it would even if it were torn to pieces.

5. You'll tell me that this feeling is an imperfection. Why doesn't the soul simply conform to the will of God, since it is so surrendered to Him?

So far as she could, she has—and has spent her life doing so. But not now, because her reason is in such a state that she is not really in charge or able to think of anything but the cause of her suffering. Since she is absent from her Good, why does she want to live? She feels a strange loneliness, because there's not a creature on the whole earth who can keep her company—in fact, I don't think even any heavenly creatures could; only the One she loves [would be able]. Everything torments her. But she sees that she's like a person hanging, who can't settle and rest on any earthly thing *or* go up to heaven. Parched with this thirst, she can't reach the water. And I don't know that she can bear it; it's a thirst that nothing will quench—and she doesn't want it to be quenched, *unless* it's with that water our Lord spoke of to the Samaritan woman, but that's not given to her.

PRECIOUS PAIN AND ITS EFFECTS

6. Ah, God, help me! Lord, how You afflict Your lovers! But everything is small in comparison with what You give them later. It's right that great things should cost a lot. Especially if it purifies this soul so that it might enter the seventh dwelling place, just as those who are to enter heaven cleanse themselves in purgatory…then this suffering is no more than a drop of water in the sea. And more than that, despite all this torment and affliction, the soul feels that this pain is *precious*—even though I believe there's no greater pain on earth (this person had gone through many trials, both physical and spiritual, but everything seemed like *nothing* to her in comparison). The soul understands well that [this precious pain] is so valuable that it could never deserve it. But this awareness isn't felt in a way that brings relief; still, with this understanding, the soul suffers willingly, and would suffer all its life long if God so willed. Although, it must be said, this would be like constantly dying instead of dying once, for truly the suffering is no less than this.

7. And now, sisters, let's consider those who are in hell: they don't have this conformity [to God's will], nor the contentment and pleasure that God places in the soul. They cannot see that their suffering is doing them any good, but constantly suffer more and more. (I mean more and more in terms of accidental pains, for the torment of the soul is so much harsher than the pains of the body.) And the pains that such souls have to endure are beyond comparison to what we've talked about here. They see that

they'll be suffering in this way forever and ever; what will become of these unfortunate souls? And so what can we do—or suffer—in such a short life that will matter *at all* if it means freeing ourselves from such terrible and eternal torments? I'm telling you, it's impossible to explain to anyone how sensitive the soul is to suffering, and how different it is from that of the body, if one hasn't gone through it. The Lord Himself *wants* us to understand this so that we might be more conscious of how much we owe Him for bringing us to a state in which—by His mercy—we have hope that He will set us free and forgive our sins.

8. Well, let's get back to what we were discussing, for we left this soul in great pain. In this intensity, the pain only lasts a short time—it'll be at most three or four hours, in my opinion, because if it lasted a long time, it would be impossible not to suffer natural weakness unless saved by a miracle. It happened once that it lasted for only a quarter of an hour, and yet left the soul in pieces. In fact, that time, the person completely lost consciousness, and lay prostrate. It happened while she was in a conversation on the last day of Easter, and she'd been so spiritually dry all of Easter that she almost didn't understand what "Easter" was or meant. But it came just through hearing some words about "life not ending." So, imagine thinking that you can resist! It's no more possible than if you wanted to make a flame without enough heat to burn you. It's not a feeling that you can hide; those who are present understand the great danger the soul is in, although they can't be witnesses of what's going on within. It's true that they are some sort of company to her, like shadows—just as all earthly things appear to be.

9. And so that you can see, in case you ever have this experience, that it's possible for your weakness and human nature to be of help to you, I'll tell you this: at times, when such a soul is dying to die, with the grievous desire oppressing it so much that the soul appears at the very point of leaving the body, she is truly afraid and would like to loosen the grip of the pain so as not to die. It's evident that this fear is a natural weakness, for it doesn't remove its desire—and it's not possible to have a remedy that *removes* this pain until the Lord Himself does it. And He does do this, ordinarily through a deep rapture, or with some kind of vision, in which the true Comforter comforts and strengthens her so that she wants to live for as long as He wills.

10. This is a painful experience, but the soul is left with wonderful effects, losing at once its fear of any trials that might happen to it. For, compared with the feelings of deep anguish that it has felt, they seem to be nothing. So that these effects might be taken advantage of, the soul would be glad to suffer this again and again; but there's no way for it to experience this again until the Lord wills it, just as there's no way to resist it or take it away when it *does* come. The soul is left with much greater contempt for the world than before, because it sees that no worldly thing was of any help to it in that torment. And it's much more detached from creatures because it sees that it can only be comforted and satisfied by the Creator. The soul is also left with greater fear and care not to offend Him, because it sees that He can torment as well as comfort.

11. It seems to me that there are two things on this spiritual road that put a person in danger of death. One is this pain, which is truly a danger—and not a small one; the other is excessive joy and delight, which can be carried to such a great extreme that it truly seems the soul faints, and that it would take very little to make it leave the body; in truth, this would be no small happiness for her.

Here you'll see, sisters, if I've been right in saying that *courage is necessary*, and that if you ask the Lord for these things, *He* will be right to ask you what He asked the sons of Zebedee: "Can you drink the cup?"[208]

12. I believe all of us, sisters, will answer yes—and with good reason. Because His Majesty gives strength to those He sees need it, and He defends these souls in every way; He stands up for them in persecutions and gossip, as He did for the Magdalene[209]—if not through words, through actions. And finally, at last, before they die, He'll pay for everything all at once, as you'll now see. May He be forever blessed, and may all creatures praise Him. Amen.

---

208. Matthew 20:22: "But Jesus answered, 'You do not know what you are asking. Are you able to drink the cup that I am about to drink?' They said to him, 'We are able.'"

209. Luke 7:44–47: "Then turning toward the woman, he said to Simon, 'Do you see this woman? I entered your house; you gave me no water for my feet, but she has bathed my feet with her tears and dried them with her hair. You gave me no kiss, but from the time I came in she has not stopped kissing my feet. You did not anoint my head with oil, but she has anointed my feet with ointment. Therefore, I tell you, her many sins have been forgiven; hence she has shown great love.'"

Questions for Reflection

1. How do you relate and respond to the various trials that Teresa outlines as part of the spiritual journey? These include trials of reputation, praise, physical suffering, interior sufferings, and even the trial of longing for God's presence and nearness. Which ones are especially relatable? Which ones do you struggle with most?
2. Throughout the sixth dwellings, Teresa uses the image of God doing things—or giving experiences to us—to "awaken love." This is the point, she seems to indicate, for so many forms of communication from God: words or phrases that we hear, raptures and visions, the flight of the spirit. When have you felt God "awaken love" in you through these means or others? How might thinking of these phenomena primarily as ways that God seeks to "awaken love" in us change your understanding of them?
3. How do you respond and relate to the descriptions of raptures, including flights of the spirit and the visions that might be given in a state of rapture? Do such extraordinary experiences strike you as compelling, repulsive, relieving, mystifying, or in some other way?
4. How would you put in your own words the advice Teresa offers in chapter seven about not forgetting to meditate on the life and death of Jesus even as we progress in our prayer journey?
5. When have you or someone you know seemed to experience the gift of overwhelming joy in God? Is your cultural and social context supportive of such joy and praise, as Teresa's convents were, or do you feel like you would have to run away into the desert if you were given such a gift, like so many other saints have before?

SEVENTH DWELLINGS

Overview of Chapter One

As we enter the final compartment of Teresa's "castle complex," we find ourselves concerned with the very center of the soul, where God dwells. The primary metaphor and action here is spiritual marriage, or union at the center. We are returning now to the image of spiritual engagement and marriage (discussed infrequently in the sixth dwellings) that Teresa claims is the best comparison she has, despite its being imperfect and somewhat problematic. How does this union differ from the ones previously described? This is the topic of the final section, but in this first chapter, she explains that part of what is different about it is this notion of the "center," but also our sense of "seeing," awareness, or consciousness about what is happening. As she puts it: "Here, [union] happens in another way. Our good God now wants to remove the scales from the eyes, so that the soul might see and understand something of His merciful action, although this is done in a strange manner." We have been prepared to understand a bit more of what she is expressing because she says this happens through an "intellectual vision," a truth seen with the eyes of the soul. Still, for all of the elevated language and terms, what she begins to describe *does* have certain (mundane) hallmarks of an earthly marriage. The first effect she spends time describing is the feeling of consistent companionship, even when the Spouse can't be easily seen. The stability, strength, and confidence given by the best human marriages is obviously part of the dynamic with divine-human partnership, too.

Chapter One (7.1)

1. It probably seems to you, sisters, that so much has been said about this spiritual path that there can't *possibly* be anything left to say. To think this would be a huge mistake. Just as the greatness of God has no limit, there's no end to His works. Who could finish telling about His mercies and wonders? It's impossible; so don't be surprised at what has been said

and what will be said, because it's only a fraction of what there is to say about God. It's a great mercy that He has communicated these things to a person through whom we can come to know about them, too. For the more we know about His communion with us creatures, the more we'll praise His greatness. And we'll strive not to despise [or resent] a soul in whom the Lord takes such delight, because every one of us has a soul. It's because we don't value our souls as they deserve, as creatures made in the image of God, that we don't understand the great mysteries within.[210] May it please His Majesty to guide my pen, and give me understanding about how I might say *something* about the many things God reveals to those He puts in this dwelling place. I have earnestly begged Your Majesty [for this guidance and ability], because He knows my intention is to make His mercies known, so that His name might be more fully praised and glorified.

2. I'm hopeful, sisters, that He will grant me this favor—not for my sake but for yours, so that you understand how important it is not to obstruct or delay the celebration of His spiritual marriage with your souls. Because, as you'll see, it brings with it *so* many blessings. O great God! It seems that a creature as pathetic as I am rightly trembles in trying to explain something so far beyond what I deserve to understand. And if it's true that I've been greatly confused, I'm wondering if it would simply be better to end this dwelling place with a few words. For it seems that others will think that I know it from experience, and that makes me very ashamed; because, knowing myself well, that's a terrible thought. On the other hand, although [I'm afraid] you might make more of these [flattering] judgments [about me], it seems to me that this [silencing] shame is a temptation and weakness. Let the whole world cry out against me, as long as God is praised and understood a little more. Especially because I might be dead by the time this writing is seen. Blessed be He who lives and will live forever. Amen.

SPIRITUAL MARRIAGE, OR UNION AT THE CENTER

3. This soul, which our Lord has already taken spiritually as His spouse, suffers and has suffered so much out of its desire. When our Lord

210. It is very tempting to change "creatures" to "creation" because we might balk at the notion of our *souls* as creatures, and we tend to think of "creatures" in very earthly terms. But to keep with Teresa's word choice here forces us to perhaps consider more intentionality the uniqueness of our human creation, which includes both physical and spiritual elements.

is pleased to have mercy, He brings it into His dwelling place—which is this seventh—before the spiritual marriage is consummated. Because, just like in heaven, He must have a room in the soul where only His Majesty dwells; let's call this another heaven. We must take great care, sisters, not to think of the soul as something dark. Since we don't see the soul, it's very common for it to *seem* dark—to think that there isn't any interior light, but only the [exterior] light we can see, and that within our soul is some kind of darkness.

About those who are not in grace, I confess this is so—but not because of any fault of the Sun of Justice, who is in her and giving her being. It's only because such a soul is incapable of receiving the light, as I think I described in the first dwelling place.[211] Based on the understanding of a certain person, it's as if these unfortunate souls are in a dark prison, tied hand and foot, unable to do any good that will help them merit [further grace], and both blind and deaf. We can rightly feel sorry for them—realizing that, for some time, we ourselves were like this—and ask the Lord to have mercy on them.

4. Let's be especially careful, sisters, to pray for this mercy of God [for such souls], and not neglect to do so. To pray for those who are in intentional sin is a very generous act of charity—much better, even, than if we were to release a Christian whom we saw tied up to a post with his hands bound behind him, someone who was dying of hunger...not because of a lack of food, since right next to him are the most delicious things to eat, but because he can't take them and put them into his mouth, and he's exhausted and sees that he is about to die an eternal death, not just a bodily one. Wouldn't it be extremely cruel to just stand looking at him and not put the food he needs into his mouth? Well, what if you could remove his chains through your prayers? You see what I mean. For the love of God, I ask you to always remember such souls when you pray.

5. We're not talking about them now, though, but about those who (by God's mercy) have repented of their sins[212] and are in a state of grace. So, we're not considering something limited, restricted, cornered, but an entire inner *world*. Within it are so many beautiful dwelling places, as you've seen,

---

211. See sections 1.2.1–3.
212. Literally: "have done penance for their sins."

and this is rightly so, because it also contains within it a dwelling place for God.

Now, when His Majesty wants to grant this soul the favor of this divine marriage, He first puts her in His dwelling. And His Majesty wants this to *not* be like other times when she's been put there in the [described] raptures. Even though I truly believe the soul is united with Him then, and also in the prayer of union, in those cases the soul feels called to its "higher" part and doesn't feel like it's being called to enter its own *center*—as it does here in this dwelling place. It doesn't really matter, because [in those previous cases,] the Lord unites her to Himself in one way or another, but He makes her blind and mute, like He made Saint Paul at his conversion.[213] He prevents any sense of *how* or in what way the favor comes that she is enjoying—there's great delight that the soul feels in being conscious of being so close to God. Yet when He joins it to Himself, the soul doesn't understand anything; the powers of its faculties are lost.

6. Here [in the seventh dwelling place], it happens in another way. Our good God now wants to remove the scales from the eyes, so that the soul might see and understand something of His merciful action, although this is done in a strange manner. The soul is put into this dwelling by an intellectual vision: a certain representation of the truth, in which the Holy Trinity is shown to him in all three persons. First, the soul's spirit is enkindled as if by a cloud of great clarity, and the soul sees these persons [of the Trinity] distinctly. Yet by an admirable knowledge given, the soul understands as a profound truth that all three persons are one substance, one power, one knowledge, and one God. So then, what we hold by faith, there the soul grasps and understands by sight, we might say—although it's not seen with the eyes of the body, because it's not an imaginary vision. Here all three persons communicate to the soul, speaking to the soul and making it understand those words the gospel [of John] attributes to the Lord: that He and the Father and the Holy Spirit would come to dwell with the soul who loves Him and keeps His commandments.[214]

---

213. Acts 9:8: "Saul got up from the ground, and though his eyes were open, he could see nothing; so they led him by the hand and brought him into Damascus."
214. John 14:23: "Jesus answered him, 'Those who love me will keep my word, and my Father will love them, and we will come to them and make our home with them.'"

7. Oh, God help me! There's such a difference between hearing and believing these words, and being led to understand *how* true they are in this way! And, every day, this soul becomes more amazed because she feels that They have never left her. She perceives quite clearly, in the way mentioned, that They are deep inside her soul. *Very* deep inside, in the most interior depths (because of a lack of learning, she doesn't know how to explain it), she feels this divine company.

CONSISTENT COMPANIONSHIP

8. You might think, given this, that such a person would be "out of her mind" and so absorbed that she can't focus on anything else. But no: much more than before, the soul is occupied with serving God; and when the busyness ends, she's left with that pleasant companionship. And if the soul doesn't fail God, He will never fail to make His presence clearly known, in my opinion. She has strong confidence that, since God has given her this favor, He will not now leave her and cause her to lose it. She can indeed think this, although this doesn't stop her from walking more carefully than ever—so as not to displease God in anything.

9. You should understand that this presence is not always felt so fully—I mean so clearly—as when it's first revealed to him,[215] or other times when God wants to give this gift. Because, if it were, it would be impossible to think of anything else, or even live with other people. And yet, although it's not always seen with such vivid clarity, he's always *aware* that he's with this company. It's like being with others in a very bright room, and then suddenly the shutters are closed and everyone is left in the dark. The light by which the others could be seen has been taken away, and so we won't be able to *see* them until the light is turned back on, and yet this doesn't stop us from understanding that they're there. It might be asked if, when the light comes back on, and you want to see them again, you actually can see them. This is not in our power, but only happens when our Lord wants to open the window of understanding. It's a great mercy the Lord gives, in never leaving the soul and wanting that to be understood so well.

215. In this section, Teresa goes back and forth between the masculine and feminine pronouns, sometimes in the same section. To keep this balance and yet assist with clarity, I alternate but keep consistency within a paragraph.

10. Here it seems that the Divine Majesty wants to prepare the soul for more through this wonderful companionship. Because clearly it will be a tremendous help in every way for moving onward, toward perfection—and she will lose the fear that she sometimes had of the other gifts He gave her, as was said. And so it was [for the person given this gift]: she improved in every way, and it seemed to her that no matter how many trials and business worries she had, the essence of her soul never moved from that dwelling place. In some way, it seemed to her that her soul was divided [between the active and contemplative parts], and when she was going through significant and trying work just a short time after God granted her this favor, she complained about her soul, just as Martha complained about Mary.[216] Sometimes she would say that it was always enjoying itself in the pleasures of stillness, while she was left with so many trials and occupations that she couldn't keep it company.

11. Maybe this seems like nonsense to you, daughters, but it truly happens like this. Although of course we know that the soul stays all together, what I've said is not just a strange notion, but a very common experience. Earlier,[217] I said that interior things can be observed in such a way that its clearly understood that there *is* a difference—a well-recognized one—between the soul and the spirit, even though they are ultimately one. There's such a subtle division that sometimes it seems one functions differently than the other, and that the Lord wants to give them different "flavors."[218] It also seems to me that the soul is a different thing from our natural capacities,[219] and that they're not entirely united. There are so many—and such subtle—things in the interior life that it would be bold for me to try to explain them. We'll see it all on the other side of the veil, where we'll understand these secrets if the Lord grants the mercy of taking us there.

216. Luke 10:40: "But Martha was distracted by her many tasks; so she came to him and asked, 'Lord, do you not care that my sister has left me to do all the work by myself? Tell her then to help me.'"

217. 6.4.1 and 6.4.9.

218. Although one might initially think this is a typo for "favors," it's not! Teresa speaks here as we do when we talk about "different flavors" of ice cream or people—using a food and taste word to describe variation.

219. Literally: "faculties," but this word is not often used in common discourse anymore.

Overview of Chapter Two

After introducing the concept of spiritual marriage in the first chapter, Teresa continues her explanation and exploration of this idea. Although she rhetorically tries to distance herself, we know from other sources that she employs her own experience here. The pivotal moment and intellectual vision came for Teresa just after she had received Communion one day, which was accompanied by the communication from Christ that "it was time for her to consider what belongs to Him as her own, and that He would take care of what was hers—along with other words that are more for feeling and understanding than for repeating and sharing." Knowing that we still might struggle to understand the difference between this and the other divine gifts previously described, Teresa can do no more than return to her central metaphor: "The difference between spiritual engagement and spiritual marriage is as great as the difference between two people who are engaged and those who can no longer be separated," she writes.

Now, the soul *always* remains with God in its center; she compares this state to the water of a stream that flows into the ocean—it's impossible to "re-separate" the stream. As the metaphor suggests, there is then a shift in one's very nature, with the most notable change being a resulting peace in the center. This doesn't mean that our whole life is "but a dream," however: there is a distinction between the central reality and our "outer" experience. As she says, "It shouldn't be thought that the faculties and senses and passions are always in this peace, although the soul itself is. The other dwellings don't stop having times of conflict and work and fatigue, but not in such a way that takes away from the soul's peace and position of stability—at least not as a general rule." Struggling to explain this inner and unshakable peace even in the midst of day-to-day turmoil, she laughingly compares it to a king in his palace who doesn't leave his post, even as he's aware of the many wars going on. Those parts of ourselves still in the "battle" are strengthened by this inner stability and steadfastness.

Chapter Two (7.2)

SPIRITUAL MARRIAGE, CONTINUED

1. Well, now let's deal with the divine and spiritual marriage. However, it must be said: this great gift can't be fulfilled *perfectly* in our lifetime, because if we were to turn away from God, this great blessing would be lost. The first time God does this merciful action,[220] His Majesty wants to reveal Himself to the soul through an imaginary vision of His most sacred humanity, so that the soul clearly understands and isn't ignorant of the fact that it's receiving such a paramount gift.[221] For other people, it will happen differently. But for this person we're talking about, the Lord appeared to her just as she had finished taking Communion. He appeared in the form of great brilliance and beauty and majesty, just as after the resurrection, and told her that it was time for her to consider what belongs to Him as her own, and that He would take care of what was hers—along with other words that are more for feeling and understanding than for repeating and sharing.

2. It might seem like this was nothing new, since, at other times, the Lord had revealed Himself to this soul in this way. But it was very different, in a way that left her very confused and scared: first, because this vision came with great force; second, because of the words He said to her, and also because He was revealed in the interior part of her soul, where she had not seen any other visions except the previous one [mentioned in chapter one of this dwelling, regarding the Trinity]. You must understand that there's a huge difference between all the other visions mentioned and the ones of this dwelling place. The difference between spiritual engagement and spiritual marriage is as great as the difference between two people who are engaged and those who can no longer be separated.

---

220. Once again, we are dealing with the word *merced*: a mercy, favor, or gift, but also here Teresa uses the verb "to do" or "to make," not the verb for "to give."
221. The word translated here as "paramount" is literally "sovereign."

3. As I've already said, even though I use these comparisons because there aren't any that work better, it should be understood that here there's no more thought of the body than if the soul were not in it—but just spirit. And in spiritual marriage, there's even *less* [connection to the body] because this secret union takes place in the very interior center of the soul, which must be where God Himself dwells. I don't think there's any need for a door to enter it. I say that there's no need for a "door" because everything that I've said and described up to this point seems to go through the senses and our natural capacities, and this appearance of the Lord's humanity must also. But then, what happens in the union of spiritual marriage is very different. The Lord appears in the center of the soul in an intellectual vision, not an imaginary one (although this is even more subtle than the one already mentioned).[222] It's like how He appeared to the apostles without entering the room through a door, when He said to them, "*Pax vobis.*"[223]

What God communicates here to the soul in an instant is such a great secret, such a great mercy and gift—and the delight the soul experiences is so intense—that I simply don't know what to compare it to. I can only say that, in that moment, the Lord wants to show her the glory that's in heaven, which is more sublime than any spiritual delight or vision. It's impossible to say more than this: as much as we can understand, the soul—I mean the spirit of the soul—is made one with God. Since His Majesty is also a spirit, He has willed to show the love He has for us by making some people understand the extent of that love, so that we might praise His greatness. For He wants to be united with this creature in such a way that they become like those who [are married and] *can't* be separated; He doesn't *want* to be separated from her.

4. The spiritual engagement is different, because in this the two often separate. The same in the case of union, also: because even though union is the joining of two things into one, in the end they can be separated, and each remains its own thing. Indeed, as we usually see in [union], the merciful gift passes quickly, and afterward the soul is left without that

222. See 6.8 for her treatment of intellectual visions versus imaginary visions.
223. Again, *Pax vobis* means "Peace be with you." This is a reference to John 20:19, 21: "When it was evening on that day, the first day of the week, and the doors of the house where the disciples had met were locked for fear of the Jews, Jesus came and stood among them and said, 'Peace be with you.'... Jesus said to them again, 'Peace be with you. As the Father has sent me, so I send you.'"

companionship—or at least without an *awareness* of it. In this other merciful gift of the Lord, that is not so: the soul always remains with its God in that center.

Let's say union [introduced in the fifth dwellings] is like two wax candles joined together [at the point of the flame] so fully that all the light was one (or at least the wicks, the wax, and light were all one), but, afterward, the one candle can be separated from the other, and they remain two candles, with two wicks. Here, it's like rain falling from the heavens into a river or a fountain; there is nothing but water there, and you're no longer able to divide or separate the water belonging to the river from the water that fell from the sky. Or it's like a small stream flowing into the sea; there's no way it can then separate itself or "get away." Or, [put another way,] like a large amount of light coming into a single room through two windows: even though the light enters "divided," it becomes all one light inside.

5. Maybe this is what Saint Paul means in saying, "He who draws near to or is joined to the Lord becomes one spirit with Him."[224] Perhaps he's referring to this ultimate marriage,[225] which presupposes that His Majesty has already reached the soul through union. And Paul also says, "For to me, living is Christ and dying is gain."[226] I think the soul can say that here, since this is where the little butterfly that we've been talking about dies, and does so with great joy because Christ is now its life.

THE RESULTING PEACE IN THE CENTER

6. This is better understood as time passes through the effects [of this life in Christ]. For it's clearly understood, through certain secret inspirations, that God is the One who gives life to our souls. These inspirations are often so lively and intense that they can't be doubted, because the soul feels them very strongly. Although it doesn't know how to explain it, this feeling is so overwhelming that sometimes it can't keep from saying some of the loving expressions they induce: "Oh, life of my life! Strength that sustains me!"[227] and things like this. For it seems that

---

224. See 1 Corinthians 6:17.
225. The adjective rendered here as "ultimate" is literally "sovereign."
226. Philippians 1:21; Teresa includes these words in Latin in the original manuscript: *Mihi vivere Christus est, mori lucrum.*
227. This is literally "sustenance that sustains me," but so few people use the word "sustenance" these days that a synonym, however imperfect, seemed called for.

God is constantly sustaining the soul through those divine breasts: out of them streams of milk flow, bringing comfort to all the people in the castle. It seems the Lord wants them to enjoy, somehow, how much the soul enjoys. As such, from time to time, a surge comes out of the mighty river that has consumed this tiny fountain and is directed toward those who have to serve the Bridegroom and the bride in the body in order to sustain them. And just as a person who's suddenly bathed in water would feel it—and couldn't help but feel it, no matter how oblivious she might be—the same can be said with even greater certainty about these operations I'm describing. For just as a great stream of water could never fall on us without coming from some source, as I've said, it's just as obvious that there is someone inside the soul who shoots these arrows and gives life to this life. It's clear that there's a *sun* from which this great light comes, sent to our faculties from the interior of the soul. The soul, as I've said, doesn't move from that center, nor lose its peace; because the same One who gave peace to the apostles when they were all together can also give peace to her.[228]

7. It has occurred to me that this greeting of the Lord must have meant much more than it sounds like on the surface; the same with His telling the glorious Magdalene to go in peace.[229] For the words of the Lord are like actions or works done in us, and so they must have produced an effect in those who were already prepared [and ready for this moment]: everything worldly is removed, leaving the soul as pure spirit, so that it might be joined in this heavenly union with the uncreated Spirit. For it's quite certain that, in emptying ourselves of all that is creaturely, and getting rid of it for the love of God, that same Lord fills us with Himself. And thus, once when Jesus Christ our Lord was praying for His apostles (I don't know where this takes place), He asked that they might be one with the Father and with Him, as Jesus Christ our Lord is in the Father and the Father is in Him.[230] I don't know what greater love there can be than this! And no one will be stopped from entering here; all of us are included, because His Majesty said, "Not

228. See John 20:19, 21; see footnote 222.
229. Luke 7:50: "And he said to the woman, 'Your faith has saved you; go in peace.'"
230. John 17:21: "That they may all be one. As you, Father, are in me and I am in you, may they also be in us, so that the world may believe that you have sent me."

only do I pray for them but also for *all* those who will believe in me";[231] He says, "I am in them."[232]

8. Oh, God help me! What true words! And how well they are understood by the soul that sees this for itself in this state of prayer! And how well we would *all* understand this, if not for our own fault—because the words of Jesus Christ our King and Lord cannot fail! But because *we* fail by not being available, and by not turning from everything that can hinder this light, we don't see ourselves in this mirror that we're contemplating, where our image is engraved.[233]

9. Getting back to what we were saying: the Lord puts the soul into this dwelling of His, which is the center of the soul itself. And just as they say that the highest heaven[234] (where our Lord is) doesn't *move* like the other heavens, it seems that when this soul enters here, there are none of the usual movements in it—those movements that usually exist in the faculties and imagination, harming her or taking away her peace.

It might seem like I'm saying that when such a soul reaches this place, and God gives this particular mercy, then she is sure of her salvation and certain never to fall again. I'm not saying that: whenever I address this topic and say the soul seems to be "secure," you should understand me to mean that this is true as long as she remains in the hand of the Divine Majesty and doesn't offend Him. At least I know for sure that, even when the soul seems to be in this state, and has been for many years, she doesn't consider herself safe. Instead, this soul walks with much more trepidation and caution than before, guarding against any small offense against God. At the same time, she has such great desires to serve Him, as I'll explain

231. John 17:20: "I ask not only on behalf of these, but also on behalf of those who will believe in me through their word."
232. John 17:23: "I in them and you in me, that they may become completely one, so that the world may know that you have sent me and have loved them even as you have loved me."
233. In the Stanbrook edition of *The Interior Castle*, the translators note that this idea is explored further in a poem by Teresa. Their enlightening footnote (n. 417) on this section reads: "Such is the power of love, O soul, To paint thee in my heart No craftsman with such art Whate'er his skill might be, could there Thine image thus impart! 'Twas love that gave thee life— Then, fair one, if thou be Lost to thyself, thou'lt see Thy portrait in my bosom stamped— Soul, seek thyself in Me." See https://ccel.org/ccel/teresa/castle2/castle2.xi.ii.html.
234. Literally: "empyrean heaven," an aspect of Christian cosmology referring to the highest part of heaven, the source of all light.

later, and is regularly pained and confused to see how little she can do and how much service she owes. This is no small cross for the soul to bear, but a very serious penance. [For you have to understand] that, for this soul, the greater the penance is, the greater its delight. The *true* penance is when God takes away your health and strength, and you're no longer able to do penance.[235] I've described elsewhere the great pain this inability causes, but it's much greater here. All of this must be due to the roots, where the tree of this soul is planted. A tree planted by streams of water is more fresh [and verdant] and gives more fruit, and so why would we marvel at the desires of this soul? Because its true spirit has become one with the heavenly water we mentioned.

10. Okay, returning to what I was saying: it shouldn't be thought that the faculties and senses and passions are always in this peace, although the soul itself is. The other dwellings don't stop having times of conflict and work and fatigue, but not in such a way that takes away from the soul's peace and position of stability—at least not as a general rule. This *center* of our soul, or spirit, is something so difficult to describe—and even to believe. I think, sisters, that I won't give you the temptation of not believing what I say simply because I don't know how to explain myself. How can I say that there are works and sorrows, and yet, at the same time, that the soul is in peace? It's a difficult thing. I want to give you a comparison or two; I pray to God that they illuminate something [of this mystery] to you; but, if not, I still know that there's truth in what I've said.

11. [Imagine it's like] a king who's in his palace: there are many wars in his kingdom and a lot of distressing things going on, but that doesn't mean he leaves his post. So it is here: although in the other dwelling places there is much chaos and many poisonous beasts—and you can hear the noise—no one enters and forcefully removes the soul from this center. And even though the things heard do cause some pain, it's not in a way that disturbs the soul or takes away its peace, because the passions have already been mastered. So, they're afraid to go in there because, if they do, they come out more exhausted. [Or think of it like this:] our whole body may hurt,

235. I think again that Ruth Burrow's concept of penance as sacrificial generosity is helpful here, because whether or not we are part of a religious order with disciplines of standard penance, we know (or can imagine) the pain of not being *able*, physically, to give sacrificially on behalf of those we love.

but if our head is healthy, the fact that the body is in pain won't make the head hurt, too. I'm laughing at myself over these comparisons; they don't satisfy me, but I don't know others [to explain this]. Think what you want; what I've said is true.

Overview of Chapter Three

In this third chapter, Teresa is remarkably focused on the transformative effects of this central union. She wants us to see as clearly as we can not only what the effects of this central union are (as far as she understands, she humbly notes), but also how they differ from the effects of all the previous dwelling places. Some of the ways that transformation can be seen are: self-forgetfulness; a desire to suffer for God only as God wills; joy in persecution and a love for "enemies"; the desire to live in order to serve the Lord; fearlessness about death; and a great detachment from all earthly things. Because we are still human, sometimes the soul *does* become distracted. Yet God takes particular care to recall this soul to the divine presence within, just as he has before, and Teresa says these continued awakenings to love alone are worth all the trials of the contemplative prayer journey leading up to this point: "If there were nothing else to be gained from this way of prayer except understanding the particular care God has for us in communicating with us, begging us to abide with Him (for these experiences don't seem to be anything else), then I would say that all the trials endured would be well worth it. They lead to enjoying these touches of His love, so gentle and penetrating."

The second half of this chapter describes other aspects of the peace and tranquility gained in this state (including the cessation of the most dramatic raptures). The soul's peace here is so broad and deep that it can't be permanently ruined by the continued sense of deep responsibility to actively serve God in a chaotic world. Storms *do* come, she says with characteristic realism, but they "pass quickly, like a wave."

Chapter Three (7.3)

THE TRANSFORMATIVE EFFECTS OF THIS CENTRAL UNION

1. Now then, we're saying that this little butterfly has died, with great joy at having found rest, and Christ lives within her. Let's see what her new life is like and how it's different from her life before, because it's by the *effects* that we will see if what's been said is true. As far as I can understand, these are the effects:

2. First, there's a self-forgetfulness so complete that the self truly seems to no longer *be,* as was said earlier.[236] For everything is such that she doesn't know or remember that there is heaven, or life, or honor for *her*—everything is busy and occupied with seeking the honor of *God.* It seems that the words His Majesty said to her have produced their effect—namely, that she takes care of His business, and He will look after hers. And so, no matter what might happen, she doesn't worry, but instead has a strange forgetfulness. For, as I say, the soul no longer seems to *be,* and doesn't want to be anything, anywhere, except when she realizes that there may be some part for her to play that increases the glory and honor of God in some way; for this, she would very willingly lay down her life.

3. Don't understand by this description, daughters, that you stop taking into account eating and sleeping (which is no small torment), or stop doing everything that you're obligated to do, according to your state in life. We're talking about interior matters; there's little to say about external works. It's her great sadness to see that all she can do through her own strength is practically nothing. Yet everything she understands to be in service of the Lord that she *can* do, she won't fail to do, for any reason on earth.

4. Second, there's a great desire to suffer, but not in such a way that it disturbs her like it used to. Because the desire for the will of God to be done in her is so extreme that everything His Majesty does is considered for the best: if He wants her to suffer, well and good; if not, she doesn't kill herself over it like she used to.

5. These souls also have a deep interior joy when they are persecuted, and with much more peace than has been previously described. They don't

236. 7.2.4–5.

have any hostility or animosity toward those who do them wrong—or want to do them wrong. Instead, such a soul has a particular love for them. If they see them in trouble, they're deeply sorry for them and would do anything possible to help them out. They commend them to God in prayer very earnestly and eagerly, and they would be happy to lose some of the merciful gifts His Majesty has given them if such gifts might be given to these others instead—and thus prevent *them* from offending our Lord.

6. What surprises me most is this: you've already seen the trials and afflictions these souls have had because of their desire to die (and thus enjoy our Lord). Now, they have just as great a desire to serve Him, that somehow through them He might be praised; they want to help benefit some soul if they can. And so not only do they *not* want to die, but they want to *live* for many years, suffering great hardships if by doing so they might help the Lord be praised, even if in a very small way. If they knew for certain that when their soul left the body it would definitely enjoy God, it still doesn't matter to them. Not even thinking about the glory of the saints changes their attitude; they don't want to see themselves in this place. For their glory is now found in wondering if they could help the Crucified in some way, especially when they see how often people offend Him—and how few there are that really look out for His honor, detached from everything else.

7. It's true that sometimes they forget this, and the tender longings to enjoy God and escape this exile return...especially when the soul sees how little it serves Him. But then the soul turns back and looks within itself, and considers God's continual presence. With that, it is content and offers to His Majesty the desire to live—the most costly offering it can give Him. They don't fear death any more than they would fear a gentle rapture. The fact is that the One who gave those earlier desires—with such excessive torment—now gives these others. May He always be blessed and praised.

8. Ultimately, these souls no longer desire gifts or spiritual delights, since they have the same Lord [who gives them] *with* them, and it's His Majesty who now lives in them. Of course, His life was nothing but continuous torment, and so ours is made the same, at least in terms of desires. In everything else, He treats us as weaklings, although we share His strength when He sees that it's needed.

There's a great detachment from everything, and a desire to always be alone or busy with something that's beneficial to some soul. They don't have spiritual dryness or interior trials, but a remembrance of and great tenderness for our Lord, so that they never want to do anything except give Him praise.

CONTINUED AWAKENINGS TO LOVE

When the soul is negligent or distracted, the Lord Himself awakens it in the way that was mentioned. The soul sees quite clearly that the impulse—or whatever it's called—comes from the interior of the soul, as we said when talking about impulses. Here, it comes very gently, but it doesn't come from thought, or memory, or in any way that might be understood as the soul having a part to play. This is ordinary and frequent, and has thus been observed many times with great care: just as a fire doesn't cast its flame downward, but *always* up, no matter how big the fire, in the same way it's understood here that this interior movement comes from the center of the soul and awakens the faculties.

9. Really, if there were nothing else to be gained from this way of prayer except understanding the particular care God has for us in communicating with us, begging us to abide with Him (for these experiences don't seem to be anything else), then I would say that all the trials endured would be well worth it. They lead to enjoying these touches of His love, so gentle and penetrating. You've experienced this, sisters, because I think that when the soul reaches the prayer of union, the Lord begins to exercise this care over us if we don't neglect to keep His commandments. When this happens to you, remember that it belongs to this innermost dwelling place, where God is in our soul. Give Him abundant praise, because He's the one sending this to you, like a message or a letter written with such love—and in such a way that only you can understand the letter and what it asks of you. Don't fail to respond to His Majesty for any reason, even if you're busy outwardly and in the middle of a conversation with people. It will often happen in public that our Lord wants to give you this secret gift, and it's very easy to make a response inwardly: you can respond with an act or expression of love, as I've said, or say what Saint Paul did: "Lord, what do you want me to do?"[237] He will teach you there in many ways what pleases Him, and the

237. Acts 9:6: "But get up and enter the city, and you will be told what you are to do."

acceptable time. For it seems to be understood that He hears us, is listening—and this delicate touch almost always gives the soul the ability to do what was said, with determination.

10. The [defining] difference in this dwelling place has already been mentioned: there's almost never aridity—spiritual dryness—or interior disturbances like those that were with it in all the other dwelling places. Instead, the soul is almost always tranquil. And it's not afraid that this great mercy is a trick of the adversary, but remains certain that it is of God. Because, as I've said, the senses and the faculties have nothing to do with it: His Majesty revealed Himself to the soul and took it with Him into a place where I believe the adversary won't dare to enter, and the Lord won't let him. And all the merciful actions that He does here to the soul, as I've said, come without any help from the soul itself, apart from what it has already done by giving itself wholly to God.

11. Every way that the Lord helps and teaches the soul here is in such peace and quiet. It seems to me to be like the building of Solomon's temple, during which no noise could be heard. Just so, in this temple of God—in this dwelling place of His—He alone and the soul rejoice together in deep silence. There's no reason for the intellect to stir, to hustle and bustle and seek anything to aid understanding. For the Lord who created it is now pleased to calm it, and have it look [in a sense] through a small crack at what is happening. Though now and then you lose sight of this view, and [the other faculties] don't let you look, this is only for a very short time. For, in my opinion, the faculties are not *lost* here, but they don't work; it's as if they are in a daze, amazed.

12. I'm amazed, too, to observe that, in arriving here, all the raptures are taken away (that is to say, those raptures that are accompanied by the loss or suspension of one's senses). Very occasionally they're experienced, but not with flights of the spirit. They're very rare, and almost never in public, like before. There's no connection now, either, between raptures and great occasions of devotion: if they see a devotional image, or hear a sermon or music, it's almost as if it were hardly [seen or] heard. Before, the poor little butterfly was so anxious that everything scared her and made her fly away. Now, either she has found her rest, or the soul has seen so much in this dwelling place that it's not afraid of anything, or she doesn't

feel that loneliness that she used to (since she enjoys such company)...well, sisters, I don't know what the reason is, but when the Lord begins to reveal what's in this dwelling place by putting your soul there, you lose this great weakness that was such a trial and wouldn't go away before. Perhaps it's because the Lord has strengthened, enlarged, and enabled the soul—or it could be that [in the past] He wanted to make public the things He was doing with these souls in secret, for purposes only His Majesty knows. His judgments surpass everything we can imagine here.

13. God gives these effects when He brings the soul to Himself, along with all the other beneficial ones from degrees of prayer already mentioned. These are given *with* this kiss that the bride asked for; I understand this request to be fulfilled in this dwelling place.[238] Here, an abundance of water is given to this wounded deer. Here, the soul delights in the tabernacle of God. Here, the dove Noah sent out to see if the storm was over *finds* the olive branch—the sign that it has found solid ground within the waters and storms of this world.

Oh, Jesus! Who *knows* how many things there must be in Scripture to explain this peace of the soul! My God, since You see very well how much this peace matters to us, please make Christians want to seek it; and to those to whom You've given this peace, in Your mercy, don't take it away. Ultimately, until *You* give us true peace, and take us where this peace cannot end, we must always live in fear. I say "true" peace not because I think this peace isn't true, but because our state could turn to war again if we turn away from God.

14. But what will these souls feel to realize that they might lack so much, such a great blessing? This realization makes them more careful and try harder to bring strength out of their weakness. They don't want to be responsible for losing *any* opportunity that might be offered to them for pleasing God more fully. The more they are favored by His Majesty, the more they are afraid and fearful of themselves. In these grandeurs of God, they've come to know their weaknesses and limitations[239] more, and they take their sins more seriously. They often go about, like the tax collector,

238. An allusion to Song of Solomon 1:2: "Let him kiss me with the kisses of his mouth! For your love is better than wine."
239. "Weaknesses and limitations" is literally "miseries."

without daring to lift up their eyes.[240] Other times, they long to reach the end of their lives so as to see God in safety—but then, with the love that they have, they want to live in order to serve Him, as stated above; they trust everything that touches them to be of His mercy. Sometimes, the many gifts they receive leave them feeling crushed and overwhelmed, fearing that, just like an overloaded ship, they will sink to the bottom of the sea.

15. I'm telling you, sisters, that you have no lack of crosses in this state—but not to the point of becoming restless, unsettled, or causing the loss of peace. These storms pass quickly, like a wave. And then calm returns, because the presence of the Lord they carry makes them soon forget everything. May He be forever blessed and praised by all His creatures. Amen.

240. Luke 18:13: "But the tax collector, standing far off, would not even look up to heaven, but was beating his breast and saying, 'God, be merciful to me, a sinner!'"

Overview of Chapter Four

In the final chapter of the seventh dwellings, and *The Interior Castle*, Teresa wants to be sure we know that, even here, in the "ultimate" earthly state of union and companionship with God, we are still *creatures*, not divine. We must walk with continued humanity and humility. And so, she says, the effects mentioned are not always present, though they will be evident the majority of the time. To conclude this castle text, however, the saint returns to a question that she has addressed at various times in the book because it is so essential to healthy spirituality: *Why* do we think these things happen in prayer at all? What's the point, from God's perspective? She answers with her most distilled version of the reason God gives spiritual gifts, or favors, employing several biblical figures and saints to support the answer she offers: all of it is so that we might have greater strength for works of service in the world and for the reign of God, to God's greater glory. For those who are led by this path, it is simply food for the journey—nourishment for what is asked of us in terms of service. Speaking in particular to her Carmelite sisters, and to all those who are very fond of contemplative prayer and solitude, she revisits a famous gospel story about the tension between "sitting at the Lord's feet" (Mary) and "doing the dishes" (Martha), or, in more general terms, contemplation and action. She proposes joining Mary and Martha together in our own lives always: never thinking that we can "only" play the part of Mary (or Martha, for that matter). Both are required. With this balance of contemplation and action, we can be equipped for the work that God intends for us to do in the world—and then we must not neglect to do it!

Teresa's final word of encouragement is a beautiful rejoinder to those in her age and our own who feel that there is nothing "significant" they *can* do, based on their talents or life circumstances. She says that the Christian life is not about making headlines for God; it's about serving with love where and how we can. All of the extraordinary gifts of prayer she has described for us in the final four dwelling places don't change one bit the central compass of our lives; our guidepost for progress and faithfulness is still, and always will be, the self-giving love of God and neighbor.

Chapter Four (7.4)

CONTINUED HUMANITY AND HUMILITY

1. Sisters, you must not think that the effects I've described in these souls are *always* there. That's why I say "ordinarily" or "usually," at least when I remember to. Sometimes our Lord leaves them to their natural state, and then it seems like all the poisonous things from the surrounding area and in the dwelling places of this castle come together to take revenge on them for all the time they were not able to get their hands on these souls.

2. It's true that this doesn't last long: a day at most, or a little longer. And in this great commotion, usually caused by some event, it becomes clear what the soul gains from the good company it's in. For the Lord gives it great strength *not* to turn away from His service or the good resolutions it has made. Instead, its resolutions seem to grow, and the soul doesn't deviate from its determination to serve even in the slightest. As I say, this happens rarely—but our Lord wants you *not* to forget what you are.[241] One reason for [not losing this awareness] is that you remain humble. Another is that you better understand what you owe to His Majesty and what a great gift you're receiving, and thus praise Him.

3. Don't ever think that because these souls have such great desire and determination not to commit *any* imperfections—and wouldn't do so for anything in the world—that they actually stop committing *many* imperfections, and even sins. Intentionally, no: for the Lord must give such souls a very particular help in this regard. I mean less significant faults, not

---

241. Teresa literally says, "not lose the memory of your being." Some translators (like Kavanaugh and Rodriguez) have kept this vague but evocative phrase as "our Lord does not want the soul to forget its being," while others (like Peers) make it a bit more direct with "our Lord's will is for the soul not to forget what it is." In either case, the reference seems to be our being *human*, not divine.

willful and serious sins.[242] As far as they can understand, they are free from those [serious ones], though not completely immune from them. And the fact that there will be some faults and sins they are not aware of is no small torment for them.

It's also distressing for them to see so many souls being lost. And although, in some ways, they have great hope that they won't be among them, when they remember some of those that Scripture says were favored by the Lord, like Solomon (who was so close to our Lord),[243] they can't help but fear, as I've said. The one who has the greatest self-confidence should fear even more, because "Blessed is the one who fears God," as David says.[244] May God always protect us; earnestly and persistently asking Him to keep us from committing offenses is the greatest security we can have. May He always be praised. Amen.

THE REASON GOD GIVES SPIRITUAL GIFTS OR FAVORS

4. It will be good, sisters, to tell you *why* the Lord gives so many merciful gifts in this world—the point of these "favors."[245] Although you'll have understood this if you've paid attention to the effects they produce, I want to tell you again here so that no one thinks it's only to give pleasure to these souls. Such thinking would be a great mistake. For His Majesty can't do a greater "favor" than to give us a life that might imitate the life of the Son He so loved. And so I'm certain that these gifts or favors are for strengthening our weakness, as I've sometimes said here, enabling us to imitate Him in His great sufferings.

5. We've always seen that those who were closest to Christ our Lord were those with the greatest work to do. Look at the trials that His glorious mother and the glorious apostles had to pass through. And how do you think Saint Paul could endure such great hardships? Through Paul's life, we can see the effects of true visions and contemplation, when they're from our Lord (and not a product of our imagination or the deception of

242. In the text, this is a distinction between "venial sins" and "mortal sins," which I have loosely translated for those unfamiliar with this categorization of sin.
243. For Solomon's turn away from God, see 1 Kings 11.
244. Psalm 112:1: "Praise the Lord! Happy are those who fear the Lord, who greatly delight in his commandments."
245. The Spanish word for "favor," "gift," "grace," or "mercy" used throughout this paragraph is once again *merced*.

the adversary). And then, did Paul happen to hide away with these gifts, enjoying them and not engaging with anything else? No! We see that he didn't have a day of rest, as far as we know—and he didn't get much rest at night, either, because that's when he earned his living.[246] I really like the story of how, when Saint Peter was fleeing from prison, our Lord appeared and told him that He was going to Rome to be crucified again [through and with Peter]. We never recite the office of this feast (where this story is found) without my finding particular comfort in it.[247] How did Saint Peter respond to this mercy from the Lord? What did he do? He went straight to his death. And it's no small mercy of the Lord that he found someone to give this death to him.

STRENGTH FOR WORKS OF SERVICE

6. Oh, my sisters, how forgetful of your rest you must be! How little we should care about rewards, respect, and reputation;[248] how far we should be from wanting admiration in anything! For if the soul is deeply with Him, as is right, she will think little of herself. All her thoughts go toward how to best please Him, and in what ways or where she will show the love she has for Him. For this is the point of prayer, my daughters; *this* is what spiritual marriage is for: works, the continual birth of good works.

7. This is the true sign that anything, or any mercy, is of God, as I've already told you. It does me little good to be fully recollected in solitude, performing acts of devotion with our Lord—proposing and promising to do wonders for His service—if then, when I leave and I have the chance, I do everything just the opposite. Well, I wrongly said that it "does me little good," because everything and everyone with God benefits us a great deal. And although we might be too weak to fulfill these noble intentions or

246. First Thessalonians 2:9: "You remember our labor and toil, brothers and sisters; we worked night and day, so that we might not burden any of you while we proclaimed to you the gospel of God."

247. Peers notes in the fourth footnote of 7.4 that "in the old Carmelite Breviary, which St. Teresa would have used, the Antiphon of the Magnificat at First Vespers on June 29 runs: 'The Blessed Apostle Peter saw Christ coming to meet him. Adoring Him, he said: "Lord, whither goest Thou?" "I am going to Rome to be crucified afresh."'" The story has it that Saint Peter returned to Rome and was crucified.

248. In the text, what I have rendered as three words is one simple word meaning "honor," but because the rhetoric of modern Western society no longer talks about honor as something to be sought, I tried to evoke what Teresa is pointing to through words and concepts that do hold power over our desires and attention.

resolutions, sometimes His Majesty will tell us how we might do it and give us the strength we need, even if it's a heavy burden (as is often the case). For when He sees a very fainthearted soul, He gives it a very great trial, something against its will, and draws from it a profit or gain. And then, as the soul realizes this dynamic, it loses some of its fear and offers itself more fully to Him. What I meant in saying "it does me little good" is that it's little *compared* to the good that comes when we align our works with our resolutions and our words in prayer. What can't be done all at once *can* be done little by little. If anyone wants prayer to truly be of benefit, let that soul bend its will: within the nooks and corners of our lives there will be many opportunities to do so.

8. Look here: this matters much more than I even know how to tell you. Fix your eyes on the Crucified, and everything else will seem small to you. If His Majesty showed His love for us through such horrifying works and sufferings, how can you want to satisfy Him with words alone? Do you know what it means to be truly spiritual? It means becoming slaves of God—marked with His branding iron, which is the cross. Since [such surrendered souls] have already given Him their freedom, He can sell them as slaves to the whole world, as He was. In doing so, He does them no harm, and actually no small *favor*. And if they don't resolve to do this,[249] I'm afraid that they won't make much progress. For the foundation of this whole building is humility, as I've said. If you don't have true humility, the Lord will not want to raise you up very high, for your own good—since, without this sure foundation, it will all crumble to the ground. So, sisters, to build good foundations, try to be the least of all and the slave of God, looking for how and where you can delight and serve those around you. What you're doing in such service is more for yourself than for them, laying foundation stones so strong and firm that your castle won't fall.

9. I repeat: it's essential to *not* build a foundation made only of prayer and contemplation. Because unless you strive after the virtues, practicing and exercising them, you'll always remain dwarfs. And then, pray to God that it's not *just* a lack of growth that's the problem, because you already know that whoever doesn't grow actually decreases. For I consider it impossible for love, when present, to stay content with just "being there."

---

249. Teresa seems to be referring to the act of surrendering oneself to God, and in the process becoming a humble servant of others, as Jesus was.

10. It might seem to you like I'm only talking to those who are beginners, and that later on, souls can rest. Yet I've already told you: the peace such souls have is *inside*; on the outside, they get less and less peace, nor do they want it. What do you think those inspirations are for? Those inspirations I talked about, which might instead be called *aspirations*—those instructions that the soul sends from its inner center to the people outside the castle, and to the dwelling places outside of where she is...[are they sent] so that they can go to sleep?[250] No, no, no! The soul wages more war from the center than it did when it was outside the center with the others, suffering—so that the faculties and senses and everything to do with the body won't be idle. Because then it didn't understand the huge gains that trials bring. They might have even been the way that God brought the soul to the center, and the company she now has gives her much greater strength than ever. For if, as David says, *with* the saints we will become saints,[251] there's no need to doubt that if we are made one with the Strong, we will be strengthened through such a full union of spirit with spirit.[252] And, in this way, we'll understand the strength the saints had, enabling them to suffer and die.

11. It's very certain that this strength that adheres to the soul in the center also goes forth to *all* those who are in the castle, and even the body itself. It seems that, often, this strength is not felt; but the soul *is* strengthened by drinking the wine of this wine cellar where the Spouse has brought it (and doesn't let it go).[253] Strength flows out into the weak body, just as here on earth the food placed in the stomach gives strength to the head, and every part. And so this soul has plenty of misfortune while he's alive, because no matter how much he does or accomplishes, the inner strength is far greater. Thus, the "battle challenges" given [from within] increase, too, such that everything he does seems like nothing at all. This must be

---

250. It's helpful to remember that Teresa is now employing the whole self as a landscape with a castle that includes many dwelling places. "The people" are not other people apart from the soul, but those aspects of ourselves that are "outside the castle," or inhabiting different dwelling places.

251. Psalm 18:26: "With the pure you show yourself pure; and with the crooked you show yourself perverse."

252. The adjective for the union of the soul to God, here rendered as "full," is once again literally "sovereign."

253. Another allusion, as in the fifth dwellings, to Song of Solomon 2:4: "He brought me to the banqueting house, and his intention toward me was love."

where the great penances of the saints come from, especially the glorious Magdalene (who was raised in such luxury). It's the origin of that hunger our father Elijah had for the honor of his God, and that Saint Dominic and Saint Francis had for drawing souls so that God could be praised. What I'm telling you is that forgetting themselves actually cost them a lot.

JOINING MARY AND MARTHA

12. This is what I want us to try to achieve, my sisters. Let us desire and occupy ourselves in prayer, not for our own enjoyment but to have this kind of strength to serve. We *don't* want to go down a path not taken, for in doing so we'll get lost at the most opportune time. It would be very strange to think that we might have these graces of God by any other road than the one traveled by Jesus and all His saints. May the thought not even pass through our minds. Believe me, Martha and Mary must join *together* in order to welcome the Lord and have Him stay with them always—and not, in effect, give Him terrible lodging by not giving Him food. How can Mary, always sitting at His feet, give food to Him if her sister won't help her? His food is that we reach souls in every possible way, so that they can be saved and praise Him forever.

13. You'll tell me two things: one, Jesus said that Mary had chosen the better part.[254] The response is that she had already done a "Martha-like job," showing her love for the Lord by washing His feet and drying them with her hair.[255] And do you think it was an insignificant humiliation for a woman like her? To go through the streets, perhaps alone, because in her fervor she didn't care about how she got there? And then to enter into a house where she'd never been before and take the snide remarks of the Pharisee,[256] among many other things she had to endure? The townspeople saw a woman like her change so much, and she was in the midst of such malicious people. It was enough for them to see that she was friendly with

---

254. Luke 10:42: "[Jesus said,] 'Few things are needed—indeed only one. Mary has chosen the better part, which will not be taken away from her.'"
255. Luke 7:37–38: "And a woman in the city, who was a sinner, having learned that he was eating in the Pharisee's house, brought an alabaster jar of ointment. She stood behind him at his feet, weeping, and began to bathe his feet with her tears and to dry them with her hair. Then she continued kissing his feet and anointing them with the ointment."
256. Luke 7:39: "Now when the Pharisee who had invited him saw it, he said to himself, 'If this man were a prophet, he would have known who and what kind of woman this is who is touching him—that she is a sinner.'"

our Lord—whom they so hated—and then *add* to it the thought of the life she'd lived...and that now she wanted to become holy (because she would, of course, have changed her style of dress and everything else). If today we gossip about people who aren't even so notorious, what would have been said then? I tell you, sisters, that "the better part" came to her after hard work and humbling acts.[257] Even if there was nothing more than seeing her Master so hated, it must have been an intolerable trial. And consider the many trials that happened later, in the death of our Lord and the years that she lived without Him afterward—which would have been a terrible torment. I personally think that the reason she wasn't given martyrdom is that she had already suffered that fate through witnessing the Lord's death. You can see that she was not always enjoying the gift of contemplation at the feet of the Lord.

SERVING WITH LOVE WHERE AND HOW WE CAN

14. The other thing you'll say is that you can't bring souls to God because you don't have any way to do so. You'll say that you would *gladly* do this, but since you're not preachers or teachers, like the apostles, you don't know how. I've answered this objection in writing a few times, but I'm not sure if I've addressed it in this castle manuscript. Nevertheless, since it's something that I think does occur to you (with the desires that the Lord gives you [to serve]), I won't fail to say it here: I've already said elsewhere that sometimes the adversary gives us grandiose desires and ambitions, so that instead of using what we have at hand to serve our Lord in *possible* things, we are content with having *desired* the impossible. Other than praying for people—through which you *will* help a lot—don't try to help everybody, but instead focus on those who are actually in your company. Your work will be more significant because you are more committed and bound to them.[258] Do you think that your deep humility and subjugation—serving

257. The word for "humbling acts" is literally "mortification," the same word used in the sentence about Mary's going through the streets. Although I chose not to use the word because it has fallen out of use, it richly evokes the notion of being so embarrassed or humbled that your ego or sense of social "reputation" being important must die.

258. The verb rendered here as "committed and bound" is literally "obliged," but this term has fallen out of use and common understanding. It's difficult to know if Teresa was referring to the *obligations* or duties that are a part of actual relationships, or the reciprocal nature of being in someone's debt because they have done a favor or service for you. Either way, the term points to the ongoing, active, and practical demands of life with others.

everyone with great love toward them—alongside your contagious love of the Lord—kindling the fire of faith in those around you—is of little benefit? You awaken them with these and the other virtues you always follow. This service is not small but great, and very pleasing to the Lord. By your doing the work that you *can* do, His Majesty will understand that you *would* do much more [if you could]; He will reward you as if you had won many souls for Him.

15. "Such service doesn't convert any souls," you'll say, "because all the sisters we deal with are already good." Who made you the judge of that, and what does that have to do with anything?[259] The better they are, the more pleasing their praises will be to the Lord, and the more their prayers will benefit their neighbors.

In short, my sisters, my conclusion is that we must not build towers without foundations—"castles in the air." The Lord doesn't look so much at the *greatness* of what we do but instead at the *love* with which we do it. And if we do what we *can*, His Majesty will enable us to do more and more each day. We must not grow weary. During the short time that this life lasts—and perhaps it will be even shorter than you think—let us offer to the Lord the sacrifices that we can, both in the interior *and* the exterior. His Majesty will unite it with His offering to the Father on the cross for us. Then, even if the works are small, they have the value given to them by the offering of *our* loving will.

16. May it please His Majesty, my sisters and daughters, to have us *all* meet where we forever praise Him, and give me grace enough to actually *do* some of what I tell you, through the merits of His Son, who lives and reigns forever and ever. Amen. I tell you, I'm filled with confusion myself, and so I ask you through the same Lord not to forget this pitiful wretch in your prayers.

259. The Spanish here for this little question is very sparse, and translations vary in terms of what Teresa is implying: that we are not to judge, or if the problem is that even if they are "good," we should not complain about our "working conditions" in and for the kingdom of God. Either way, her answer seems to be, "So what? That's no excuse!"

Questions for Reflection

1. How do you respond to the metaphor of spiritual marriage? What do you think is at the heart of this metaphor for Teresa and in Scripture? Which parts of it make sense or appeal to you, and which parts are difficult to relate to? How would it change your understanding of the life of faith to consider Christ to be not only your "friend," but also your "Spouse"?

2. How do the stated effects of this spiritual marriage, or union in the center, differ from other versions of "mature spirituality" or "Christian faithfulness" that you have been taught or have perceived? Does this type of union seem desirable to you at this point in your journey? Why or why not?

3. How would you describe, in your own words, why God gives unforgettable and often unexpected gifts in the life of prayer? When have you seen this dynamic of "strength for service" at work in your own life or the life of others? Teresa says not everyone receives these gifts because not everyone needs them. What are your thoughts about why our experiences with prayer vary so greatly?

4. Is your tendency in life to favor the Mary role or the Martha role? What would a balance or *joining* of the two look like?

5. Where do you feel Teresa's call to service meets your current life and circumstances? What is the "possible" thing you might actually be able to do in the coming days, weeks, or months to love God and neighbor?

Overview of the Epilogue

In her final words to the reader, Teresa admits that she ended up enjoying this dreaded project of obedience more than she thought she would. And she acknowledges once more, in retrospect, that we can't exactly "explore" every dwelling place of this castle she's described. God must lead us or draw us into certain spaces; for some places, divine action is required, and we shouldn't try to force entry. At the same time, she reiterates that there are many more dwellings than those described here; this is not an exhaustive map by any means! With characteristic self-deprecation, she places herself under the authority of church doctrine and asks for readers to pray for the Roman Catholic Church, for the Lutherans who had broken away from that church, and for herself, a strong, extraordinary woman as well as a teacher aware of her own faults to the very end.

Epilogue

1. When I started writing what I've put down here, it was with the reluctance I mentioned at the beginning. And yet, after finishing the work, I must say that it has given me much gladness, and I consider the work well spent—though I confess it didn't cost me much. Considering how strictly confined you are, how few opportunities for entertainment you have, and the fact that some of your monasteries are of insufficient size for your numbers, I think it will be a consolation for you to delight in this interior castle. For without any permission from your superiors, you can enter and walk through it at any time.

2. It's true that no matter how great your strength seems to you, you won't be able to enter *all* the dwellings through your own efforts: the Lord of the castle Himself must bring you to some. That's why I warn you: if you encounter any resistance, don't try to force it. In doing so, you'll anger Him, and He may never let you enter them. He's a close friend of humility.

By considering yourself undeserving of even entering the third dwelling places, you'll more quickly get the will to reach the fifth. This happens in such a way that you can then serve Him from there, continuing to go through the dwellings many times, until He brings you into the very dwelling place He has for Himself. From there, you'll never leave, unless you are called away by the prioress. (This great Lord wants you to fulfill her will for you as if it were His own.) And yet, even if you are away a lot due to her commands, when you return, the door will always be open for you. Once you've been shown how to enjoy this castle, you'll find rest in all things, even those that are a lot of work. For you'll always have the hope of returning to it, and no one can take that away.

3. Although I've written here of no more than seven dwelling places, in each of them there are many more, below and above and all around, with beautiful gardens and fountains and labyrinths and things so delightful that you'll want to dissolve in praises of the great God who created the soul in His image and likeness. If you find anything good in this book that helps you to know Him better, know truly that it was His Majesty who said it in order to give you happiness; anything bad that you might find has been said by me.

4. Because I have a strong desire to be of *some* help to you in serving my God and Lord, I personally ask you to do the following whenever you read this: praise His Majesty greatly, and ask Him for the growth of His Church, for light for the Lutherans, and that He might forgive me my sins and take me out of purgatory. Perhaps I will be there, by the mercy of God, when this is given to you to read. (If it is available to be seen at all, after being reviewed by learned men.) And if I'm in error about something, it's because I don't understand it; in everything, I subject myself to that which is held by the holy Roman Catholic Church. In this church I live, and declare my faith, and promise to both live and die. May God our Lord be praised and blessed forever. Amen, amen.

5. This writing was finished in the monastery of Saint Joseph of Ávila, in the year 1577, on the eve of the Feast of Saint Andrew, to the glory of God, who lives and reigns for ever and ever. Amen.

FURTHER READINGS

This brief further readings list aims to point interested readers toward more work *by* Teresa of Ávila, *about* her, or *in conversation* with her. Most of the works cited are intended for a broad (not *primarily* academic) audience, though some of the authors are indeed scholars of spirituality, and this saint in particular.

More by Teresa of Ávila

Teresa of Avila. *The Collected Works of St. Teresa of Avila*. Translated by Kieran Kavanaugh, O.C.D., and Otilio Rodriguez, O.C.D. 3 vols. Washington, DC: ICS Publications, 1976.

———. *The Interior Castle: Study Edition*. Translated by Kieran Kavanaugh, O.C.D., and Otilio Rodriguez, O.C.D. Washington, DC: ICS Publications, 2020.

———. *The Life of Saint Teresa of Avila by Herself*. Translated by J. M. Cohen. New York: Penguin Classics, 1988.

More About Teresa of Ávila

Du Boulay, Shirley. *Teresa of Avila: An Extraordinary Life.* New York: BlueBridge, 2004.

Medwick, Cathleen. *Teresa of Avila: The Progress of a Soul.* New York: Doubleday, 1999.

Sackville-West, Vita. *The Eagle and the Dove: Teresa of Avila and Therese of Lisieux.* London: Vintage, 2018.

Williams, Rowan. *Teresa of Avila.* New York: Continuum, 2000.

More in Conversation with Teresa of Ávila and Her Work—especially The Interior Castle

Ahlgren, Gillian T. W. *Entering Teresa of Avila's Interior Castle: A Reader's Companion.* Mahwah, NJ: Paulist Press, 2005.

Bielecki, Tessa. *Holy Daring: The Earthy Mysticism of St. Teresa, the Wild Woman of Avila.* West Hartford, CT: Adam Kadmon Publishing, 2016.

Burrows, Ruth, O.C.D. *The Interior Castle Explored: St. Teresa's Teaching on the Life of Deep Union with God.* Mahwah, NJ: HiddenSpring, 2007.

Burney, Claudia Mair. *God Alone Is Enough: A Spirited Journey with Teresa of Avila.* Brewster, MA: Paraclete Press, 2010.

Don, Megan. *Meditations with Teresa of Avila: A Journey into the Sacred.* Novato, CA: New World Library, 2011.

Dubay, Thomas. *Fire Within: St. Teresa of Avila, St. John of the Cross, and the Gospel—On Prayer.* San Francisco: Ignatius Press, 1989.

Humphreys, Carolyn. *From Ash to Fire: A Contemporary Journey Through the Interior Castle of Teresa of Avila.* Leominster, UK: Gracewing Publishing, 2006.

Mathewson, Laurel. *An Intimate Good: A Skeptical Christian Mystic in Conversation with Teresa of Avila.* New Kensington, PA: Whitaker House, 2024.

McLean, Julienne. *Towards Mystical Union: A Modern Commentary on the Mystical Text "The Interior Castle" by St Teresa of Avila*. London: Saint Pauls, 2004.

Muto, Susan. *Where Lovers Meet: Inside the Interior Castle*. Washington, DC: ICS Publications, 2008.

Starr, Mirabai. *St. Teresa of Avila: Passionate Mystic*. Boulder, CO: Sounds True, 2013.

About the Author

Baptized as Teresa Sánchez de Cepeda y Ahumada (1515–1582), Teresa of Ávila was a prominent Spanish mystic, Roman Catholic saint, Carmelite nun, author during the Counter Reformation, and theologian of contemplative life through mental prayer. She was a reformer of the Carmelite Order and is considered to be a founder of the Discalced Carmelites, along with John of the Cross. In 1970, the saint—also known as "Teresa of Jesus"—was the first woman to be declared a Doctor of the Church, honoring her achievements in theological teaching. Her books, which include her autobiography and her seminal work, *The Interior Castle*, are an integral part of Spanish Renaissance literature, as well as Christian mysticism and Christian meditation practices.

About the Editor

Laurel Mathewson is the author of *An Intimate Good: A Skeptical Christian Mystic in Conversation with Teresa of Avila*. She has written award-winning work for *Sojourners* magazine, *Geez* magazine, and *The Christian Century*. She and her husband, Colin, co-pastor St. Luke's Episcopal Church, a multicultural community in San Diego where the Lord's prayer might be heard in English, Arabic, or Swahili, depending on the Sunday. As an "elder millennial" mother and pastor, Laurel is passionate about preaching, teaching, pondering the ever-surprising love of God with a diverse and multigenerational audience of serious skeptics and serious believers, parenting her three children, ocean swimming, and well-made cookies. Her essential vocation, in the end, is as an interpreter: of texts, traditions, and contemporary experience; between Catholic and Protestant strands of Christianity; and between seemingly incongruous or unintelligible perspectives, even across the centuries.